D1432159

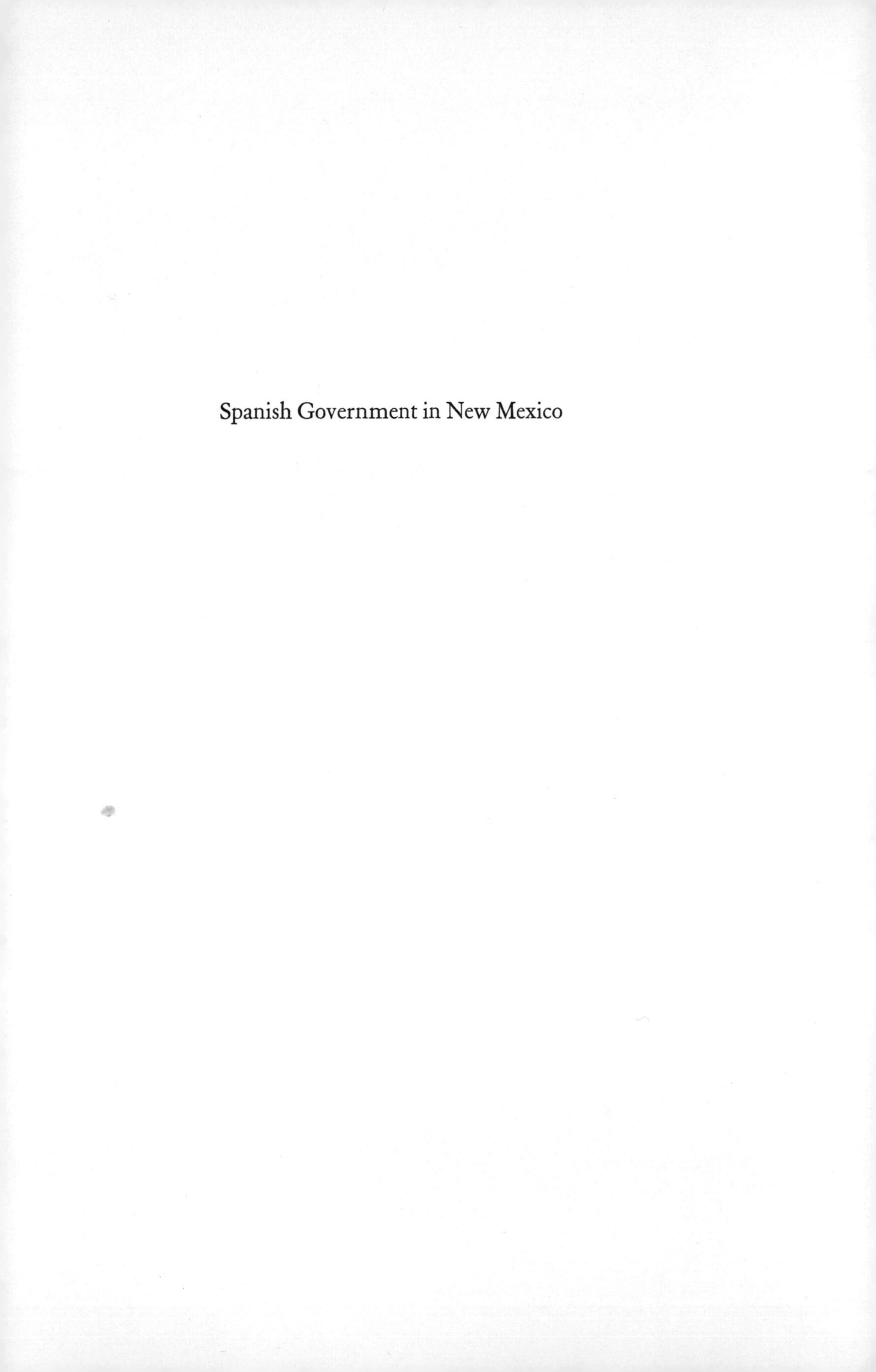

Spanish Government in New Mexico

Spanish Government in New Mexico

MARC SIMMONS

THE UNIVERSITY OF NEW MEXICO PRESS

 Manufactured in the United States of America by the University of New Mexico Printing Plant. Library of Congress Catalog Card No. 68-23021.

To My Mother and Father

PREFACE

THIS BOOK is the result of research carried out over a period of several years. The principal work was done in the Spanish Archives at the State Records Center in Santa Fe and in the Coronado Room of the University of New Mexico Library, Albuquerque. In these two places is found a wealth of material in the form of original documents and photocopies and microfilms of archival collections from Spain and Mexico. A great deal of information from these sources still remains unused, and occasionally a long-buried treasure will turn up. As this book was going to press, for example, the author discovered a previously unreported plan of the presidio of Santa Fe, which is now published herein for the first time.

The author anticipates that this detailed account of Spanish government in New Mexico will serve as a guide and reference for all those interested in colonial history. Furthermore, it should prove useful as a case study, illustrating the administrative development of one of Spain's provinces in the New World.

Dr. Myra Ellen Jenkens, Senior Archivist of the New Mexico State Records Center and Archives, first suggested the need for an intensive study of political institutions and administrative procedures, and her continuing assistance and encouragement were highly valued. Mr. Joseph Halpin, Director of the State Records Center, extended many courtesies. The following professors read the manuscript and offered suggestions for its improvement: Donald C. Cutter, Troy Floyd, and Stanley Newman. Professor Luís Navarro García, Dr. Ward Alan Minge, Bruce Ellis of the Museum of New

Mexico, and photographer Bart Durham for their aid all deserve my thanks. Finally, I must acknowledge my debt to Dr. France V. Scholes who aroused my original interest in Spanish institutions and who remains an abiding source of inspiration and a model for high standards of scholarly endeavor.

MARC SIMMONS

CONTENTS

INTRODUCTION

A MISTAKEN NOTION which prevails today is that the essential outlines of colonial New Mexican history are well known and that only here and there a few details remain to be added to complete the story. Popular taste, which delights in accounts of adventure and tragedy, long ago led scholars to explore in depth the activities of the conquistadores, the circumstances of the Pueblo revolt of 1680 and the subsequent reconquest, and the military campaigns against the plains and desert Indians in the eighteenth century. In the rush to examine the more spectacular sides of what, in truth, was an exciting and colorful history, investigators have often neglected the seemingly more prosaic, though nonetheless fundamental, aspects of the colonial story. One area of that neglect is treated in this book—political administration in the late eighteenth and early nineteenth centuries.

New Mexico's civil government in the seventeenth century has been skillfully described by France V. Scholes, as may be observed by references to his work later in the present study. Because the population of the province was relatively small and the number of settlements few, the organs of political administration remained essentially simple. Even in the first half of the eighteenth century, government in New Mexico was characterized by its lack of complexity. This situation was fundamentally altered, however, during the last fifty years of the colonial regime. Reforms emanating from Spain touched the farthest reaches of the empire, even the remote province of New Mexico. New legislation worked changes in all areas of political administration, as did the turbulent sequence of events in Spain during the early nineteenth century.

Such basic documents as the Order of Intendants and the Spanish Constitution of 1812 have been familiar to historians for some time, but in relation to the New Mexico story, they have been used imperfectly or not at all. Other important pieces of legislation, as those concerned with creation and administration of the commandancy system, and the vital presidial *Reglamento* of 1772, have been unknown to or neglected by most New Mexican writers. All of these materials, in addition to others of greater or lesser merit, have been drawn upon extensively in the present study. A brief commentary on sources appears at the beginning of the bibliography. Note should be taken also of the list of abbreviations, which follows this introduction, and of the glossary preceding the bibliography.

The primary objective of this study is to set forth a description of political government in New Mexico during the last fifty years of its existence as a province of Spain. The central theme is the expansion and elaboration of the administrative system, the overriding characteristic of political activity in New Mexico.

Many topics presented here—the organization of the Santa Fe presidio and the urban militia, the postal system, the administration of the tobacco monopoly, and the judicial procedure, to name only a few—have, hitherto, received little or no attention in the general histories. All areas of government are explored in some depth with the exception of affairs concerned with the Church. Ecclesiastical matters, nevertheless, do figure in some measure in the analysis of related subjects.

In a project of this scope, deficiencies within some areas are bound to appear. Additional years could have been well spent in combing through archival collections in search of further material, and a fuller and more authoritative account of government would have been the result. Alternately, concentration on a single topic, as military organization or the alcalde system, would have permitted a definitive essay within a limited field.

The present approach was adopted because a larger survey appears the most logical, especially since all spheres of government within the Spanish system are, to some degree, interdependent, and one facet of administration may not be comprehended without reference to the others. Enough documents were viewed, the author believes, to establish the general pattern, and while some particulars may, no doubt, be added or corrected in the future, the basic structure should stand as here described.

The chapters which follow are arranged in three parts. Part One describes New Mexico's relationship to the immediately superior government, i.e., the commandancy general. Chapter I is concerned with the origins of the reforms instituted in northern New Spain, and Chapter II deals with the circumstances occasioning the creation and organization of the commandancy general. The third chapter analyzes the operation of this government in the years 1776 to 1792. The following chapter discusses the intendancy system and its connection with New Mexico, while Chapter V recounts the developments within the commandancy system from 1792 to independence.

The intent in these five chapters is to picture in precise terms the manner in which New Mexican officialdom was dependent upon the authorities of New Spain. Abundant consideration is given to the question of succession in the office of commandant general. This has never been clearly presented in the New Mexico histories, and consequently it has remained impossible in a number of cases to ascertain exactly to whom the governors of the province were responsible.*

Part Two deals with New Mexico's provincial government. In Chapter VI the office of governor is examined to show the manifold powers and duties connected with it. The next chapter probes the financial affairs of the province, while Chapter VIII surveys the military organization.

The concern of Part Three is with the district and municipal government in New Mexico. Chapter IX discusses the *alcaldes mayores*

* Two important works bearing upon this subject and written by Luís Navarro García appeared in Spain as the present work was nearing completion. They are: *Don José de Gálvez y la comandancia general de las Provincias Internas del norte de Nueva España* (Sevilla, 1964); and *Las Provincias Internas en el siglo XIX* (Sevilla, 1965).

and their assistants, the *tenientes alcaldes,* and the authority which they exercised over district affairs. Then follows a chapter on the nature and extent of municipal government in the later colonial period. Finally, Chapter XI offers a few brief conclusions which appear warranted from the material presented.

ABBREVIATIONS

AGI	Archivo General de Indias, Sevilla.
Guadalajara	Sección de Audiencia de Guadalajara.
México	Sección de Audiencia de México.
AGN	Archivo General de la Nación, México.
Historia	Ramo de Historia.
Prov. Int.	Ramo de Provincias Internas.
BSCEH	*Boletín de la sociedad Chihuahuense de estudios históricos.*
NMHR	*New Mexico Historical Review.*
SANM	Spanish Archives of New Mexico, Santa Fe.

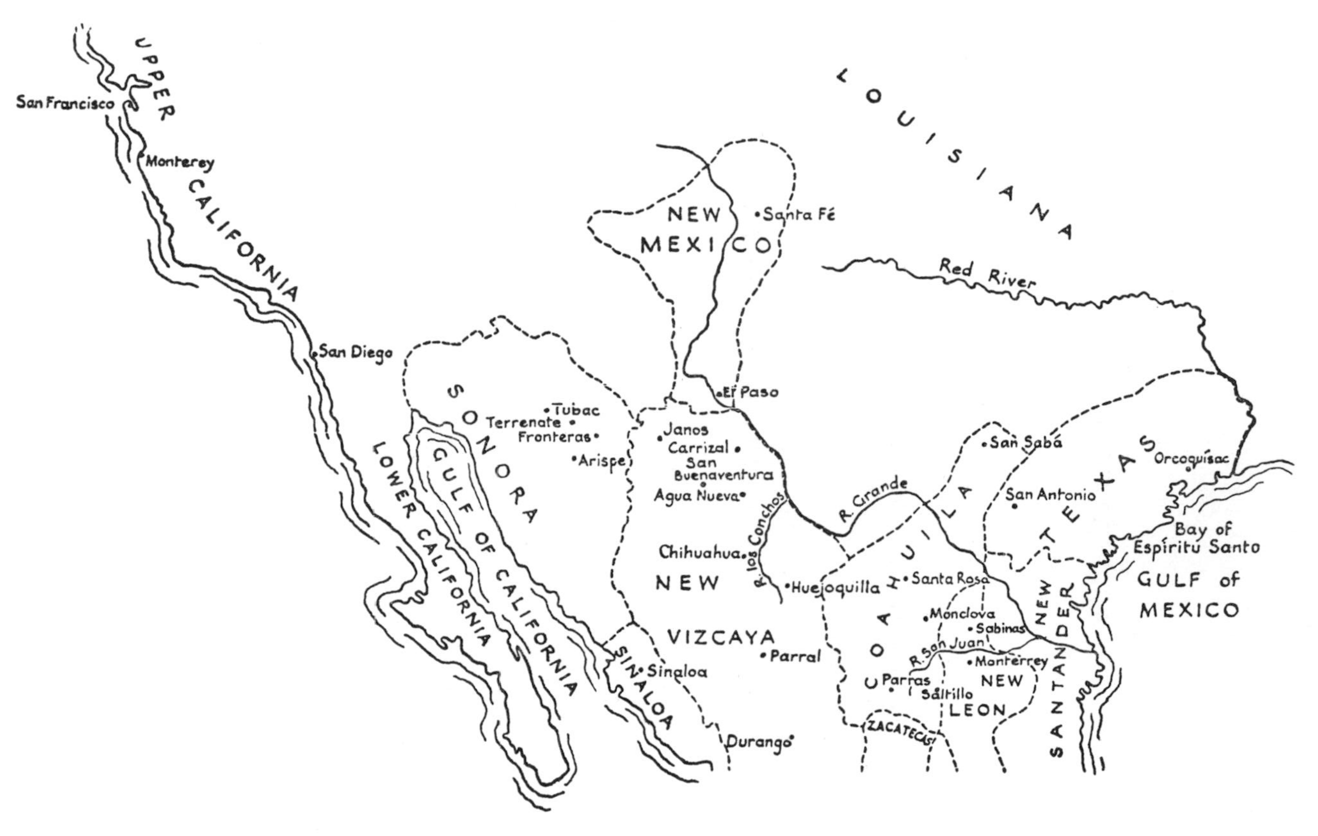

Internal Provinces of New Spain

MIGUEL LA GRUA TALAMANCA

Y BRANCIFORTE, de los Príncipes de Carini, Marqués de Branciforte, Grande de España de primera clase, Caballero de la Insigne Orden del Toyson de Oro, Gran Cruz de la Real y Distinguida de Cárlos Tercero, Comendador de Bienvenida en la de Santiago, y de Torres y Canena en la de Calatrava, Caballero de la de San Juan, Gentil Hombre de Cámara de S. M. con exercicio, Consejero del Supremo Consejo de Guerra de continua asistencia, Capitan de la Real Compañia Italiana de Guardias de Corps, Teniente general de los Reales Exércitos, Virrey, Gobernador y Capitan general de N. E. Presidente de su Real Audiencia, Superintendente general Subdelegado de Real Hacienda, Minas, Azogues y Ramo del Tabaco, Juez Conservador de éste, Presidente de su Real Junta, y Subdelegado general de Correos en el mismo Reyno.

SIENDO el principal objeto de las piadosas Soberanas intenciones de nuestro Católico Monarca (que Dios guarde) la felicidad de sus amados Vasallos, se ha dignado S. M. en Real Orden que me comunicó el Exmô. Señor Don Diego de Gardoqui, con fecha de 12 de Octubre último, libertar á la Provincia del Nuevo México, una de las Internas de este Reyno, del pago del derecho de Alcabala de sus frutos y producciones por el tiempo de diez años contados desde aquella fecha; y á fin de que llegue á noticia de todos los habitantes de estos Dominios la expresada Real benigna disposicion, mando se publique por Bando en esta Capital y demás Ciudades, Villas y Lugares de la comprehension del Virreynato, remitiéndose exemplares al Señor Comandante general de Provincias Internas para el mismo efecto en los respectivos de su mando. Dado en México á 31 de Agosto de 1796.

Æl Marqués de Branciforte.

Por mandado de S. Exâ.

Viceregal proclamation of a royal decree exempting the Province of New Mexico from the *alcabala,* or sales tax, for a period of ten years. Issued in Mexico City, August 31, 1796, and endorsed by Commandant General Nava on September 24 of that year. Spanish Archives of New Mexico, Orders and Decrees, vol. I, p. 99.

REGLAMENTO

E INSTRUCCION

PARA LOS PRESIDIOS

QUE SE HAN DE FORMAR

EN LA LINEA DE FRONTERA

DE LA NUEVA ESPAÑA.

RESUELTO POR EL REY N. S.

en Cédula de 10 de Septiembre de

1772.

Title page of the original *Reglamento e Instrucción para los Presidios,* from a copy in the Spanish Archives of New Mexico.

A leather-jacketed presidial soldier of the late colonial period. Photograph courtesy of the Archivo General de Indias, Sevilla.

831.

Acompaño a Vm. la adjunta Copia
de dictamen que ha expuesto el Asesor
de la comandancia General, y con que
me he conformado por decreto de este
dia, para que en su consecuencia pro
ceda Vm. a hacer la reforma, y
minoracion de Misiones que propu
so en su oficio de 6 de Mayo n.o 232,
y a formar el Plan circunstancia
do que indica el referido dictamen,
dandome cuenta de los resultas.

Dios gue. a Vm. m.a a.
Arispe 15 de Sept.e de 1781.

El Cav.ro De Croix

Sr. D. Juan Bap.ta
de Anza

Letter of the Commandant General, The Caballero de Croix, to Governor Juan Baptista de Anza, written at Arizpe, Sonora, on September 15, 1781, regarding the reduction of the number of missions in New Mexico. Spanish Archives of New Mexico, doc. 831.

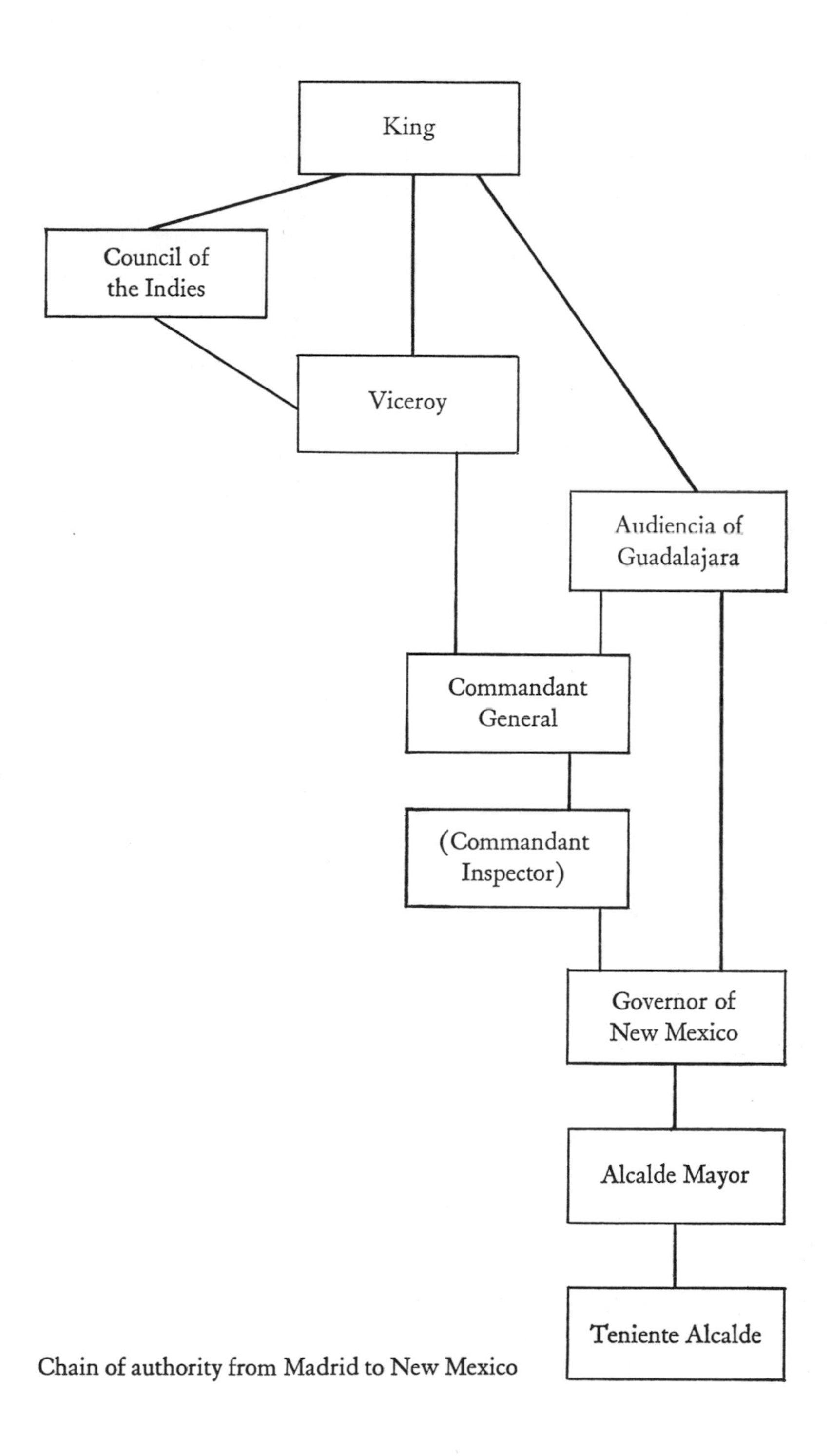

Chain of authority from Madrid to New Mexico

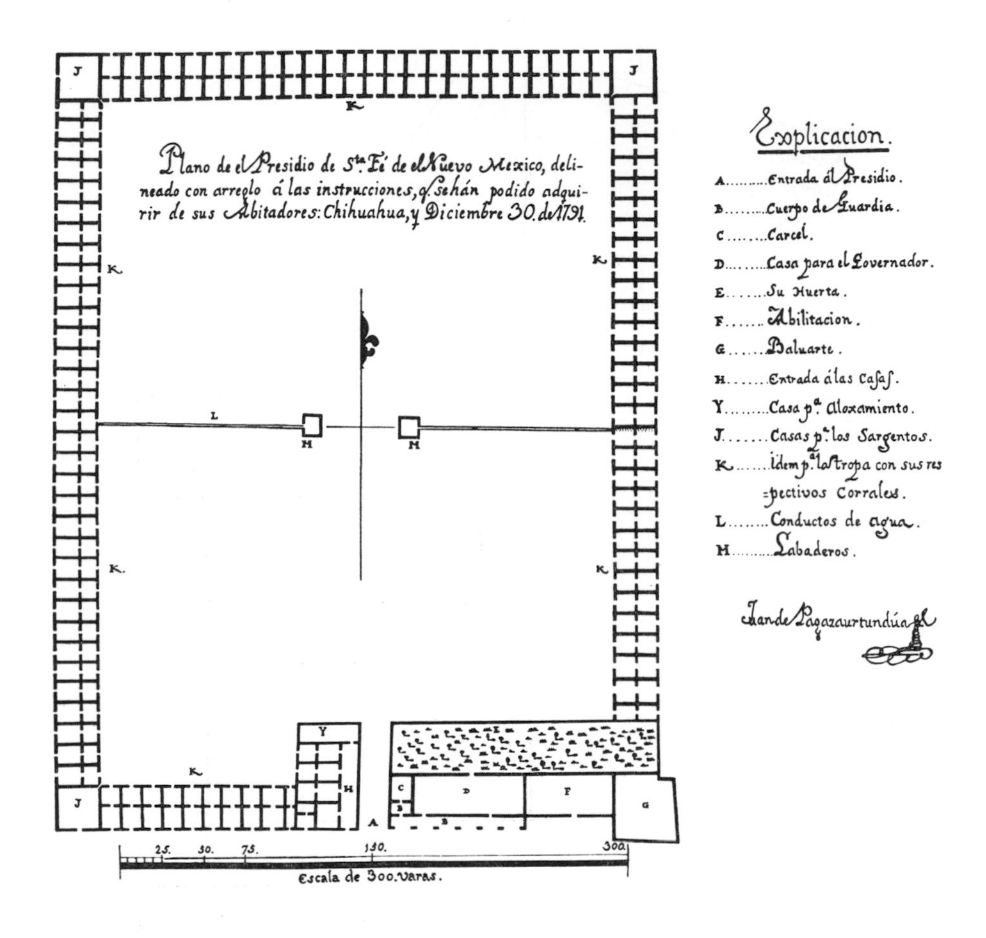

PLAN OF THE PRESIDIO OF SANTA FE, 1791

Legend: A, Entrance to the Presidio; B, Guard room; C, Jail; D, Governor's residence; E, Garden; F, Supplymaster's office; G, Bastion; H, Entrance to the residences; I, House for quartering troops; J, Sergeant's quarters; K, Troop quarters with their respective corrals; L, Water channels; M, Lavatories; Juan de Pagazaurtundúa

[Prepared for photographic reproduction by Jack Mills, Museum of New Mexico, from a copy in the Archivo General de la Nación, Mexico, Provincias Internas, 161.]

PART ONE

Chapter I

ORIGINS OF REFORM

Political organization in northern New Spain during the eighteenth century was closely linked to frontier defense, military organization, and boundary expansion. Indians assailed the European settlements with impunity since the few soldiers in the feeble presidial garrisons were incapable of striking retaliatory blows. To Spain's Indian troubles were added threats of encroachment upon her borders by European rivals France, Great Britain, and Russia. The Louisiana cession of 1762 effectively removed the French manace, but this was largely offset by the new confrontation with the more aggressive English along the Mississippi River.

Spain's humiliating defeat by England in the Seven Years' War prompted a bit of introspection, especially with regard to economic and defense policies at home and in the colonies. The vigorous Charles III, looking abroad and viewing the unsettled state of the northern borderlands, embarked upon a program of reorganizing and strengthening the old military frontier while expanding his settled dominions through the occupation of Louisiana and Alta California. In the new scheme to revitalize the old northern provinces, the matter of military reform assumed major importance.

Don Pedro de Rivera had made a detailed report of the northern outposts of New Spain in the years 1728 to 1730, but since that time no comprehensive inspection had been ordered by the government.[1]

1. The results of the Rivera inspection are embodied in his report: Vito Alesio Robles, ed., *Diario y derrotero de lo caminado, visto y observado en la visita que hizo a los presidios de la Nueva España septentrional el Brigadier Pedro de Rivera* (Mexico, 1946). His findings resulted in the formation of the first Regulation of Presidios which prevailed until the Reglamento of 1772. On Rivera see also, Ted J. Warner, "The Career of Don Felix Martínez de Torrelaguna" (unpublished Ph.D. dissertation, University of New Mexico, 1963), chap. VII, and Navarro García, *José de Gálvez,* pp. 74-78.

The result was an inevitable decrease in efficiency and an increase in corruption on the part of presidial commanders who were in the habit of charging exorbitant prices for commodities sold to their troops. In 1763 a hard look at reality showed northern New Spain to be defended by a handful of ragged and ill-equipped presidial soldiers whose few successes in encounters with Indians had invariably proved ephemeral.

The need for a new and general inspection of presidios had been recognized for some time, but it was not until August, 1765, that the king issued orders for an investigation to be conducted by the Marqués de Rubí. He was commissioned "to report on the status of each presidio, its location, condition of its garrison, the price of commodities . . . , and to make suitable recommendations."[2] Arriving in Mexico early in 1766, Rubí conferred with the Viceroy, then left the capital to begin his review of government affairs from Texas to California. The set of formal instructions he carried included particular provisions for New Mexico. The administration of Governor Tomás Vélez Cachupín was to be investigated with special reference to his Indian policies, and information was to be assembled on the condition of the garrisons at El Paso and Santa Fe.

On July 14, Rubí and his party reached Carrizal, the southernmost outpost of the jurisdiction of New Mexico, having traveled by way of Zacatecas, Durango, and Chihuahua. Here was stationed a detachment from the El Paso presidio consisting of an officer and ten men whose duty was to afford protection to the small settlement and to travelers along the Chihuahua road. Moving north the inspector reached the Rio Grande at El Paso and ascended its valley to Albuquerque and Santa Fe. In the capital he surveyed the town and its garrison of eighty men,[3] then retraced his route to Carrizal to continue his task in the remaining provinces.

The activities of the Marqués de Rubí were to have far-reaching

2. Carlos E. Castañeda, *Our Catholic Heritage in Texas* (7 vols.; Austin, 1936-1958), IV, 223.

3. Before the inspection of Rivera in 1726, the Santa Fe troop had numbered one hundred men, but upon his recommendation, it was reduced to eighty. Frank D. Reeve, *History of New Mexico* (3 vols.; New York, 1961), I, 384.

consequences for the future development of the northern frontier. Highly critical of existing conditions, he singled out the presidial commanders, accusing them of contributing to the misery of the soldiers by cheating on supplies and illegally employing the men for duty as escorts for merchants of the Chihuahua trade. The twenty-four presidios were scattered haphazardly across the landscape with no thought given to a co-ordinated defense program utilizing mutual support. Morale among the soldiers was low, owing to the injustices committed by their commanders, and because there were no regulations governing the term of enlistment or providing pensions and rewards.

Among recommendations looking toward stabilization of the frontier, Rubí proposed reduction of the northern outposts to fifteen, along a line drawn from the coast of the Gulf of California to the mouth of the Guadalupe River in Texas, following the thirtieth parallel.[4] An exception had to be made in the case of New Mexico which jutted far to the north. The Santa Fe presidio was to remain, and the founding of a new garrison was recommended for Robledo, a point twenty leagues north of El Paso. Urged also was the removal southward to the vicinity of Carrizal of the El Paso presidio, Rubí believing that the five thousand inhabitants at this point on the Rio Grande were capable of defending themselves. Further, he suggested a tightening of Indian policy which would necessitate exercising a skeptical attitude whenever the savages made peaceful overtures. A new *Reglamento é instrucción para los presidios,* proclaimed in a royal *cédula* of September 10, 1772, was an outgrowth of these enlightened proposals conceived by the Marqués.[5]

4. Castañeda, *Our Catholic Heritage in Texas,* IV, 244.

5. The full title was *Reglamento é instrucción para los presidios que se han de formar en la linea de frontera de la Nueva España.* The copy consulted by the writer was printed in Mexico in 1834 and is in the Bancroft Library. For complete bibliographical data, consult H. R. Wagner, *The Spanish Southwest,* 1542-1794 (2 vols.; Albuquerque, 1937), II, 467-70. While this paper was in progress, a copy of the original appeared and was placed on loan to the State Archives by Mr. and Mrs. Ted Otero of Santa Fe. According to Wagner, only four other copies of the original 1772 printing are known to exist in the United States. Two translations of the document have recently been made and published. John Galvin, ed., *The Coming of Justice to California: Three Documents* (San Francisco, 1963), pp. 2-47, and Sidney B. Brinckerhoff and Odie B. Faulk, *Lancers for the King* (Phoenix, 1965).

At the same time that Rubí was inspecting the military organization of the frontier provinces, the king dispatched the Visitor General José de Gálvez to New Spain with authority to implement sweeping reforms in administrative and financial affairs of the viceroyalty. Although the missions of these two men were essentially independent, each performing his particular function within the general framework of the reform program, it is clear that Gálvez carried secret instructions to inform himself of military matters, and this he proceeded to do in his capacity as Intendant of the Army (*Intendente del Exército*).[6] The all-embracing problem of the Apache barrier was indeed of such magnitude that the crown was contemplating a drastic overhaul of the administrative as well as military structure of the entire northern periphery. The powers of so exalted an official as the visitor general necessarily extended to some consideration of this latter question.

In the course of his investigation, Gálvez formulated the details for two great administrative reforms. One was the establishment of the *comandancia general,* or frontier military district, and the other was the organization of the intendancy system. The plan for the latter was approved by the king in August, 1769, with the proviso that it would be well to allow sufficient time for the choice of suitable men in whom to entrust the new administrative positions. Sufficient obstacles arose to delay actual establishment until 1786. The case of the commandancy general is somewhat different, for by late 1776, the motions were under way to put this measure into operation. And it is this phase of Bourbon reform that bears most heavily on the subsequent history of New Mexico.

A preliminary step was the appointment of a commandant inspector to direct and co-ordinate military affairs.[7] He held the rank of colonel at least, he was a direct subordinate of the viceroy, and when the king should see fit to appoint a commandant general for

6. María del Carmen Velázquez, *El Estado de guerra en Nueva España,* 1760-1808 (Mexico, 1950), p. 85.

7. The title of commandant inspector actually was in use in the northern provinces prior to 1772.

the internal provinces as recommended by Gálvez, the inspector was to come under his authority. This officer was to establish his residence at whatever place seemed most convenient for carrying out his responsibilities. He was prohibited from holding a governorship or the captaincy of a presidio within his jurisdiction (the *comandancia inspección*), since this might interfere with his other obligations. To aid him, two assistant, or adjutant inspectors (*ayudantes inspectores*) were designated, each with the rank of at least captain and an annual salary of three thousand pesos. The commandant inspector received eight thousand pesos yearly. The duties of the inspector were broad in scope, enabling him to exercise direct and forceful supervision in all military and related matters. He was enjoined to implement the specific articles of the Reglamento which looked to amelioration of conditions within the presidios of his jurisdiction. His authority extended over instruction and discipline of troops, and over financial expenditures, including supply and maintenance of garrisons and pay of soldiers.

Presidios were to be visited annually by either the commandant inspector or by one of his two adjutants. Special inquiry was to be made into the conduct and affairs of presidial officers, especially the commandant of the garrison, and any irregularities were to be reported to the viceroy. This regularization of inspections was intended to mitigate the abuses that the Marqués de Rubí had found prevalent among these officials.

In his capacity as commandant of all presidios, the inspector was empowered to determine the number, objective, and time of patrols and to plot the routes of detachments that were to operate in the spaces between garrisons. When some beleaguered outpost called for aid, or when it became necessary to take the field and attack the Indians in their rancherías, he was to unite the detachments into one or more divisions and outline the strategy of the campaign. In addition, he was authorized to suspend hostilities against the enemy if they sought a truce, and to begin preliminary peace negotiations. On such occasions, he was to make clear to the chiefs that arrangements must receive the confirmation and approval of the viceroy.

Prisoners were to be treated kindly, and any officers, soldiers, or civilians who abused them were to be severely punished.[8]

To put into effect the new regulations, the king appointed Don Hugo O'Conor as Commandant Inspector of Presidios. O'Conor had served as a sergeant major on the Texas frontier, and the energy and ability he displayed in dealing with the Indians had made him a likely candidate for the new office. Antonio Bonilla and Roque de Medina were named adjutant inspectors.

With alacrity O'Conor set about to secure a more efficient military service and to fashion the new cordon of presidios. Viceroy Bucareli ordered the governors of the several northern provinces to furnish the commandant with whatever assistance he might seek.

By 1776 the revised presidial line was established, and the Indians had felt the sting of Spanish resistance. Nevertheless, the fundamental difficulties remained and no final solution to the defensive problem was in sight. Presidial commanders were roaming farther afield with their troops, but this left the settlements near the presidios more exposed. Small war parties continually swept away the horse herds, leaving the garrisons afoot. This problem was so acute in New Mexico that the royal treasury was forced to appropriate money for 1,500 horses to replace those stolen from the citizenry and soldiers.[9] Well-trained officers remained scarce, and the troops, in spite of reinforcements, never reached the number necessary to provide continual and effective policing of the vast region. Although much graft and corruption had been eliminated, allowing supplies to flow more freely, the difficulty of the terrain and the isolation of many of the outposts hindered efficient distribution of vital weapons and ammunition.

8. *Reglamento para los presidios,* título 15. The title of "commandant of presidios" mentioned above antedated that of commandant inspector. The former was created by a royal order of August 7, 1765, and was first extended to the Marqués de Rubí. Brigadier Hugo O'Conor acquired it in 1770, and retained the designation when he became commandant inspector in 1772. Francisco R. Almada, "Los Apaches," *Boletín de la sociedad Chihuahuense de estudios historicos,* II (1939), 7.

9. Viceroy Bucareli to Julían Arriaga, November 26, 1775, in R. Velasco Ceballos, *La administración de D. Frey Antonio María de Bucareli y Ursua* (2 vols.; Mexico, 1936), I, 283.

Chapter II

THE COMMANDANCY GENERAL ESTABLISHED

Militarily speaking, the commandancy general was a direct outcome of the recommendations made by José de Gálvez. Eight years elapsed, however, before Gálvez was in a position of power that permitted him to see personally to the carrying out of his plan. In January of 1776 Julián de Arriaga died, and his place as Minister General of the Indies—the highest office in Spain responsible for overseas affairs—was soon afterward granted to José de Gálvez, now the Marqués de Sonora, who at once set about to erect the commandancy general of New Spain's interior provinces.[1]

Considerable optimism on the part of the Spanish government greeted the creation of the new military department, for it was hoped that this effort would at last bring some measure of peace to the troubled frontier. In such event this colonial problem child could be made secure, and significant economic development could get under way. Spain would be released, at least partially, from the terrible burden of defending the area, and the provinces could assume the responsibility of paying a share of their own expenses.

It might be supposed that the viceroy of New Spain would resent the reduction of his jurisdiction and powers which the new scheme entailed. Thomas, indeed, implies that maladministration of the frontier by Viceroy Bucareli was a prime factor animating the crown in its course of action.[2] If such was the case, the viceroy must have harbored considerable displeasure at the turn of events, for

1. Charles E. Chapman, *A History of California: The Spanish Period* (New York, 1921). p. 319. The term "internal" or "interior" provinces was commonly used from the early eighteenth century to refer to the northern provinces, because they were interior with reference to Mexico City, the capital of New Spain. H. H. Bancroft. *History of the North Mexican States and Texas* (2 vols.; San Francisco, 1884), I, 636.

2. Alfred Barnaby Thomas, *Teodoro de Croix and the Northern Frontier of New Spain*, 1776-1783 (Norman, Okla., 1941), p. 16.

these could only reflect upon his competence and reputation in the eyes of the crown. Bernard E. Bobb, in the absence of documentary evidence, dismisses the supposition that any failure on the part of Bucareli influenced the royal decision to separate the interior provinces.[3] The fact remains, nevertheless, that almost from the onset Bucareli and Teodoro de Croix, the first commandant general, found themselves on unfriendly terms, and more than one viceroy in subsequent years discovered opportunities to criticize the existence of a separate northern jurisdiction.[4]

Organization. The commandant general was the highest royal official in the Provincias Internas. He communicated directly with the king through the Minister of the Indies. He was virtually independent of the Viceroy of New Spain, except that he was required to keep that officer abreast of developments in the North so that the viceroy might offer the proper assistance when the circumstances required.[5] The annual salary of the commandant was set at twenty thousand pesos, a sum deemed sufficient to permit him to maintain himself properly.[6]

The title commandant general indicated that military duties were the uppermost consideration. The commandant inspector and his two adjutants retained the duties delegated to them by the Reglamento of 1772, but these were now performed under immediate supervision of the commandant general. Below the inspectors were the governors of the several provinces who acted as military commanders in their respective districts. With the appointment in 1776 of the commandant general, who was designated simultaneously captain general, the governors lost this latter title, which they had

3. *The Viceregency of Antonio María Bucareli in New Spain,* 1771-1779 (Austin, 1962), p. 146.

4. See, for example, Conde de Rivilla Gigedo II, *Instrucción reservada que dió a su sucesor en el mando, Marqués de Branciforte sobre el gobierno de éste continente en el tiempo que fué su virrey* (Mexico, 1831), art. 720.

5. *Instrucciones a Teodoro de Croix,* AGN, Prov. Int., 241, art. 2; and also printed in Velasco Ceballos, *La Administración de Bucareli,* pp. 332-42. As will be noted shortly, in the matter of finances, the commandancy was subject to the accounting office in Mexico City.

6. *Ibid.,* art. 7.

previously held. The governors usually corresponded directly with the commandant general, their only relations with the inspectors occurring when one or the other of these directed a military campaign or conducted an inspection within their jurisdiction. The more important provinces, New Mexico excluded, often had an official called the *comandante de armas* who served under the governor and relieved him of the more burdensome military matters.

Military. The military forces of the commandancy general included the presidial garrisons, the mobile companies which patroled the more remote areas, a citizens' militia, and special companies of Indian auxiliaries.[7] Over these was the commandant general, who spent much time in the field, particularly in the first years, attending personally to the direction of military matters. For this he had a personal guard of twenty men. Periodically he dispatched to Spain reports and memorials to keep the king and his minister informed of frontier activities and to seek advice on problems of great moment.

Beyond this a host of prosaic duties under the heading of military responsibility fell to the commandant general. Supply and maintenance of troops was a constant worry, and the commandants in the course of time experimented with several methods in an effort to devise an efficient system. Soldiers were paid through the various treasury offices within the internal provinces, but the commandant general was ultimately responsible for disbursement of salaries through the supply masters of the various companies. Further, the commandant was the final arbiter in granting or disallowing pensions to widows, orphans, the disabled, and retired soldiers, and rewards for special or lengthy service. Moreover, he made all military appointments and promotions for lesser offices, usually acting upon recommendation of the governors or presidial commanders. He himself suggested to the king candidates for the more important positions for which the crown reserved right of appointment.

7. *Ibid.*, art. 13. Of the Indian troops, the Opatas were regarded as the bravest and most loyal. A number of them served in campaigns against the Apaches in southwestern New Mexico.

Civil Government. Administrative concerns the commandant general left, as much as possible, in the hands of local officials and his own staff of assistants. In practice this was not always feasible since the structure and character of Spanish government discouraged initiative and independent action on the part of lesser functionaries. The peculiar exigencies of frontier command, however, permitted a wider latitude of movement among officers than in most other areas of the realm.

An especially cumbersome duty for the commandant general was the direction of affairs of the royal treasury, or *real hacienda.* As superintendent general of financial matters, he kept watch over the several treasury offices (*cajas reales*), the most important of which, initially at least, was that of Arizpe, Sonora. In this city the commandant maintained his headquarters. Croix's instructions enjoined him to construct there a royal mint (*casa de moneda*) to remedy the shortage of coin which was injuring commerce.[8] With transfer of the capital of the commandancy to Chihuahua in 1792, Arizpe lost its fiscal pre-eminence. The town continued, however, in possession of the mint, its treasury office, and the *pagaduría,* or head paymaster's office. The commandant general, as a matter of course, came to rely upon the treasury office of Chihuahua and the new mint which was placed in that city.

As superintendent general the commandant regulated the conduct of affairs within the royal treasury and its various *ramos,* or branches. His powers in this regard were defined broadly as supervisory, and actual details of administration were handled by regular agents of the colonial exchequer. There was no separate accountant's office for the Provincias Internas, so all books were audited by the accountant (*contador*) of the tribunal of accounts (*tribunal de cuentas*) in Mexico City. This tribunal, which had been established in New Spain in 1605, was the final court of audit where all the treasury officers (*oficiales reales*) of New Spain received their quittance. The commandant general was required to submit a state-

8. Art. 12.

ment of the financial conditions of his jurisdiction to the king every six months, and to see that all accounts of the various treasury branches were properly and promptly submitted at the end of each year to the tribunal of accounts. With proclamation of the Order of Intendants, in 1786, significant modifications were interposed in this system, but withal, the commandant remained the crown's chief fiscal agent in the northern provinces.

It had been intended that administrative reorganization of the frontier provinces would lead to their financial independence from the Viceroyalty of New Spain. Unfortunately, the recurring Indian problem, which necessitated increasing military expenditures and which hindered economic development, precluded realization of this goal. A treasurer's report prepared at Arizpe in January, 1784, may be taken as fairly typical of the financial situation which prevailed throughout the period. The report indicated that a shortage of 135,130 pesos would have to be remedied so that the treasury of that city could meet its obligations for the coming year. Figures showed a similar deficit existed at the same time for the treasury office of Chihuahua.[9]

The major disbursements of the several treasury offices throughout the commandancy general were for administrative and military expenses and for salaries *(sínodos)* of the missionaries. Chihuahua's treasury office, for example, provided the support for the presidios of Nueva Vizcaya and New Mexico, the salaries for officers and men of the several mobile companies, the salary of the governor at Santa Fe and the lieutenant governor stationed at El Paso, and the salaries of the friars in New Mexico and northern Nueva Vizcaya. Moreover, the responsibility of paying the commandant general and his subordinates soon devolved upon it, as did the duty of supplying the funds for pensions of retired and disabled soldiers, and of widows and orphans.[10] Other expenses included support, after 1791, of the

9. AGN, Prov. Int., 78.

10. Report of the Treasury Office of Chihuahua, October 10, 1788, AGN, Prov. Int., 46. Before creation of treasury offices in the northern provinces, New Mexico had been dependent upon the Caja de Guadalajara. Navarro García, *José de Gálvez,* p. 64.

Hospital Real Militar in Chihuahua, administrative costs of the treasury itself, and various extraordinary expenses.

The sources of revenue which supplied the royal treasury with funds were numerous, the people of New Spain paying some forty-odd varieties of taxes. Many of them were not collected in the frontier provinces because of the poverty of the region. Even so, as Priestley points out,

> the intervention of the royal treasury in every phase of life of the individual was incessant. It made the old colonial régime so odious that law breaking became the usual practice. . . . The burden was not that taxes were unbearably high . . . but that they were so multifarious and so visible.[11]

Many of the special taxes were administered by the treasury proper. Others formed separate branches or ramos within the royal treasury, with their own sets of officials who were responsible for collection of a particular revenue. Prior to the inspection of Gálvez, the tendency had been to farm out tax collection to individuals or to the governments of leading cities who then took it upon themselves to assemble the revenues for a share of the proceeds. After 1768 the job was largely taken over by regular treasury officers, and direct government administration continued to the end of the colonial period.

A major source of wealth for the treasury offices of the internal provinces were the various duties attached to the mining and working of precious metals. Levying of these taxes was normally in the hands of an assayer (*ensayador*).

Indian tribute, which elsewhere in New Spain produced considerable income for the king, was practically nonexistent on the frontier. Humboldt commented at the beginning of the nineteenth century that in the provinces of Nueva Vizcaya and New Mexico, not a single tributary individual could be found.[12]

The *alcabala* or sales tax was levied on most articles at both first

11. *The Coming of the White Man* (New York, 1929), p. 190.

12. Alexander von Humboldt, *Ensayo político sobre el reino de la Nueva España* (4 vols.; Mexico, 1941-1947), II, 321.

and later sales. Invariably freedom for a term of years from the alcabala was included among the privileges conceded to newly established colonies or to those which maintained a precarious existence. Among items exempted from this tax were bread, coin, books, horses, and weapons.[13] In spite of this, the measure bore heaviest upon the citizenry, and was the most detested of all taxes. The rate of the alcabala varied from two to fourteen per cent on goods sold or exchanged, but in the troubled northern provinces of New Spain it remained fixed at two per cent.[14]

The crown reserved for itself control of a number of industries as monopolies through which it realized a handsome profit. The most lucrative of these in the Provincias Internas were the monopolies of tobacco, salt, gunpowder, quicksilver, playing cards, and stamped paper.[15]

The tobacco monopoly, established by the Visitador José de Gálvez, involved closing out all private interest in the manufacture, sale, and production of this commodity except in certain favored districts where the government bought the entire crop. Sale of tobacco emerged as one of the richest sources of public income in America and produced, between 1765 and 1809, 120 million pesos' revenue.[16] The regard with which this branch of the treasury was viewed is perhaps indicated by the fact that among the many titles of the commandant general, that of Superintendent of the Office of Tobacco was given a prominent place. Monopolies of lesser commodities were maintained by the crown in the more important northern provinces, but not in such places as New Mexico.

Other sources which provided treasury receipts of some significance were the *cruzada* (sale of indulgences) and the tithes, both ecclesiatsical revenues. The bulk of this income always went for re-

13. C. H. Haring, *The Spanish Empire in America* (New York, 1947), pp. 287-89.

14. Juan N. Rodríguez de San Miguel, *Pandectas Hispano-Megicanas* (2 vols.; Mexico, 1852), II, 192.

15. Treasurer's Report, Durango, November 19, 1794, AGN, Prov. Int., 12.

16. Herbert Ingram Priestley, *José de Gálvez, Visitor-General of New Spain,* 1771-1779 (Berkeley, 1916), pp. 142-55.

ligious purposes, so that the royal treasury was not appreciably benefited.[17]

Another method employed for extracting money for the treasury was the *media anata,* or payment representing usually half of the first year's salary of newly appointed officials. By a special decree in 1791, the commandant general was exempted from paying this tax.[18]

As implied by the deficits in the Arizpe and Chihuahua treasury offices referred to above, the revenues, as a rule, were insufficient to meet the financial obligations of the commandancy general, hence the internal provinces continued their dependence upon the viceroyalty. The treasury office of Guanajuato, made rich by the mines in its area, supplied funds for a number of years to the offices in Durango, Chihuahua, and Arizpe. Before 1793 this amounted to 240,000 pesos annually to Chihuahua alone.[19] As late as 1814, the viceroy ordered the intendant of San Luis Potosí to permit the treasury officials in the Provincias Internas to make withdrawals against the office of his district whenever the need arose and funds on hand would permit.[20] The large sums were transported northward by mule trains every three, four, or six months, under heavy military escort.

A set of treasury officials administered the affairs of each office. Chihuahua possessed a director of the treasury who accepted an annual salary of two thousand pesos. He was assisted by a senior and a junior officer (*oficial mayor* and *oficial segundo*) and by an officer of the mint.[21] After introduction of the intendancy system in 1786, a treasury minister subordinate to the intendant of Durango was placed at Chihuahua.[22]

17. Haring, *The Spanish Empire in America,* p. 285.

18. AGN, Prov. Int., 157. Although other sources of revenue may be noted in the Provincias Internas, only those which had special significance, as indicated by the treasury reports, have been cited here.

19. Pedro de Nava to Viceroy Revilla Gigedo II, Chihuahua, November 7, 1793, AGN, Prov. Int., 12.

20. Manuel de Acevedo to Viceroy Calleja, San Luis Potosí, May 23, 1814, AGN, Prov. Int., 129.

21. Report of the Treasury Office of Chihuahua, 1788.

22. Priestley, *José de Gálvez,* p. 295.

Judiciary. Superior justice in the Provincias Internas was in the hands of the Audiencia of Guadalajara. This court of law possessed jurisdiction in most of western and northern New Spain. As its principal duty, it heard and decided appeals from inferior judges and tribunals within this area. When plans were being formulated in 1760 for the erection of a separate viceroyalty, it was proposed that the new government be composed of the provinces within the jurisdiction of the Audiencia of Guadalajara. For practical and economic reasons, the idea of a military department which contained only the northern periphery prevailed. Notwithstanding, the commandancy after 1776 continued to be thought of as a preliminary step in establishing a viceroyalty which would include the audiencia. The idea was not abandoned until the introduction of the intendancies ten years later.

The Audiencia of Guadalajara, with so many provinces under its jurisdiction, encountered considerable difficulty in fulfilling its obligations. It was suggested by Viceroy Marqués de Croix (uncle of Teodore de Croix) and by Gálvez himself in 1767 that either a separate chamber to hear criminal cases or two more judges be added to the audiencia.

For a brief period before the commandancy was inaugurated, Gálvez appears to have assumed that an entirely new audiencia would be created within its boundaries.[23] Although this failed to materialize in 1776, other prominent individuals urged in subsequent years that this measure be undertaken, both to relieve the court in Guadalajara and to expedite judicial proceedings in the northern provinces. Felipe de Neve, who became commandant general in 1783, and his successor, Jacobo Ugarte y Loyola, strongly urged the creation of a separate audiencia. Ugarte frequently mentioned this pressing need and submitted to the crown on one occasion a plan for establishing a brandy monopoly, which could provide the sums needed for operating expenses of the proposed court.[24] That

23. (José de Gálvez), *Informe general que entregó el Señor Marqués de Sonora al Virrey D. Antonio Bucareli y Ursua,* December 31, 1771 (Mexico, 1867), p. 11.

24. Brief on the State of the Provincias Internas, Ugarte y Loyola to Viceroy Flores, Arizpe, December 10, 1787, AGN, Prov. Int., 253.

the urgings of these and other officers had no effect is evidenced by the fact that New Mexico's representative to the Spanish Cortes in 1812, Pedro Bautista Pino, in the report on conditions in his province, was compelled to continue the old argument for placing an audiencia in Chihuahua.[25]

Below the Audiencia of Guadalajara the machinery of justice was subdivided to an extraordinary degree. Broadly speaking, two channels of judicial procedure lay open: one, the *justicia ordinaria,* or the regularly established courts; and the other, the *justicia privilegiada,* or special courts operating under their own *fueros.* At the head of the former stood the Audiencia of Guadalajara with final jurisdiction in all criminal cases and in all but the most important civil suits which could be reappealed to Spain. Below this court were the various inferior magistrates as the governors and alcaldes, and after 1786 the intendants and their *subdelegados.* In minor cases the alcaldes acted as judges of first instance (*jueces de primera instancia*) and the governors as judges of second instance (*jueces de segunda instancia*). Theoretically appeal was possible, thereafter, to the audiencia, but in practice, it seldom occurred. In important cases the alcalde referred matters directly to the governor who served as judge of first instance, and who was required to permit appeals to the audiencia which served as the court of second and usual final instance.[26] When the intendants were named to office, they assumed the administration of justice in the first instance for important cases since they replaced the governors in Sonora, Nueva Vizcaya, and elsewhere. In the few areas which remained outside the mainstream of the intendancy system, as New Mexico, the governors and alcaldes continued to function as before.

The workings of the various fueros, or privileged courts, were extremely complex, and there existed frequent conflict of jurisdiction

25. Pedro Bautista Pino, *Exposición sucinta y sencilla de la provincia del Nuevo México* (Cádiz, 1812), p. 28 [reproduced in H. Bailey Carroll and J. Villasana Haggard, trs., *Three New Mexico Chronicles* (Albuquerque, 1942), pp. 211-261].

26. Croix to Anza, February 21, 1782, Spanish Archives of New Mexico, Santa Fe, document 837. These numbers follow those of Ralph Emerson Twitchell, *The Spanish Archives of New Mexico* (2 vols.; Cedar Rapids, Iowa, 1914), Vol. II.

with the ordinary tribunals. The most important fueros were those belonging to the military, the Church, and the royal treasury. In addition, certain occupations possessed the fuero in civil suits pertaining to their sphere of administration, or to which their officials or employees were a party. Among these were the merchants', miners', and grazers' guilds, and the medical profession.[27] Only the *fuero militar* and the *fuero eclesiástico* ultimately had any significant bearing on events in New Mexico, hence description here will be confined to these two.

The military fuero granted persons who came within its jurisdiction—the regular troops and, with certain limitations, the militia—the privilege of recourse to their own courts. This prerogative often extended to both civil suits and criminal actions. Only after 1763 did the military magistracy constitute a significant part of the legal structure of New Spain, for prior to that time, regular troops were few in number and the militia was in an early stage of development.[28] Rapidly, thereafter, the fuero assumed such magnitude that the astute Viceroy Revilla Gigedo II was led boldly to express his dissatisfaction and warn of its dangers.[29]

The commandant general of the interior provinces constituted the court of first instance for most cases arising under the fuero in the northern district and involving the regular troops. In actual practice such cases were adjudicated by the *auditor de guerra,* owing to his superior knowledge of judicial affairs. For the provincial militia the court of primary jurisdiction was formed by the commander of the local unit.[30] This officer was to have a legal assistant to advise him in the manner of the auditor de guerra, but on the remote frontier, such a lawyer was seldom available.[31] Appeals by militiamen were taken to the commandant general via the governor who might append his *dictamen,* or opinion.

27. Haring, *The Spanish Empire in America,* p. 133.

28. Lyle N. McAlister, *The "Fuero Militar" in New Spain, 1764-1800* (Gainesville, Fla., 1957), pp. 7-10.

29. *Instrucción reservada,* arts. 92, 117.

30. McAlister, *The "Fuero Militar,"* p. 9

31. The nature of the office of the *auditor* will be described below.

The Catholic clergy had a special legal institution of its own under the canonical law with church tribunals and class privileges. As Revilla Gigedo II observed, the ecclesiastical fuero was at one time the most extensive in New Spain.[32] Toward the end of the colonial period, however, it was limited by the establishment of competency of crown courts in all cases under criminal law, and with the declaration that cognizance of those cases involving pious funds and foundations for support of clergymen should be taken into the secular courts.[33] Apart from the fuero, the Holy Office of the Inquisition possessed judicial authority through New Spain in matters of faith and morals.

Finally, in the administration of justice, another court of general jurisdiction whose authority included the internal provinces should be mentioned. This was the *acordada,* at once a rural police force and a tribunal whose purpose was to deal with cases of highway robbery in outlying districts.[34] Audiencias were often far removed from these sources of trouble, so to combat banditry promptly and effectively, the acordada was brought forth as an independent sphere of criminal jurisdiction.

Patronage. The *patronato real,* or royal patronage, was vested in the commandant general by the instructions of 1776. This privilege consisted of the rights which the sovereigns of Spain possessed over the Church in America and which derived from papal grants of the early sixteenth century. The concession of the tithes and the right to nominate all ecclesiastical officials had been obtained by the crown so that, in a very real sense, the Church became another branch of the royal government.

The commandant general, as vice-patron, was empowered to nominate persons for vacant curacies and benefices, and these were to be approved by the respective diocesan prelates, or in their absence, by the cathedral chapters (*cabildos*). Moreover, he was con-

32. *Instrucción reservada,* art. 94.

33. Priestley, *José de Gálvez,* p. 65.

34. Francisco Banegas Galván, *Historia de México* (3 vols.; Mexico, 1938-1940), I, 33-34.

ceded premission to delegate this function to provincial governors so that ecclesiastical affairs might be expedited. His authority in these matters was to extend over both the secular and regular clergy.[35]

Actual administration of Church affairs, particularly on purely religious matters, lay with the bishops and other religious officers in the Provincias Internas. The jurisdiction of the Bishop of Durango extended to all of Nueva Vizcaya and New Mexico. In the latter province, continued hopes for the founding of a bishopric at Santa Fe were not realized until 1853, although, like the erection of an audiencia at Chihuahua, it was proposed on several occasions.[36]

Administrative Assistants of the Commandant General. To support the commandant general in performing military tasks, a corps of officers from the commandant inspector to the local presidial commanders existed, as has been described. In the sphere of civil government, the commandant enjoyed the services of a small staff of administrative officials who acted as advisers and who relieved him of many petty and burdensome chores. The most important of these were the *asesor general* and the secretary of the commandancy, both of whom received their appointments directly from the king.

The assessor was a man trained in law (a *letrado*) who acted as the legal adviser of the commandant general. Strictly speaking, an assessor handled matters relating to civil and criminal cases, and a separate functionary, the auditor de guerra, had jurisdiction over military cases.[37] Both offices, however, were often combined in a single person within the internal provinces. Pedro Galindo Navarro was designated by the king as the first assessor and auditor de guerra to assist Teodore de Croix.[38] His salary was set at three thousand pesos yearly.[39]

35. Instrucciónes a Teodoro de Croix, art. 4; also Irving Berdine Richman, *California under Spain and Mexico, 1535-1847* (Boston, 1911), p. 432.

36. AGI, Guadalajara, leg. 561.

37. For a discussion of the distinct nature of these two officials, see Manuel Josef de Ayala, *Diccionario de gobierno y legislación de Indias* (2 vols.; Madrid, 1929), I, 350.

38. Bancroft, *North Mexican States,* I, 638-42. Navarro served until 1790 when he was transferred to the *asesoría general* of Mexico.

39. Report of the Treasury Office of Chihuahua, 1788.

While the assessor acted chiefly in an advisory capacity, he seems to have served as something of a judge in civil and criminal cases arising within his immediate district. When the commandant general received the proceedings in a case from a subordinate jurisdiction, as New Mexico, these were customarily submitted to the assessor for an opinion before being passed on to the Audiencia at Guadalajara. With cases involving the military fuero in which the commandant had final jurisdiction, he relied heavily upon the advice of the assessor acting in his capacity as auditor de guerra. In areas of the commandancy which lacked an assessor, or someone versed in legal matters to advise the provincial authorities, recourse was had to the assessor general, who freely gave assistance through formal opinions. In 1805, for example, the assessor sumitted to the governor in Santa Fe an opinion prescribing proper legal procedure for judicial matters in New Mexico.[40]

Working closely with the commandant general was his secretary, with the title of *secretario de cámara y gobierno,* who was employed in writing the letters, dispatches, and periodical reports relating to government business and in preparing and certifying the official records. Captain Antonio Bonilla, former adjutant inspector of presidios under O'Conor, was the first appointee to hold this office in the new administration. He continued with the same salary of three thousand pesos, which he drew in conformity with the Reglamento.[41] Bonilla's experience in frontier affairs added to his competence and usefulness to the commandant, and, among other achievements, he was credited with organizing the archives of the commandancy general in Sevilla.[42]

Several other assistants of lesser stature were attached to the commandancy, but their titles and functions, as well as salaries, were altered from time to time. Originally two notaries had been named

40. Trial of Three Indians and a Genízaro for Sedition, SANM, doc. 1931.

41. Instrucciónes a Teodoro de Croix, art. 10; and Viceroy to Real Audiencia de Guadalajara, Mexico, February 24, 1777, AGN, Prov. Int., 74.

42. Alfred Barnaby Thomas, "Antonio de Bonilla and Spanish Plans for the Defense of New Mexico, 1772-1778," In *New Spain and the Anglo-American West* (2 vols.; Lancaster, Pa., 1932), I, 190.

to the staff, but in 1788, there was only one.[43] By this date also appeared three officers known as the *oficial mayor,* the *oficial segundo,* and the *oficial tercero.* The first enjoyed an annual salary of one thousand pesos, the latter two hundred pesos. The exact nature of their duties is unknown. A report of 1795 observed that the skeleton staff of the commandant general could not fulfill the many clerical tasks assigned to it with the result that the commandant himself was called upon to assist, his attention thereby being diverted from more urgent matters.[44]

The Capital of the Provincias Internas. An early plan for the commandancy general proposed Durango as the site for the capital. This location José de Gálvez judged to be too far from the Indian frontier and from the new settlements in California which were his primary concern. As a consequence, the capital came to be at Arizpe, Sonora, because that post lay midway between Nueva Vizcaya and the Californias, though far to the west of the geographical center of the new commandancy.[45] The designation of Arizpe as provisional headquarters was embodied in the original instructions to Teodoro de Croix and was confirmed by a royal order dated February 12, 1782. Nevertheless, some writers have mistakenly assumed that this officer had no fixed residence in the first years but traveled around from place to place.[46] The itinerant nature of his military duties perhaps created this erroneous impression. A cédula of 1782 raised the town of Arizpe to the status of a *ciudad* and announced that a new bishopric for Sonora would be located there.[47]

In subsequent years the commandants general became dissatisfied with their location at Arizpe and petitioned the crown for a change.[48]

43. Instrucciónes a Teodoro de Croix, art. 10; and Report of the Treasury Office of Chihuahua, 1788.

44. Report on Conditions in the Provincias Internas, Governor Fernando de la Concha to the Viceroy Marqués de Branciforte, Mexico, January 20, 1795, AGN, Prov. Int., 15.

45. Chapman, *History of California,* p. 319. Caborca mission also was briefly considered for the site of the capital. Richman, *California under Spain and Mexico,* p. 122.

46. Mathew G. Reynolds, *Spanish and Mexican Land Laws, New Spain and Mexico* (St. Louis, 1895), p. 28.

47. Bando of Teodoro de Croix, June 15, 1783, SANM, doc. 864.

48. Brief on the State of the Provincias Internas, 1787.

The reasons for this attitude are not altogether clear, but in part it must reflect the fact that the Indian problem, centered in Nueva Vizcaya and New Mexico, assumed greater relative importance than the threat of European interlopers in California. Arizpe may have been considered somewhat removed from the main field of activity. In 1787 the commandant general suggested that the capital be transferred to Ures, a point south of Arizpe. In the same year, however, the viceroy sent instructions from the king to the effect that the commandant was to have no fixed residence but was to move about visiting towns and outposts where his services were most needed.[49]

In spite of this provision, Commandant General Ugarte y Loyola informed the governor of New Mexico in 1788 that the state of affairs in Nueva Vizcaya was forcing him to establish his residence in the Villa of Chihuahua.[50] This town, thereafter, served more as a base of operations, the commandant actually passing most of his time in the field. A royal order of 1792 returned officially to the idea of a permanent capital, designating in this case the Villa of Chihuahua, a declaration which legalized a *fait accompli*.[51] For seven years after 1813, the capital existed at Durango, but in the year before independence, it was returned to Chihuahua.

49. Decree of Flores, Mexico, December 3, 1787, AGN, Prov. Int., 160.

50. Ugarte to the Governor of New Mexico, Arizpe, January 23, 1788, SANM, doc. 995.

51. *Real Orden,* November 23, 1792, AGN, Prov. Int., 241.

Chapter III

THE PROVINCIAS INTERNAS, FIRST PHASE

On May 16, 1776, Charles III appointed Teodoro de Croix, nephew of the former viceroy, the Marqués de Croix, as the first commandant general of the Provinces Internas. The provinces of Coahuila, Texas, Sonora, Sinaloa, Nueva Vizcaya, New Mexico, and the Californias, to which were later added Nuevo Santander and Nuevo León, were detached from the viceroyalty and placed under Croix's jurisdiction by a royal cedula of August 22, 1776. Instructions to the new commandant, issued on the same date, conferred upon him practically viceregal powers—direct dependence upon the king, authority over the political governors, treasury officers, and judicial authorities, and exercise of the royal patronage.[1] Withal, as Bancroft observes, Croix's command was to be pre-eminently a military one. His first duty was to systematize the frontier defenses and to wage war on savage foes.

The creation of the commandancy general of the internal provinces in 1776 was clearly an experimental measure and it is not surprising that it underwent a number of successive changes. Alterations in administrative structure and policy were invariably designed to fill gaps which appeared in the over-all defense system. The frequency of these suggested that no real panacea for the problems of the frontier had been devised—instead, stopgap measures were employed as momentary expedients to be abandoned when they proved useless or whenever some seemingly more efficient technique or method appeared.

In spite of the Reglamento on presidios and the efforts by Hugo O'Conor to impose reform, Teodoro de Croix, upon assuming his post as commandant general, observed that weaknesses remained

1. Thomas, *Teodoro de Croix,* p. 18.

in the presidial cordon. His energies, thereafter, were concentrated on eliminating these and strengthening the provinces in general. In conceiving a policy of action, his aims came to be centered on (1) rearranging the cordon to render the presidios more effective; (2) establishing a secondary line of frontier settlements from which militia could be drawn to support military campaigns and provide supplies for the presidios; (3) protecting the presidial horse herds from Indian raids; and (4) introducing needed reforms in the internal administration of the presidios.[2]

In late 1777 and well into 1778, Croix proceeded upon a comprehensive inspection tour of much of his new jurisdiction. In the process he promoted three councils of war which helped to crystallize in his mind the aims just stated. Moreover, a general policy was evolved which indicated that flexibility was to be the keynote of Spanish action. As described by Bobb, "alliance, war, and peace with various Indian groups were all to be part of the Spanish method, both as coexisting and sequential policies."[3]

Although Croix was vigorous in his approach, like O'Conor before him, he enjoyed only partial success. In the years before 1781, significant achievements were registered, including several notable victories against the Indians and the successful promotion of local militia units. A massacre of a Spanish garrison by the Yumas and complaints against Croix by absentee *hacendados* who held lands around Saltillo and Parras, tended to mar his record in the final years he served as commandant general.

On the purely administrative level, Croix's years in office were singularly free of friction with subordinate officials. He had been admonished to adopt a conciliatory attitude toward nonmilitary individuals and to consult freely and in a friendly manner with civil and ecclesiastical officers. In June, 1778, he wrote to Minister José de Gálvez from Chihuahua recommending division of the Provincias Internas into two distinct and independent jurisdictions. The

2. Ibid., pp. 47-48.
3. *The Viceregency of Bucareli,* p. 153.

eastern sector was to include Coahuila, the districts of Parras and Saltillo, Texas, Nuevo León, and Nuevo Santander, while the remaining provinces were to compose the western. Croix reasoned that it was nearly as impracticable to direct the affairs of Texas and Nuevo Santander from Arizpe as from Mexico.[4] His suggestion, nonetheless, was not immediately followed.

Croix served at his post until 1783 when Charles III rewarded him with the choicest office in the overseas empire—that of Viceroy of Perú. Felipe de Neve, formerly governor of the Californias, had been named commandant inspector in the previous year, and with Croix's departure, he became commandant general by a royal order of February 15, 1783.[5] Although in delicate health, Neve continued to carry the war to troublesome Indians. A campaign to the Rio Gila, in which he and the two adjutant inspectors participated, produced a number of successful skirmishes.[6] Neve served only a short while before he died on August 21, 1784.[7] His successor was José Antonio Rengel, the commandant inspector who assumed charge ad interim under the supervision of the Audiencia of Mexico which was ruling because of the sudden death of Viceroy Matías de Gálvez.[8]

By a real cedula of October 6, 1785, the king appointed Jacobo Ugarte y Loyola, then governor of Puebla, to the office of commandant general.[9] Ugarte was a reasonable choice in view of his wide experience in frontier matters, having earlier been governor first of Coahuila and then of Sonora.[10] By this time, however, the crown was moving toward a revamping of the governmental structure of the internal provinces. The welter of administrative changes which

4. Bancroft, *North Mexican States,* I, 639, Decree of Flores, 1787.

5. AGN, Prov. Int., 77. Neve's elevation to the superior office was officially proclaimed in Santa Fe on March 6, 1784, SANM, doc. 857a.

6. Alfred Barnaby Thomas, *Forgotten Frontiers* (Norman, Okla., 1932), pp. 244-56.

7. AGN, Prov. Int., 46.

8. Rengel to the Governor of New Mexico, Chihuahua, November 30, 1784, SANM, doc. 898.

9. SANM, doc. 936.

10. For a brief biographical sketch of Ugarte y Loyola, see Thomas, *Forgotten Frontiers,* p. 384n.

ensued provides a complex and often confusing history, offering further indication that Spain possessed no frontier policy with a predetermined coherence.

In 1785, Bernardo de Gálvez, nephew of José de Gálvez and son of Matías de Gálvez, Viceroy of New Spain, succeeded to the viceregal office upon the death of his father. Because of the special competence of Bernardo in frontier matters—he had previously been a military commandant in Coahuila and governor of Louisiana—his authority was extended over the Provincias Internas. His new relationship with the commandant general was detailed in an *Instrucción* sent to Ugarte y Loyola on August 26, 1786.[11] The commander of the internal provinces was to continue in use of the ample powers conceded to his predecessors, but with the understanding that he was now immediately subordinate to the orders of the viceroy. Since the defense and tranquility of the provinces were to be the preferred objects of his attention, Ugarte was cautioned to concentrate on operations of war and to leave judicial details entirely to the governors, subdelegating to them in the same manner the powers of the patronato.

Remembering the complaint of Croix that the provinces were too large for one man to govern, and his own experiences assuring him of the need of a split command, Gálvez provided Ugarte with two assistant officers. Juan Ugalde, colonel of infantry, was assigned military jurisdiction over the eastern provinces. José Rengel, reappointed commandant inspector after having served briefly as provisional commandant general, was placed in charge of the central provinces of Nueva Vizcaya and New Mexico. Ugarte y Loyola retained direct management of the remaining western provinces of Sonora and the Californias. The two aides were still under orders from the commandant general, but they were permitted to correspond directly with the viceroy. Article 13 of the *Instrucción* pro-

11. Donald E. Worcester, ed., *Instructions for Governing the Interior Provinces of New Spain,* 1786 (Berkeley, 1951). An original copy of this document may be found in AGN, Prov. Int., 129.

vided that they should act freely in whatever concerned operations against the enemy and peace with those who asked for it. Specifically they were required to obey the commandant general's orders insofar as they did not oppose those given them directly by the viceroy.

José Rengel, although he now had a new facet added to his military duties, continued to act as inspector of all the troops of the commandancy general. Whenever the demands of this office compelled him to be absent from Nueva Vizcaya, he was instructed to leave the interim military command of the province to the officer enjoying his greatest confidence, devolving it, if possible, upon the one of highest grade and most service in rank. Regarding matters strictly relating to the *inspección,* Rengel was ordered to deal directly with the commandant general and to correspond with the viceroy only through this official. Because of the inaccessibility of New Mexico, the governor of that province carried on as subinspector of the troops within his district in order to avoid, whenever possible, visits by the commander inspector and his aides.[12]

This new form for the internal provinces was not precisely in keeping with the earlier recommendations of Croix. The government essentially was still a single unit under the commandant general and a sizable chunk of the northern frontier persisted in demanding his attention. Moreover, friction developed between Ugarte and Ugalde on a number of issues, and when appeal was made by both to the viceroy, that official became involved as the third member in a contentious triangle. Further, the division of the commandancy into three departments precipitated rather than solved difficulties in dealing with the Indians.

Bernardo de Gálvez succumbed suddenly to a fever in 1786 and the Provincias Internas briefly enjoyed their old independence in the short interval which elapsed before the appointment of another

12. *Ibid.,* pp. 30-33. As may be adduced from what has been said, the *ramo de inspección* was that branch of the military concerned with administration, supply, and discipline.

viceroy. In March, 1787, the authority of the new viceroy, Manuel Antonio Flores, over the commandant general was declared by a royal cedula to be the same as that of his predecessor.[13]

Affairs stood thus until December 3, 1787, when Flores under royal authorization issued a decree abolishing the three separate commands and consolidating the northern jurisdiction into two independent commandancies general as in the original suggestion of Croix.[14] The Provincias Internas del Poniente, or western provinces, remained under Ugarte y Loyola and included the Californias, Sonora, Nueva Vizcaya, and New Mexico. The jurisdiction of José Rengel as commandant inspector was restricted to the latter three provinces, and two of the adjutant inspectors, of which there were now three, were assigned to the same area. Once again, therefore, Rengel found himself subordinate in all matters to the commandant general.

The Provincias Internas del Oriente, or eastern provinces, were organized anew under Juan Ugalde, who was elevated to the rank of commandant general with an annual salary of six thousand pesos. This office, in view of the restrictions imposed by the crown, was practically devoid of political responsibility. Ugalde was explicitly admonished to devote himself to purely military matters, using as his guide the presidial Reglamento of 1772.[15]

As noted, the limited authority of Viceroy Flores was extended over the commandancy in the manner prescribed in the Gálvez instructions of 1786. Rather quickly, however, this order was superseded by a new cedula of March 11, 1788, which restored full viceregal authority.[16] Following close upon this mandate was a royal order of May 15 which combined the offices of commandant general of the West and commandant inspector.[17] With the reduced load

13. Herbert E. Bolton, *Guide to Materials for the History of the United States in the Principal Archives of Mexico* (Washington, D.C., 1913), p. 76.

14. Decree of Flores, 1787. The governor of New Mexico was notified of the change by Ugarte in a letter of January 23, 1788, SANM, doc. 996.

15. Decree of Flores, 1787, art. 12.

16. Bolton, *Guide,* p. 76.

17. Ugarte y Loyola to the Governor of New Mexico, September 2, 1788, SANM, doc. 1017.

carried by the former, doubtless it was concluded that he could perform with ease the functions of inspector. In reality, logic should have dictated even earlier the practicability of such a measure. José Rengel, since his post was being absorbed by Ugarte, was transferred to Sonora where he became *comandante de armas*.[18]

Ugarte y Loyola was promoted to the intendancy of Guadalajara in 1790, leaving Colonel Antonio Cordero as interim commander. Brigadier General Pedro de Nava subsequently received the permanent appointment as commandant general of the western provinces on March 7, 1791. Ugalde at the same time, broken down by years of hard service, was relieved of the eastern jurisdiction and returned to Spain. Nava temporarily assumed control of these provinces until Ramón de Castro was appointed to serve as Ugalde's replacement.[19]

As the final act in the first historical phase of the commandancy system, the king issued orders on November 22, 1792, reuniting the Provincias Internas and placing them, as originally provided in 1776, under a single commandant. This directive was in opposition to the recommendation of Viceroy Revilla Gigedo II, who had forcefully argued, after making a visit to the area concerned, for the full extension of his power over the northern region.[20] By the November 22 ruling, Pedro de Nava was confirmed as commandant over the "restored" internal provinces at a yearly salary of fifteen thousand pesos. A jurisdictional provision separated the Californias, Nuevo León, and Nuevo Santander, attaching them to the viceroyalty. The Provincias Internas, in revised form, were composed of the five provinces of Sonora, Nueva Vizcaya, New Mexico, Texas, and Coahuila.[21]

With the attaining of independence by Nava from the viceroy, the office of commandant general regained the civil and administrative

18. *Comandante de armas* appears to have been the title denoting the ranking military commander in a province where the political and military powers were separated.

19. Carroll and Haggard, *Three New Mexico Chronicles*, p. 171n.

20. *Instrucción reservada*, art. 719; Donald E. Smith, *The Viceroy of New Spain* (Berkeley, 1913), p. 155.

21. Conde del Campo de Alange to the Viceroy of New Spain, San Lorenzo, Spain, November 23, 1792, AGN, Prov. Int., 241.

functions originally conceded to it, and of which it had been deprived in successive stages. With this event the pendulum had retraced its crescent within a span of seventeen years. At the beginning the commandant was virtually a viceroy in all but name. From this lofty position, he had been reduced by 1785 to a command which, in truth, included no more than Sonora and the Californias. Officers who ruled the central and eastern provinces were only nominally subordinate to him. At the lowest ebb, he became completely subject to the viceroy in 1788.

The circumstances which encouraged such indecision and vacillation on the part of the crown may be suggested in no more than the broadest terms. A meticulous study of the Provincias Internas' sections of the Spanish and Mexican archives will be necessary to reveal the frequently occult motives which influenced the Spanish government in its course of action.

The opening lines of the Gálvez instructions to Ugarte indicate that the king was fully aware of the persistence of fundamental weaknesses affecting this far corner of his realm. It was declared bluntly: "The unhappy state of the Provincias Internas is well known." The reasons as set forth lay in the rigors of war, pestilence, and hunger which neither the zeal of the commandants nor increases of troops and presidio equipment could alleviate. To these expected sources of trouble were added the dissensions among the officers who constantly jockeyed for added power and prestige. A particularly critical state was reached in 1789 with a vigorous attempt by the commandant to make himself independent of the viceroy. This circumstance was a major factor in arousing the ire of Revilla Gigedo II, as noted previously. The sum total of these and other problems not yet fully understood served to confuse the crown, promote discord in colonial offices, and defeat the original intent of the commandancy general.

Chapter IV

THE INTENDANCY SYSTEM

Establishment and Organization. The reforming zeal of the Spanish Bourbons resulted in the comparatively bold innovation of the commandancy system. A more sweeping reform, to which reference has already been made, was the Ordinance of Intendants for New Spain implemented in 1786.[1] Designed to curb rampant corruption, to halt lax obedience to royal and viceregal orders, and to promote greater administrative efficiency, this measure came to have a profound effect on local political affairs. With the announced purpose of improving fiscal administration and augmenting royal revenues, the Order swept away the governors, alcaldes mayores, and other civil officers whose peculations had imposed a serious drain on the treasury. In their place were appointed twelve governor-intendants to manage the newly created intendancies, or districts, of New Spain. These officials were selected by the king, and their powers extended to the departments of justice, general administration (*policía*), finance, and war. Within the area presided over by the intendant (*intendente*), divisions known as *partidos* were made and placed in charge of subdelegates (*subdelegados*) who were nominated by the intendents but appointed by the viceroy. This regularization of provincial government greatly reduced the total number of officials, lowered expenses, increased royal revenues through more efficient collection, and relieved the viceroy and the commandant general of a portion of their multitudinous duties by virtually creating a separate financial department.

In the north, the Intendancies of Durango and Sonora were en-

1. A translation of this Order may be found in Lillian Estelle Fisher, *The Intendant System in Spanish America* (Berkeley, 1929).

tirely within the jurisdiction of the commandancy general and that of San Luís Potosí partially so. The Intendancy of Sonora had actually been created during the time of Viceroy Bucareli when it was thought that the exceptional mineral wealth and revenues from tribute of that province could be more effectively handled by an intendant. Although Sonora endured for a number of years prior to 1786 as the only intendancy in New Spain, for several reasons it was not successful.[2] Teodoro de Croix, nonetheless, in his *Informe general* of 1781, proposed the appointment of an intendant for Nueva Vizcaya who, being "skillful, disinterested, zealous, and loyal, might arrange the political and economic government of the pueblos. . . ."[3] With promulgation of the Order of Indendants, Sonora remained as an independent jurisdiction, and Nueva Vizcaya was set up as an intendancy with its capital at Durango. In all, New Spain was divided into twelve intendancies plus the separate department of the Californias administered by the commandant general.

The duties of the new intendants extended to collection of revenues, civil administration and cases of justice, and all economic matters. In these areas they served as assistants of the viceroy or commandant general to whom they were directly subordinate. These two superior officers experienced at the onset a curtailment of their powers in fiscal matters by the appointment of an intendant general (*superintendente general de real hacienda*) who resided in Mexico City and through his agents, the intendants, took full cognizance of financial affairs. As Smith has observed:

> A new council, officially termed the *junta general de real hacienda,* was established at the capital with the superintendent-general as its president. This new chief of the financial end of the government became, not an official subordinate to the viceroy, but a co-ordinate ruler over what was in some ways the most important branch of government.[4]

2. Luís Navarro García, *Intendencias en Indias* (Sevilla, 1959), pp. 53-54.
3. Thomas, *Teodoro de Croix,* p. 131.
4. *The Viceroy of New Spain,* p. 117.

The intendancies, however, had only been fairly established when the viceroy was himself made superintendent general and hence had all his old powers returned to him.[5]

In the Provincias Internas the intendants of Sonora and Durango were under immediate direction of the commandant general in all military matters, and he as subdelegate of the royal treasury was their supervising agent in fiscal affairs. In the departments of justice and general administration, the two intendants were under authority of the Audiencia of Guadalajara.[6] In actual practice they enjoyed considerable freedom of action, particularly since their immediate superior, the commandant general, concentrated his attention on military business. Although the intendants possessed military functions within their so-called war department, or *causa de guerra,* these were in effect limited to the maintenance and provisioning of provincial troops in peace and war, and to a monthly review of soldiers stationed within their respective provinces.[7]

The Intendancy System and New Mexico. Lansing B. Bloom once wrote that the intendancy system need not concern students of New Mexico history directly since this province never was erected as a separate intendancy.[8] One need only peruse the Order of 1786 to see that this statement is misleading. Although it must be admitted that New Mexico never became a co-equal unit within the new machinery of government, it should be recognized that the Order contained many general provisions, especially in regard to the functioning of local or municipal government, applicable to all New Spain. Moreover, the role of New Mexico as a military province attached to the intendancy system is clearly set forth in Article 10 within the Order, and this must necessarily be absorbed into any account of provincial government in the late colonial period. Furthermore, random pieces of correspondence which survive in the

5. *Ibid.,* p. 272.
6. Navarro García, *Intendencias en Indias,* p. 71.
7. Fisher, *The Intendant System,* p. 297.
8. *New Mexico History and Civics* (Albuquerque, 1933), pp. 140-41.

Spanish archives at Santa Fe suggest that some tenuous, though very real and heretofore undescribed, relationship existed between the governor of New Mexico and the intendant of Durango.

Although writers in the past have concluded that Upper California, Lower California, and New Mexico remained outside the intendancy system as separate military systems, this was not true for New Mexico.[9] Article 1 of the Order of Intendants states unequivocally, "In order that my will may have its prompt and proper effect, I command that the territory of that empire [New Spain], *exclusive of the Californias,* shall be divided for the present into twelve intendancies."[10] Absence of reference to New Mexico here is conspicuous.

Further insight is provided by Article 10, the first paragraph of which reads as follows:

> The political and military administrations of Yucatàn, Tabasco, Vera Cruz, Acapulco, the New Kingdom of León, Nuevo Santander, Coahuila, Texas, and New Mexico shall continue. Consequently they must keep the divisions of justice and general administration united to the military authority in their respective territories or districts, except the branch belonging to municipal finance and to community funds of the towns, which must be [under] the exclusive power of the intendants, with subordination to the *junta superior de hacienda.*[11]

It is clear from this that New Mexico was to be regarded in a manner similar to a number of other frontier or exposed provinces, all of which heretofore have been considered as loose appendages of one or another intendancy. The Californias are not mentioned because they were completely divorced from association with any intendant. The provinces named were made practically independent by virtue of their particular military missions. Only with regard to municipal funds might the intendant interpose his authority; and in the case of New Mexico, where the poverty of most citizens spelled the almost total absence of community revenues, even this

9. See, e.g., Fisher, *The Intendant System,* p. 26; Haring, *The Spanish Empire in America;* Twitchell, *The Spanish Archives,* II, 258.

10. Fisher, *The Intendant System,* p. 98. The italics are inserted by this writer.

11. *Ibid.,* p. 105.

avenue of action was closed. This is not to say, however, that New Mexico was entirely freed from the hand of the intendant of Durango. While this province had never been an integral part of Nueva Vizcaya, it was, nonetheless, joined in close association, and though not incorporated officially into the new government, the intendant of Durango seems to have regarded New Mexico as belonging to his jurisdiction within certain shadowy and ill-defined limits.

The governor of New Mexico was both the chief military and the chief civil officer of his jurisdiction, with emphasis definitely on the first of these responsibilities. Practically all matters in either sphere might be construed as of ultimate military significance since whatever promoted the welfare of the province served to shore up its capacity to resist enemies. At the same time, civil administration existed as a substratum of government directed, likewise, by the governor who united in his person the divisions of justice and general administration with the military authority.

The fact is that there was not a great deal of difference between the new intendant governor of Durango and the governor of New Mexico. The former enjoyed greater stature, having come from Spain and ruling over a larger and more important area, but both were in charge of general administration and justice within their respective districts and both exercised the vice-patronage of the Church. The intendant had little jurisdiction in matters of war since the interior of his province was relatively tranquil, and in the north, where agitation was prevalent, the commandant general was on hand to subdue tumult. While matters of defense preoccupied the governor of New Mexico, he had, in contrast to the intendant, few financial responsibilities since his area was not a producer of significant revenues. The commandant at Chihuahua frequently addressed general orders to "the intendants and governors of the Provincias Internas," indicating that each was roughly co-equal within his appropriate sphere of jurisdiction.[12]

That the intendant of Durango possessed some superiority over

12. See, e.g., Bando of Commandant General Nemesio Salcedo, Chihuahua, April 10, 1804, SANM, doc. 1716.

New Mexico's governor, at least in the conduct of certain financial business, is indicated by two official letters in the Spanish Archives at Santa Fe. The first, from the Intendant Bernardo Bonavia and dated January 29, 1798, is a notice addressed to the Gobernador del Nuevo Mexico informing him of a *real provisión*[13] issued by the Audiencia of Guadalajara which contained a royal cedula annulling all exemptions from tithe payments, including those made previously to clerics and soldiers. In closing, Bonavia states that his assistant legal adviser (*teniente letrado y asesor*) reported his official opinion as to how the measure should be applied. This was sent to the governor, and the intendant requested that its receipt be acknowledged.[14] The second piece of correspondence was penned by Governor Real Alencaster on April 1, 1806, and is a reply to an earlier official letter from the intendant. Alencaster reports that there is no real estate (*fincas urbanas ni rústicas*) in the hands of benevolent organizations within his area.[15]

It was the duty of the intendants to enforce royal decrees relative to finances, and the two instances just cited indicate that the power of the intendant of Durango extended in such matters to the province of New Mexico. Beyond this he probably held jurisdiction in certain cases involving public revenues. Suits and legal cases connected with the monopolies of tobacco, the alcabala, *pulque,* gun powder, and playing cards were decided in the first instance by the intendant or one of his subdelegates, and it may be assumed that if any such proceedings arose in New Mexico, they were carried to Durango.[16] It is certain that various criminal and civil cases originating in New Mexico found their way into the hands of the inten-

13. The term *real provisión* could apply to a cedula from Spain, or to a decree of the viceroy or audiencia proclaimed in the king's name.

14. SANM, doc. 1414. It was recommended in 1789 that the asesoría of Durango be abolished as its expense was an excessive burden on the treasury. Apparently this suggestion was not carried out. Intendant of Durango to the Viceroy, October, 1789, AGN, Prov. Int., 26.

15. SANM, doc. 1982.

16. Fisher, *The Intendant System,* p. 45.

dant's assessor.[17] By Article 15 of the Order of 1786, this lawyer was made legal adviser in all business of the intendancy.[18] Since New Mexico in the late colonial period was chronically short of men trained in law, cases which were appealed from the local courts to the Audiencia in Guadalajara frequently went via the legal adviser in Durango so that he might have an opportunity to attach his opinion. Thus, another real, albeit inconspicuous, example is provided of New Mexico's limited dependence on the Intendancy of Durango.

Fisher suggests that initially it was the crown's intention to bring most of the military provinces, which had been set aside originally as military departments and which included New Mexico, into full participation in the intendant system.[19] Within a brief time after creation of the new frame of government, this actually occurred in the eastern interior provinces which were effectively incorporated into the Intendancy of San Luís Potosí, though remaining under the military control of the commandancy.[20] This left New Mexico, since the Californias are excluded, as the only remaining military department in the north, and suggests why some writers have mistakenly concluded that this was the situation embodied in the original plan.

At the beginning of the nineteenth century, Baron von Humboldt expressed surprise that after two centuries of colonization, New Mexico was not yet considered ready for annexation by the intendancy of Nueva Vizcaya (Durango).[21] The answer resided in the fact that disruptions produced by pillaging Indians demanded the presence of a military governor who could act swiftly and decisively in hours of emergency. Also, because of its geographical isolation

17. See, e.g., Isidro Rey to Governor Alencaster, El Paso, July 21, 1805, SANM, doc. 1862.

18. Fisher, *The Intendant System,* p. 111.

19. *Ibid.,* p. 29.

20. Navarro García, *Intendencias en Indias,* p. 119n. The suppression of the separate Gobierno de Texas took place in 1788, and presumably similar action ensued in Coahuila, Nuevo León, and Nuevo Santander at approximately the same time.

21. *Ensayo político,* II, 331.

imposed by intervening deserts and wasteland, inconvenience and confusion could have been the only outcome if a subdelegate dependent on the intendant had been imposed upon New Mexico.

Last Years of the Intendancy System. A number of problems arose with regard to the new intendancies, so that early expectations came to be only partially realized. Designed to regularize political government in New Spain, the system fell short of its goal when at the onset certain districts had to be kept separate as military departments. Moreover, there existed an obvious lack of uniformity among the intendancies—comparison of area and population showed considerable variance. Viceroy Revilla Gigedo II was particularly critical on this account, and he further complained that men of inferior caliber had been appointed to office.[22]

If the intent of the measure was to secure a more efficient government for the colonies and to improve conditions of life there for all classes of the inhabitants, then it was misdirected. By and large, the aim of the Order of Intendants was not inclined toward fundamental reform which would serve the interests of the colonists. Benefits accruing to them were always incidental to the increment of Spain's greatness and financial prosperity. Here perhaps lay the key which will explain in general terms the failures in Spanish overseas policy.

Foreign wars and exigencies at home required the crown to economize after the launching of the intendancy project, thus frustrating efforts by qualified persons on the scene to have some of the larger jurisdictions divided into smaller units under a sufficient number of properly paid officials. Revilla Gigedo II argued without avail in 1790 for creation of a new intendancy to comprise the eastern Provincias Internas.[23] The politically astute and ambitious Miguel Ramos Arizpe raised the demand again before the Spanish Cortes in 1813, but his efforts were equally unsuccessful.[24]

22. *Instrucción reservada,* arts. 835, 836.

23. Letter of the Viceroy to Valdés, Mexico, March 31, 1790, cited by Navarro García, *Intendencias en Indias,* p. 124.

24. *Ibid.,* p. 141.

Although some alterations were made in the system from time to time, as for example in an Ordenanza of 1803, these had little or no effect on conditions in New Mexico.

With the liberal reforms in Spain in 1812 and 1813 resulting in the appointment of a Minister of Interior and the founding of political governments and provincial deputations, the intendant's powers were reduced to those relating to the treasury. The skeleton of the intendancy structure, however, persisted for three years after the independence of Mexico, not being finally abolished until September of 1824.[25]

25. Rodríguez de S. Miguel, *Pandectas,* II, 219.

Chapter V

THE PROVINCIAS INTERNAS, SECOND PHASE

Pedro de Nava was succeeded as commandant by General Nemesio Salcedo y Salcedo, who received his appointment by an order dated August 26, 1800.[1] The original commission instructed the new commandant general to take the oath of office from the viceroy of New Spain, and it declared the the king would order the appropriate intendant immediately to begin paying him his salary of fifteen thousand pesos a year. Salcedo was delayed in assuming control until November 4, 1802.[2] From then on he continued to serve at his post until he was relieved in 1813, thereby remaining in office longer than any other commandant.[3]

The relatively long administration of Salcedo was crowded with events of great moment. In the spring of 1804, the crown became convinced anew that the combined Provincias Internas were too large and unwieldy for a single executive to administer efficiently. Accordingly, a royal order of May 30 proclaimed a return to the system of 1787, whereby the area was partitioned into two divisions, each ruled by a separate commandant general. The fulfillment of

1. Royal Cedula of Charles IV: Commission to Brigadier Salcedo, SANM, doc. 1499a.

2. Bancroft, and others following him, have apparently been confused about the order of succession at this time. Salcedo was in his jurisdiction by the date just noted as he addressed a letter on that day to Governor Fernando de Chacón in Santa Fe, announcing his induction into office. SANM, doc. 1625.

3. According to Bancroft, Nava retained charge until 1804 when he gave way to Colonel Pedro Grimarest, who in turn was shortly replaced by Salcedo. General Salcedo, he states, held office until 1812 when Alejo García Conde assumed charge. *North Mexican States,* II, 581-82. See also Bolton, *Guide,* p. 76. Some of these changes appear actually to have been ordered in regulations which provided for territorial reorganization of the internal provinces in 1804 and 1811. Though such may have been the case, they never took effect, for Salcedo, as indicated by extensive correspondence in the Santa Fe Archives, was continuously at his job until 1813. His last known letter to the governor of New Mexico was dated from Chihuahua on June 28 of that year. SANM, doc. 2501.

this mandate was delayed for more than eight years because of the political upheavals in Spain occasioned by the Napoleonic War and the ensuing independence movements which burst upon the colonies. In the meantime, Salcedo continued to govern the united provinces.

The administrative modifications made in 1804 were revived on May 1, 1811, and confirmed by a royal order on July 24, 1812.[4] The regency which was governing Spain at this time in the name of the king provided for two commandancies of equal rank, dependent upon the viceroy and designated as *oriente* and *occidente*. To head the western provinces, the council of regents named Brigadier Bernardo Bonavía y Zapata, who, since 1796, had been serving as governor-intendant of Durango. Alejo García Conde, then intendant of Sonora and Sinaloa, was ordered to Durango to fill the post vacated by Bonavía.[5] In the east, command was first bestowed upon Colonel Simón de Herrera, who was subsequently slain by filibusters in Texas. Field Marshall Félix Calleja, later made viceroy, was offered the position, but he declined to accept, and it was finally given to Colonel Joaquín de Arredondo.[6]

General Salcedo must have greeted the news of Bonavía's appointment with some relief for he himself was in declining health and desirous of returning to Spain.[7] In July of 1813, Bonavía reported that the superior office had been turned over to him and he was in full command.[8]

The new commandant general experienced some immediate frustration. His appointment had originated with the order of May 1, 1811, but beyond this there seemed to be no instructions to guide him. With the relinquishing of power by Salcedo, the provinces as-

4. AGN, Prov. Int., 129; and Bancroft, *North Mexican States*, II, 582n.

5. Salcedo to the Viceroy, Chihuahua, May 31, 1813, AGN, Prov. Int., 129.

6. Carroll and Haggard, *Three New Mexico Chronicles*, p. 171. With regard to some points, these authors are confused on the order of succession. See also Humboldt, *Ensayo político*, II, 422-23.

7. Salcedo to the Viceroy, Chihuahua, September 10, 1812, AGN, Prov. Int., 129.

8. Bonavía to the Viceroy, Durango, July 26, 1813, AGN, Prov. Int., 129. According to Navarro García, *Las Provincias Internas*, p. 76, Salcedo divided the archive of the commandancy at this time, turning over part to Bonavía and remitting the remainder to Arredondo.

sumed their new status as appendages of the viceroyalty, but the specific relationship between the two commandancies and Mexico City remained unclear. Bonavía sought information by posing two questions. Which provinces were under his jurisdiction? In precisely what manner was he dependent upon the viceroy? With regard to the first, he noted that the order of May 11 had made reference to ten provinces, but he contended that ten could not even be counted for both the eastern and western divisions. As for the matter of his relation to the viceroy, Bonavía explained that this needed to be spelled out in exact terms so that he would not exceed his authority or neglect duties which rightfully belonged to him.[9]

Apparently Colonel Arredondo in the east was as bewildered as his fellow commandant. Late in 1814, the viceroy addressed to him a set of instructions outlining in detail the commandant's duties and powers.[10] Presumably a similar document was dispatched to Bonavía, for the revised arrangement, when clarified, showed that he had within his jurisdiction the four provinces of Sonora, Sinaloa, Nueva Vizcaya, and New Mexico. The western internal provinces retained the old secretariat, auditor, and other administrative officers, while a new corps of civil servants was created for the eastern.[11]

The confusion produced by the initial lack of instructions to the commandant general did lead to one problem which was not resolved during Bonavía's years in office. This concerned the location of the capital of the western provinces. As remarked earlier, the capital came to be placed permanently in the city of Chihuahua, although the commandant was frequently absent from his place of residence attending to affairs elsewhere.

When Bonavía came to office, he apparently felt very comfortable in Durango where he had served for so many years as intendant. In the absence of any special directive ordering his removal to Chihuahua, and feeling no inclination to effect the transfer on his own

9. *Ibid.*
10. Arredondo to the Viceroy, Monterrey, February 28, 1815, AGN, Prov. Int., 129.
11. Viceroy to the Minister of War, Mexico, July 31, 1819, AGN, Prov. Int., 129.

initiative, he settled down to administer his new command from Durango. A cry was raised by the indignant municipal officers of Chihuahua's town council (*ayuntamiento*) who lodged a vigorous protest with the viceroy.

In a formal denunciation of Bonavía's inaction, they declared:

> The residence of the commandant general of these provinces, established unofficially in Durango, is a subject of such importance and gravity that the ayuntamiento feels compelled to make known the incalculable injuries which will be the result. . . .[12]

The aggrieved parties went on to point out that Durango's geographical position in the extreme south was distant from Chihuahua by 170 leagues and from the capital of New Mexico, the most northern outpost of the command, by 450 leagues. The commandant, they argued, could not hope to direct the defense of the area since he was so far removed from the scene of action. In all events, the viceroy was reminded that the royal order fixing the residence in Chihuahua was still in force, and Bonavía should be ordered to comply with it.

The viceroy was sympathetic with the remonstrances and early in 1814 wrote to the commandant general at some length, ordering him to proceed with his staff to Chihuahua as soon as possible. This decision was based upon the following reasons: 1) this was the law under the existing royal orders; 2) Chihuahua was about equidistant from the other provincial capitals; 3) from there he could better direct policy against the barbarous Indians; and 4) he would be closer to the affairs of New Mexico which should command his particular attention since the United States had designs on the province.[13]

The municipal council in Chihuahua expressed its pleasure at the viceregal order which it felt was essential to the city's welfare and

12. Ayuntamiento of Chihuahua to Viceroy Calleja, October 12, 1813, AGN, Prov. Int., 186, Nueva Vizcaya, Misc. Papers. See also José M. Ponce de León, *Reseñas históricas del estado de Chihuahua* (Chihuahua 1913), pp. 104-16.

13. Viceroy Calleja to Bonavía, Mexico, February 14, 1814, AGN, Prov. Int., 186, Nueva Vizcaya, Misc. Papers.

prestige.[14] General Bonavía, however, was a man of some determination. In a message to Viceroy Calleja, he manifested his disinclination to comply with the superior demand. In defense of his position, he noted that in spite of Durango's southern location, he had not been prevented from traveling widely within the Provincias Internas in attending to affairs of state. Moreover, his situation in the south rendered communication with the viceroy and with the commandancy of the east easier and more rapid.[15]

In mid-1815, García Conde, the new intendant at Durango, complained to Viceroy Calleja that Bonavía was giving no sign of departing. The tone of his letter suggests that the commandant was becoming a nuisance by interfering in the affairs of the intendancy.[16] In spite of this remonstrance, General Bonavía succeeded, by one means or another, in maintaining his position at Durango until he went out of office in 1817.

While the commandant general continued to rule from the southern city, the two adjutant inspectors who remained to him, the third one having gone to the eastern provinces, were placed over the northern presidios—one directing those in Sonora and Sinaloa, and the other those in Nueva Vizcaya and New Mexico from a seat in Chihuahua. These inspectors were directly over the presidial commanders in their respective districts and were responsible for seeing that the orders of the commandant general were carried out.[17]

The governor of New Mexico continued to communicate directly with the commandant, but in business relating to the military inspection, he customarily went through the adjutant inspector in Chihuahua, who served as something of an intermediary. This inspector supervised the release of funds from the treasury office to presidial commandants and troop captains or their representatives, the supply-

14. Ayuntamiento of Chihuahua to the Viceroy, April 26, 1814, *ibid.*

15. Bonavía to the Viceroy, Durango, April 13, 1814, *ibid.*

16. García Conde to the Viceroy, Durango, August 19, 1815, *ibid.*

17. Circular to the Ayudantes Inspectores from Bonavía, Durango, October 9, 1815, SANM, doc. 2632.

masters. This duty ordinarily belonged to the commandant inspector who, after 1788, was the commandant general. But with Bonavía remaining in Durango, the adjutant inspector assumed immediate direction of this and other functions pertaining to maintenance of frontier forces.[18] On November 28, 1817, Bernardo Bonavía relinquished his office to return to Spain, and his place was assumed by the intendant García Conde who held the post until independence.[19]

The Commandancy General and Independence. In 1818 a royal order provided for the final major administrative alteration of the commandancy system by the Spanish government. The two commandant generals were deprived of what special functions remained to them and were reduced to the level of any other provincial military commander.[20] Some duties of civil government they retained, but these were to be no greater than those which belonged to other governors.[21] Again in this instance, the royal directive failed to be explicit and the commandants experienced the usual confusion regarding their new status.

In military matters they were subject to the subinspector general in Mexico City, but otherwise to the viceroy. No explanation was made as to the future position of the adjutant inspectors. Were they to continue as subordinates of the commandants, or were they now subject directly to the subinspector general as well? Further, were the commandant generals to retain their old secretariats, or were

18. Bonavía to the Governor of New Mexico, Durango, December 12, 1815, SANM, doc. 2632. The "circular" referred to in the previous citation is contained within this document. See also Governor Allande to the Ayudante Inspector de Presidios de Nueva Vizcaya, Santa Fe, April 10-May 13, 1818, SANM, doc. 2718.

19. The transition between the administrations of Bonavía and García Conde is somewhat confusing. Francisco R. Almada, in "*La Comandancia General de Provincias Internas,*" BSCEH, I (1938), p. 40, states that the transfer of power occurred on November 28 as above noted. Other sources indicate that Colonel Antonio Cordero served briefly as commandant general ad interim in 1818. See, e.g., Alfred B. Thomas, "An Anonymous Description of New Mexico, 1818," *Southwestern Historical Quarterly,* XXXIII (1929), p. 50.

20. *Real Orden,* Madrid, October 16, 1818, AGN, Prov. Int., 129.

21. Officials of the Audiencia of Guadalajara to the Viceroy, November 29, 1819, *ibid.*

these to be abolished?[22] The viceroy himself could not provide answers to these and other questions; hence, information was sought from Spain.[23]

It seems certain that the order of 1818 was never fully implemented. Alejo García Conde, on becoming commandant general, continued to direct the western provinces from Durango, though he spent much time in the field, particularly in Sonora. Late in 1819 he transmitted to the governor of New Mexico a dispatch from the subinspector general of the troops of New Spain[24] indicating that at least the portion of the new ruling which placed the commandant under that superior military official was carried into practice. The governor of New Mexico, thereby, became subordinate in his military capacity indirectly to the subinspector general, but all correspondence continued through the commandant general.[25] At the same time, the adjutant inspector continued in charge at Chihuahua, fulfilling his assigned duties as described above.[26]

When Alejo García Conde succeeded Bernardo Bonavía as commandant general, he had surrendered the office of intendant to his brother Diego García Conde. This individual managed civil affairs until 1821 with the title of Brigadier of the National Armies and Political Chief and Intendant of Nueva Vizcaya.[27] In 1820 he acted as president of a special council (*junta preparatoria*) which was convened in Durango for the purpose of formulating the procedure by which elections for new deputies to the Spanish Cortes of 1820 and

22. Arredondo to the Viceroy, Monterrey, April 7, 1819, *ibid.*

23. Viceroy to the Minister of War, Mexico, July 31, 1819, *ibid.*

24. García Conde to Melgares, Durango, November 24, 1819, SANM, doc. 2860.

25. García Conde to Melgares, Durango, June 27, 1820, SANM, doc. 2899.

26. Melgares to the Commandant at Chihuahua, Santa Fe, January 3, 1820, SANM, doc. 2874.

27. Bando of García Conde, Durango, July 5, 1820, SANM, doc. 2904. The title of political chief (*jefe político*) was commonly held by the governors of New Mexico after independence, but that it was used to designate them as early as 1820 is indicated by such a reference in this document. Bancroft, in *North Mexican States,* II, 587, declares that Antonio Cordero ruled Durango as civil and military governor for three years previous to independence. On this, see Navarro García, *Las Provincias Internas,* pp. 93-94.

1821 would take place. The set of voting instructions drawn up by the junta applied to the four western internal provinces—Nueva Vizcaya, Sonora, Sinaloa, and New Mexico.[28] The council's action was of scant importance since the winds of revolution soon swept down upon the internal provinces.

The liberal resurgence in Spain in 1820 aroused the powerful conservative factions in Mexico. Fearing for the preservation of their privileges, they cast their lot with Agustín Iturbide, a dissident officer in the royal army, who formalized his separatist intentions in the Plan of Iguala, proclaimed to the country at large on February 24, 1821.

The Plan provided a scheme whereby all the inhabitants of New Spain could unite, on a basis of mutual toleration, in establishing their political independence. Embodied within the document were three principal provisions guaranteeing 1) the Catholic religion and clerical privileges, 2) absolute independence, and 3) racial equality.[29] These became known as the Three Guarantees, and to them rallied all insurgent elements. Iturbide rapidly gained strength as royalist commanders declared in favor of his leadership, and soon most of the interior was in his hands.

A new viceroy, Juan O'Donojú, arrived from Spain in July of 1821, and shortly thereafter signed with the rebel leader the Treaty of Córdoba, which incorporated the Plan of Iguala and recognized the independence of New Spain. Iturbide, upon whom a grateful populace had bestowed the title of El Libertador, then proceeded to organize a government by forming a regency and convoking a constituent congress. Meanwhile, the Spanish Constitution of 1812, with certain modifications, continued in force.

At Chihuahua, Commandant General Alejo García Conde, no doubt lukewarm to the independence movement in its initial stages, soon fell into line and by a decree of August 27, addressed to all the people of the Provincias Internas de Occidente, called upon them to

28. Junta Preparatoria, Instructions, Durango, July 5, 1820, SANM, doc. 2903.

29. Herbert Ingram Priestley, *The Mexican Nation* (New York, 1924), pp. 247-48.

swear allegiance to the Plan of Iguala.[30] On the same day, he commanded the municipal council of Chihuahua to declare its fidelity to the system of Iturbide, and it promptly did so.[31]

Historians hitherto have concluded that the struggle for independence made little impression on the people of New Mexico.[32] This view, however, appears extreme, since it is certain that the small *rico,* or wealthy class, kept fully abreast of developments to the south and was more than passingly concerned with the outcome of events. Notice of important decrees and other actions reached the governor regularly, and these were conveyed to local officials. Copies of the Treaty of Córdoba, for example, were distributed to the alcaldes of thirteen towns in the province, and it would have been strange, indeed, if such news did not evoke considerable discussion.

On December 26, word reached Santa Fe of Iturbide's triumphal entry into Mexico City, which signaled the consummation of independence. The news produced the following display, according to the New Mexican governor: "*Vivas* resounded on all sides, patriotic harangues were heard, and never had such delight and satisfaction reigned."[33]

30. García Conde apparently transferred himself and his staff from Durango sometime around the beginning of 1821, for the first letter from the Commandant General written in Chihuahua and found in the Santa Fe Archives is dated January 18 of that year. SANM, doc. 2959.

31. Ponce de León, *Reseñas históricas,* 147-48; and Papers of the War for Independence, March 3-September 13, 1821, SANM, doc. 2970. The assertion by Bancroft in *North Mexican States,* II, 586, that García Conde was removed as commandant general because he delayed in supporting independence is completely erroneous. He seems not to have realized that there were two García Condes, and in this case, he may have confused Alejo with Diego.

32. Hubert Howe Bancroft, *Arizona and New Mexico, 1530-1888* (San Francisco, 1888), p. 308; and Ralph Emerson Twitchell, *The Leading Facts of New Mexican History* (5 vols.; Cedar Rapids, Iowa, 1911-1917), I, 480.

33. "La gaceta imperial," March 23-26, 1822, quoted by Ralph Emerson Twitchell, *Old Santa Fe* (Santa Fe, 1925), p. 179.

PART TWO

CHAPTER VI

THE OFFICE OF GOVERNOR

CIVIL AND MILITARY authority in New Mexico was vested in a governor who directed affairs of the province with the aid of his agents, the alcaldes mayores. It is difficult for the modern student to appreciate properly the complexity and enormity of the problems which beset Spain's officers in this farthest corner of the empire. The tribes which invested the frontiers on all sides engaged in alternate trade and war with the Spaniards and Pueblo Indians, exacting during times of hostility a considerable toll in human lives and suffering. The economy of the region developed slowly, because of the defense effort. The general feeling of crisis promoted by the uncertainty of life and limb was intensified by the poverty of the people. With hardship a salient characteristic of life in New Mexico, the office of governor needed a man of considerable fortitude and intelligence.

It may fairly be reckoned that the governors coming from Spain and Mexico, especially in the eighteenth century when raiders from the plains had accelerated their activities, looked with considerable misgiving upon their assignment to New Mexico. Some, such as Pedro Fermín de Mendinueta and Juan Bautista de Anza, were men of exceptional vigor who met considerable success in defeating or bargaining with the Indians. Others displayed less forceful traits of character, and some were blatantly weak and dishonest. As Scholes has succinctly remarked, "A governor's powers were wide enough to permit an honest and energetic man to maintain discipline and secure justice, or to make it possible for a self-seeking official to become a local tyrant."[1]

1. France V. Scholes, "Civil Government in New Mexico," *NMHR,* X (1935), 75.

In theory, the governor headed a battery of lesser officials who assisted in the conduct of provincial business. These included a lieutenant governor, the members of the town council, or cabildo, of Santa Fe, a secretary of government who served as notary as well as personal adviser to the governor, and a clerk. Administering the separate districts or rural subdivisions into which the region was divided were the alcaldes mayores, together with their subordinate lieutenants and an assortment of petty magistrates among the Pueblo Indians. In actual practice, the eighteenth century witnessed a decline in the number of functionaries, mainly, it seems, because of the dearth of qualified candidates to fill the various offices.

Toward the end of the century, for example, the governor was without the services of a secretary and a notary, and several districts lacked for a time an alcalde mayor. Moreover, the lieutenant governor was far to the south, administering the district of El Paso, and the municipal council of Santa Fe, which traditionally had aided the governor in the directon of provincial affairs, had ceased to exist sometime before mid-century. As a consequence, the governor came to rely upon the advice and assistance of the officers of the capital's presidial garrison.

The governor's duties encompassed directly or indirectly all affairs within his jurisdiction. As a military ruler, he was responsible for maintenance of the peace, the most demanding of all tasks. Tied to this obligation was the supply, training, and command of the regular presidial troops and the citizens' militia. Moreover, his constant dealings with the native inhabitants, both peaceful and hostile, made him, in effect, the Indian agent for the district—the personal liaison between the Spanish government and these subjects.

Outside the city of Santa Fe, few local administrative duties were in the hands of the governor since these he delegated to his agents, the alcaldes mayores. They, in addition, dispensed justice at the local level, the governor retaining supervision over their activities and sitting as a court of appeal from their decisions. Generally, his sphere of action included both civil and criminal cases and litigation involving the military fuero.

In absence of a treasury office in New Mexico, the governor was concerned with the collection of taxes and the promotion of such meager crown revenues as existed. Similarly, he encouraged the economy of the country whenever possible, although this and the administration of finances remained minor phases of his total activity.

The governor, as vice-patron of the Church, was responsible for maintenance and welfare of the entire missionary program. The work of conversion, however, was weakened after the Pueblo revolt of the late seventeenth century, and it never recovered its early vigor.

Beyond these specific obligations, the governor was impelled to foster the general welfare of his province. This implied a wide range of authority, and, in fact, empowered him to perform whatever acts were necessary to ensure the proper functioning of the governmental machinery, subject always, of course, to the approval of his immediate superiors. The governor could issue appropriate ordinances and decrees; he arranged for division of the province into lesser administrative districts; he appointed civil officials at the local level and nominated persons for military positions; he supervised the founding of new settlements, the concentration of the population for defensive purposes, and the taking of a periodic census; he controlled the assignment of land and water rights outside the Villa of Santa Fe; and he regulated public travel within the province.

The governor was empowered to maintain public buildings, including his residence (the *casa real*), the cuartel, or installations and barracks of the presidial troops, frontier outposts, supply depots, roads and communications. To insure his familiarity with the province he was expected to conduct a general inspection (*visita*) of his jurisdiction, seeking out and remedying injustices and providing necessary changes in the local administration. To all of this was added an inordinate amount of paper work, the governor being required to compose a host of reports throughout the year to be submitted in duplicate or triplicate to the central authorities.[2]

2. On the general character of the governor's office, see Priestley, *Jóse de Gálvez*, p. 60; and Scholes, "Civil Government in New Mexico," p. 76.

Appointment and Term. Appointments to the governorship of New Mexico in the eighteenth century were made directly by the king, upon recommendations of the viceroy or commandant general, submitted through the Council of the Indies.[3] If the appointee was in Spain, he took his oath of office before the Council.[4] If in the New World, it was administered to him in the presence of the Audiencia of Mexico and the viceroy until the separation of the Provincias Internas in 1776; after that the duty devolved upon the commandant general and the Audiencia of Guadalajara. Frequently the commandant general alone received the oath from the new governor, especially if the latter was already in the northern provinces, since a journey to Guadalajara would have occasioned excessive delay.

A formal title of appointment, prepared for each new governor, outlined his obligations to the crown, fixed his salary and term of office, and commanded the appropriate officials to accord him all honors, benefits, rights, immunities, and prerogatives of his office.[5]

The first governor of New Mexico, Juan de Oñate, received a lifetime appointment as governor and captain general. When he resigned his office in 1607, however, the contract into which he had entered with the crown was nullified. Thereafter, the term of the governor was regulated by prevailing colonial policy rather than by a particular contract.[6]

The normal term of office for a governor in the seventeenth century seems to have been about three years, though one official served for seven years while another remained in office only six

3. The governors were named by viceregal appointment in the seventeenth century. A curious note by Twitchell, *Leading Facts,* I, 480, provides an insight into the selection of governors just prior to independence. He states, "In the official newspaper of the City of Mexico, of March 7, 1819, the office of governor of New Mexico was declared vacant, and aspirants were notified to send in their petitions. . . ."

4. Real Alencaster to the Audiencia of Guadalajara, Santa Fe, March 31, 1805, SANM, doc. 1802.

5. Thomas, *Forgotten Frontiers,* pp. 115-16.

6. George P. Hammond and Agapito Rey, eds., *Don Juan de Oñate, Colonizer of New Mexico, 1595-1628* (2 vols.; Albuquerque, 1953), I, 48.

months.[7] In the following century, five years became the general rule, though a number of men served for briefer or longer periods.[8] The royal title of appointment conferred upon Governor Anza in 1777, for instance, specifically limited his term to "five years more or less."[9] The term itself actually began when the new governor arrived in Santa Fe and received the staff (*bastón*) of office from his predecessor or from the person who had been serving in the interval.[10] Often the retiring officer left a set of instructions to guide his successor and acquaint him with the affairs of the province.

The governor's office became vacant with the expiration of its occupant's term, or through the governor's removal for misconduct or other causes, or through his resignation or death. On occasion, an executive who became ill or otherwise incapacitated petitioned the king for permission to retire. Such an instance arose in 1803 when Governor Fernando de Chacón was relieved of his office by order of the crown.[11]

Salary. The presidial Reglamento of 1772 provided that the salary of the governor, combined with that of his position as commandant of the presidial garrison, should be four thousand pesos annually. Earlier the governor had received only two thousand pesos, but then the position of presidial commandant had been held by a separate individual.[12]

Scholes notes that in the seventeenth century the governor's yearly salary commenced with the date of his departure for Santa Fe

7. *Recopilación de leyes de los reynos de las Indias* (4 vols.; Madrid, 1681), lib. v, tit. 1, ley 10; and Scholes, "Civil Government in New Mexico," p. 74.

8. The list of Spanish governors and their terms of office may be found in Lansing B. Bloom, "The Governors of New Mexico," *NMHR,* X (1935), 154-56. This compilation is more authoritative than earlier ones by Bancroft, Twitchell, and others.

9. Thomas, *Forgotten Frontiers,* p. 117.

10. Scholes, "Civil Government in New Mexico," p. 75.

11. Order of Charles IV, August 25, 1803, SANM, doc. 1704. Chacón had been injured several times in battle and in falls from his horse.

12. Anza's title of appointment issued in 1777 assigns him only the two thousand pesos designated for the governor's job, suggesting that the royal officers who prepared the document overlooked the appropriate provision in the new Reglamento regarding this. Thomas, *Forgotten Frontiers,* p. 116.

from Mexico City.[13] Governor Anza, however, by the royal order referred to above, began receiving his pay on the day he took office.[14] Customarily the salary ended with the date of transfer of authority to a successor in Santa Fe.

The governor's salary for the first year was taxed through the *media anata* or half-annate. This tax, as noted in a previous chapter, consisted of one-half of a royal officer's regular pay earned during the initial year of his term. In 1632 a schedule had been established regulating the media anata and providing that half of the sum due the crown be paid prior to the receipt of the commission and the other half be paid in the first month of the second year after assuming office.[15]

A report of the accounting office in Mexico, prepared in 1777, indicates that the only official in New Mexico affected by the media anata was the governor, who was required to pay one thousand pesos.[16] This means that the tax was being collected only on what he was earning as political chief, his salary of two thousand additional pesos as military commander remaining exempt.[17] This custom was formalized in a royal decree of August 21, 1799.[18] Commandant General Teodoro de Croix in 1778 had been confused on this question, as other royal officers must have been before and after. It is to be presumed, however, that the order of 1799 settled the matter, although the governor of New Mexico was not notified of the king's action until 1803.[19]

13. "Civil Government in New Mexico," p. 75.

14. Thomas, *Forgotten Frontiers,* p. 116. Usually a new governor received one year's pay in advance.

15. Warner, "The Career of Martínez de Torrelaguna," p. 35n.

16. Ecclesiastics in New Spain for a while were subject to the media anata, but this seems not to have applied to the friars in New Mexico. Priestley, *José de Gálvez,* p. 334; and Croix to Anza, Arizpe, January 23, 1783, SANM, doc. 851. *Alcaldes ordinarios* and other elective municipal officers of the Provincias Internas were formally exempted from the tax in 1796, though probably few had been paying it before this time. Nava to the Governor of New Mexico, Chihuahua, October 11, 1796, SANM, doc. 1372.

17. State of the Media Anata in the Provinces, January 30, 1777, AGN, Prov. Int., 74.

18. Salcedo to the Governor of New Mexico, Chihuahua, March 14, 1803, SANM, doc. 1646; and Real Cédula, December 24, 1799, SANM, doc. 1472a.

19. Governor of New Mexico to Salcedo, Santa Fe, August 29, 1803, SANM, doc. 1672 (3).

Sometime in the early 1790's, the king issued a reglamento which required the treasury agent at Chihuahua to withhold a fifth of the New Mexico governor's salary each year.[20] It was intended that the money would serve to pay any judicial fines levied at the time of his residencia. Governor Chacón petitioned the king in 1794 to revoke the decree, arguing that the withholding of such funds caused him excessive hardship.[21] Governor Real Alencaster made a similar plea in 1805.[22]

Considering the personal expenses of a governor, traveling costs to and from New Mexico, and the media anata tax, the salary delivered to him was scarcely adequate. Moreover, several governors in the seventeenth and early eighteenth centuries actually bought their offices from the crown. The Marqués de la Peñuela paid four thousand pesos for the position in 1705, and was obligated to pay, in addition, the media anata.[23] This represented a considerable initial outlay, and it is clear that the men who thus purchased their offices expected to profit through illegal activities open to them.

The Governor as Military Commandant. The military capabilities of the governor of New Mexico were perhaps his most important assets. Officials devoted to self-aggrandizement might shirk their responsibilities in defending the province, but those who conscientiously strove to protect the citizenry and the interests of the crown often placed themselves in a hazardous position when personally leading campaigns against the enemy. Service records, which are available for a number of the governors, indicate that most came to New Mexico with a background of considerable experience in soldiering.

From the founding of New Mexico until 1768, the governor held the military title of captain general.[24] On February 24, 1768, the

20. Until the creation of the treasury branch in the northern provinces, the governor's salary had come directly from the royal exchequer in Mexico City. SANM, doc. 1795.

21. Petition, November 18, 1794, SANM, doc. 1298a. Governor Alencaster in 1805 asked that a bond be substituted for the twenty per cent salary discount. SANM, doc. 1795.

22. SANM, doc. 1795.

23. Warner, "The Career of Martínez de Torrelaguna," p. 35, and Navarro García, *José de Gálvez,* p. 49.

24. Hammond and Rey, *Don Juan de Oñate,* I, 48.

crown, upon the advice of the Council of the Indies, determined to reserve the title to the viceroy of New Spain, designating the governor simply as commander of the armed forces of New Mexico. Some time apparently elapsed before the order went into effect, for Governor Mendinueta, who left his chair in 1777, is mentioned as the last occupant who bore the rank of captain general.[25]

The governor's principal duties as military commander revolved around defense of the province. The troops available were the royal or veteran troops stationed in Santa Fe, the citizens' militia, and the Indian auxiliaries.

The governor directed the operations of war freely within his province, either leading punitive expeditions himself or delegating the task to a trusted subordinate. Occasionally a combination of troop movements with forces from Nueva Vizcaya and Sonora was arranged, in which case the governor acted in concert with the campaign commander designated by the commandant general.

The operation of the presidial garrison at Santa Fe demanded close attention. The governor, through his subordinate officers, saw to the direction, quartering, and provisioning of the royal troops. Earlier his authority in these matters had permitted him to reap considerable profit through manipulation of company funds, but beginning with the Rivera inspection, successive modifications were introduced that limited his power and deprived him of opportunities for peculation.

Soldiers were detached from time to time to serve at strategic outposts on the Indian frontier, from whence they made frequent reports to their commander. Besides deploying the troops, the governor was responsible for assigning soldiers to escort duty with the supply trains going south or with the entourages of visiting church dignitaries. He could also make recommendations concerning the establishment of new presidios.

The governor, as captain of the regular troops, submitted nomina-

25. Twitchell, *Leading Facts,* I, 447; Thomas, *Forgotten Frontiers,* p. 115.

tions for commissioned and non-commissioned officers to the commandant general.[26] These were listed in order of the governor's preference, and the service records of each man were attached to the correspondence. By law three names were offered for each vacancy, the commandant general selecting the most qualified candidate. In reality, the governor often experienced difficulty in finding worthy soldiers among the few in his charge to fill the available offices, and he customarily made only a single nomination. Occasionally he could encounter no one who was suitable, in which case he so advised the commandant general. This officer then sought out some meritorious soldier from the garrisons of Nueva Vizcaya and dispatched him to New Mexico to fill the vacant rank. All appointments by the commandant general were subject to royal confirmation. The governor as presidial commander was permitted to name corporals on his own authority.[27]

In a similar manner the governor recommended to commandancy headquarters persons for service awards, retirement certificates, and pensions. Appropriate papers prepared by the Santa Fe officials were filed with the secretariat in Chihuahua outlining each case and submitting evidence suppporting the recommendation. The governor was notified by the commandant general as to which of the awards had been approved.

He was obligated to inspect the troops monthly and to prepare an extract indicating the condition and strength of the company. The original extract remained on file at the presidio while two copies were forwarded to the commandant inspector.

The governor, because of his remote position, exercised the duties of subinspector. This was intended to relieve the commandant inspector and his assistants of the necessity of frequent inspection tours

26. Prior to 1788, the nominations were required to go through the commandant inspector, but in that year, it will be remembered, the inspector's office was absorbed by the commandant general.

27. *Reglamento para los presidios,* tit. 8. Also Salcedo to Chacón, Chihuahua, December 29, 1802, SANM, doc. 1637; and Salcedo to Real Alencaster, Chihuahua, September 4, 1806, SANM, doc. 2015.

of the province.[28] The most notable visit by a commandant inspector occurred in October and November of 1787 when Don José Antonio Rengel conducted a review of the Santa Fe presidial company and then led a successful campaign against troublesome Apaches. So far as is known, no commandant general ever paid an official visit to New Mexico.

The Residencia. The residencia was a judicial inquiry into the conduct of a royal officer made at the conclusion of his term of administration. It was a means of holding civil servants who had completed a definite term responsible for their official acts. The procedure in judgments of residencia was laid down in the *Recopilación de leyes de las Indias* in the seventeenth century[29] and was enlarged upon and somewhat modified by a royal cedula of August 24, 1799.[30]

In New Mexico it was the duty of each governor to act as a magistrate (*juez de residencia*) in taking the judgment of his predecessor. The residencia was usually begun soon after the new governor assumed office, since the retiring official was not permitted to leave the province until the inquiry was completed. If investigation showed that he was guilty of malfeasance in office, he faced a fine or, in severe cases, banishment or imprisonment according to the nature of the offense.[31]

The residencia came as a matter of routine and was made whether the individual concerned had compiled a good or bad record. Persons of all stations were invited to appear before the magistrate and offer testimony. More often than not, it could be shown in the case of the New Mexico governors that royal orders had been violated, powers abused, and subjects, particularly the Indians, mis-

28. Ugarte y Loyola to Viceroy Flores, Chihuahua, July 3, 1788, AGN, Prov. Int. 65. Under orders of the commandant general, the Ayudante Inspector Antonio García Texeda was instructed in 1805 to review the Santa Fe garrison in order to acquaint himself with the military affairs of that distant province. Salcedo to Real Alencaster, Chihuahua, February 17, 1805, SANM, doc. 1796.

29. Lib. v, tit. 15.

30. SANM, doc. 1460.

31. The character of the residencia in New Mexico in the seventeenth century has been revealed through the studies of France V. Scholes. See especially his *Troublous Times in New Mexico* (Hist. Soc. of N.M. Publ. in History; Santa Fe, 1942), chap. III, *passim.*

treated. When such was made known, however, the guilty officer was usually successful in thwarting justice by bribing the judge.[32]

In the eighteenth century, the records which are presently available indicate that some modifications were introduced in the system of residencias in New Mexico. Chief among these was the "pernicious practice" whereby governors occasionally were granted licenses by the viceregal authorities permitting them to leave the province prior to the residencia. This usually resulted in the governor escaping penalties, although he was required to leave behind an attorney to settle complaints.[33]

In another innovation, judges of residencia were sometimes named independently; that is, the new governors were not conceded investigatory authority over their predecessors, this power being delegated instead to a royal appointee sent from the South. Captain Don Antonio Bezerra Nieto, commander of the royal presidio at Janos, for example, was appointed in 1722 to conduct the residencias of former governors Valverde and Martínez.[34] Judges of this kind were often accused by the friars not only of accepting bribes but also of exploiting the local Indians for whatever profits could be gained.[35] Citizens, too, became skeptical of some of the judges. A number of New Mexicans, for instance, journeyed to Chihuahua in 1794 to render complaints directly to the commandant general against former Governor Fernando de la Concha.[36] It is difficult to believe that such a measure would have been taken had the citizens placed any faith in the normal judicial process.

It will be remembered that the Spanish king in the 1790's ordered that a fifth of the governor's salary be withheld each year so that funds would be on hand to pay the judicial fines assessed at the time of the residencia. Presumably the balance remaining after penalties were extracted was delivered over to the retiring officer.

32. Scholes, "Civil Government in New Mexico," p. 87.

33. Warner, "The Career of Martínez de Torrelaguna," p. 132.

34. *Ibid.*, p. 133.

35. Charles W. Hackett, ed., *Historical Documents Relating to New Mexico, Nueva Vizcaya, and Approaches Thereto, to 1773* (3 vols.; Washington, 1923-1927), III, 429.

36. Nava to Chacón, Chihuahua, September 12, 1794, SANM, doc. 1295.

It seems that investigation into the conduct of a retiring governor was often extended to include the activities of his immediate subordinates. This was the common practice in New Spain and was carried over, at least in the eighteenth century, to New Mexico.[37] The judge looked into the affairs especially of the alcaldes mayores who were appointees of the governor and who might be suspected of entering into illegal schemes with him to enrich themselves. In the 1600's, the governors upon assuming office usually preferred to replace the holdover alcaldes with their own favorites, thus wedding these men to their interests. The trend in the following century, particularly in the later period, was for a new governor to retain the alcaldes of his predecessor with the result that a number of men held these offices for life. Nevertheless, some alcaldes from time to time underwent a judgment of residencia along with the governor, as indicated by a document of 1750.[38]

The cedula of 1799 referred to above was received by the governor of New Mexico in July of 1800.[39] Several of its provisions shed light upon procedures followed in the residencia at the provincial level.

The testimony and papers collected by the judge in the case of a political and military governor were to be remitted to the Council of the Indies in Spain for final judgment.[40] Those of the alcaldes mayores were to pass to the appropriate audiencia, in the case of New Mexico that of Guadalajara, for review. The activities of the governor's legal adviser were to come under scrutiny during the official residencia, though as future recital will show, the governor of New Mexico in the later colonial years never enjoyed the services of such a legal adviser. By other articles of the cedula, alcaldes ordinarios, town councilmen (*regidores*), notaries (*escribanos*), and similar minor political officers were exempted from the residencia.

The civil attorney (*fiscal civil*) of the audiencia composed a questionnaire and a book of rules and instructions for use of the

37. Priestley, *José de Gálvez,* p. 113.

38. Hackett, *Historical Documents,* III, 429.

39. SANM, doc. 1495.

40. The same line was followed for viceroys, audiencia presidents, and intendants.

jueces de residencia. When an investigation was concluded, the Council or audiencia, depending upon which had ultimate jurisdiction, issued a certificate of good conduct to the official involved or imposed the appropriate penalties if infractions of the law had been proved. Without this certificate an individual was ineligible to hold future offices.[41]

The Visita. The visita or formal inspection of a specific area was a regular feature of Spanish colonial administration. It was designed to control the actions of distant officials who were constantly tempted to indulge in abuse of their powers. Frequent reference has already been made to José de Gálvez who came to New Spain as visitor general in the 1760's. His inspection, though conducted with certain objectives in view, was all-embracing in that he arrived vested with powers permitting him to examine any phase of government.

Visitas were conducted in New Mexico by the governor. By law he was strictly limited to a single general inspection (*visita general*) during his term of office unless otherwise ordered by his superiors.[42] If urgency demanded another visita, appeal could be made to the commandant general who authorized the investigation. The governor from time to time seems to have designated one of his subordinates to conduct a limited visita in some restricted area.[43] A full report of the inquiry was returned to the governor, or if he himself undertook a general visita, he submitted the account to the commandant general.[44]

According to law, the jail in Santa Fe ought to have been visited weekly by a local official. In other provinces this petty function was delegated to the alcaldes, but in New Mexico's capital the governor frequently performed the duty.[45] On occasion the alcalde mayor visited the jail in place of the governor.

In conducting a general visita, the governor was accompanied by

41. Royal Cedula on Residencia Procedure, August 24, 1799, SANM, doc. 1460.

42. *Recopilación,* lib. v, tit. 2, ley 11. Real Alencaster to Isidro Rey, Santa Fe, June 30, 1807, SANM, doc. 2063.

45. See, e.g., Warner, "The Career of Martínez de Torrelaguna," p. 34.

44. *Recopilación,* lib. v, tit. 2, ley 15.

45. Hubert Howe Bancroft, *California Pastoral, 1769-1848* (San Francisco, 1888), p. 579.

a secretary (*secretario de visita*), who acted as official recorder. Announcement of an official inspection was proclaimed a month or so in advance, in order that the people might become well acquainted with the manner by which it would be pursued and make arrangements, if they desired, to appear before the governor. The party of the inspecting officer passed from one district to the other, halting in the principal towns or Indian pueblos. At each, the original edict (*bando*) announcing the visita was read, in the native language (*voz común*) if at an Indian pueblo, after the people had been assembled by the governor's assistants. Those persons who had complaints against their local political officers appeared before the commission to submit evidence and to have their testimony entered in the official record. Often no one had a grievance, in which case an appropriate declaration to that effect was taken by the governor. Besides receiving complaints, the governor held court for the benefit of local citizens who could not travel to Santa Fe to initiate a suit or other legal proceedings.

Besides permitting citizens to confront the governor to express their dissatisfaction, the visita gave that officer opportunity to inspect local defenses and review the state of the provincial militia (the *revista de armas*). In addition the governor was required to compile a census of the places visited. Unfortunately, most of the records pertaining to the general inspection have disappeared so that no full treatment of the subject is possible at this time.

The Administration of Justice. In Part One of this study, reference was made to judicial procedure in the Provincias Internas, which were under the Audiencia of Guadalajara. A detailed examination of the functioning of the local courts will be undertaken in a succeeding chapter, and at that time the role of the governor in the legal process will be developed further. Nevertheless, some general remarks on this subject may be considered here to provide a rounded picture of the governor's office.

The governor sat as the principal civil and criminal magistrate within the province of New Mexico. As such, he was often designated as the chief justice (*justicia mayor*) or as chief alcalde (*jefe de alcaldes*), indicating that his jurisdiction extended over lesser judges of the district.[46] In minor cases, he received appeals from the rural courts with the right to render judgment in the final instance. In all cases of a serious nature, he served as judge of first instance with appeals being carried to the Audiencia of Guadalajara. Since in the late colonial period he lacked a legal adviser and even a royal notary to assist him, cases which the governor prepared often went to the legal advisers, the asesor or auditor de guerra, of the commandancy for an opinion before continuing to the superior tribunal.[47] In all cases involving Indians, the governor held exclusive jurisdiction, as well as the power to appoint defenders (*defensores* or *curadores*) in their behalf.[48] Periodically he reported to the audiencia a list of cases pending and a statement of prisoners held in the jails of Santa Fe and El Paso.

In 1754 Governor Fermín de Mendinueta expressed the opinion that the people of New Mexico as a whole were "perverse, poor, and lazy" and because of the irregularities in their conduct justice should be meted out rigorously.[49] Governor Concha almost a half-century later was found to be in general accord with this harsh judgment, and he observed that the people required a stern hand to prevent them from perverting the law to their own advantage. In two matters especially were the residents of the province guilty. The first concerned appeals to Guadalajara. Since it involved great expense to carry a case to the audiencia, parties who considered themselves wronged in some litigation merely awaited the arrival of a new governor. They then renewed their old disputes or petitions in hope

46. The general term *justicia mayor* was also applied on occasion to the *alcaldes mayores* to distinguish them from their lieutenants.

47. Cases were permitted to go direct from New Mexico to the superior tribunal in Guadalajara without the intervention of the assessor, and this, in fact, seems to have been the usual practice. See e.g. Real Alencaster to the Lt. Governor, Santa Fe, September 1, 1805, SANM, doc. 1883 (3).

48. Lansing B. Bloom, ed., "Instrucción a Peralta por vi-rey," NMHR, IV (1929), 181. Detailed instructions by the assessor general on the handling of Indian cases are contained in a trial record for the years 1805 and 1806 in Santa Fe. SANM, doc. 1931.

49. Alfred B. Thomas, *The Plains Indians and New Mexico,* 1751-1778 (Albuquerque, 1940), p. 41.

that another judgment would be more favorable to their interests. Governor Concha asserted that new governors possessed no legal authority to reopen cases decided by their predecessors, but had only the duty to advise persons of the procedure which they must follow in their appeals.

In the second matter, citizens were accustomed to circumventing their local magistrates by resorting directly to the governor, particularly in protesting new edicts. This produced much disorder in the judicial process and forced the governors to insist that litigants observe the required formalities in all legal actions.[50]

Church Patronage. No published comment exists on the powers which the governor of New Mexico exercised as vice-patron of the Church in the late colonial period. There is a dearth of information on the subject; nevertheless, some clues are provided by contemporary documents.

As previous discussion has shown, the original instructions to the first commandant general conferred upon that officer the patronage within his jurisdiction. He was permitted to select from the candidates proposed by the Bishop of Durango, or in the case of his death those proposed by the cathedral chapter, the priests who should fill vacant curacies and benefices. The commandant was allowed to subdelegate this prerogative to the various governors in the Provincias Internas so that the selection of religious ministers might be expedited.[51] Each new governor of New Mexico at the onset of his term seems to have been dependent upon a formal renewal of the vice-patronage by the commandant general. In short, the latter retained, in theory, the privilege of delegating or withholding it as he saw fit.

Prior to creation of the commandancy, the Audiencia of Guadalajara held the patronato, appointing and removing religious curates,

50. Fernando de la Concha, "Advice on Governing New Mexico, 1794," *NMHR,* XXIV (1949), 247 (trs. by Donald E. Worcester).

51. This included authority over both secular and regular clergy. Richman, *California under Spain and Mexico,* p. 432.

both secular and regular, in the northern provinces.[52] Nominations for regular curates, even in the seventeenth century, were made by the bishops, the prelates of the religious orders interposing their authority only in the matter of disciplining their members. The friars in New Spain resented this situation, though the prnciple that no clergyman might have jurisdiction over secular persons unless he was subject to the episcopal authority had been affirmed by the Council of Trent.[53]

In 1783 Commandant General Felipe de Neve notified Governor Anza that he was subdelegating the patronato to him by virtue of the authority which derived from instructions issued to the first commandant. Neve added that he was informing the cabildo of Durango (the See being vacant) of his action so that it might direct future nominations (*propuestas*) of curates to the governor.[54] He further enjoined Anza to keep the office of commandant advised of all measures undertaken involving the royal patronage.[55]

Neve gave no hint as to how the cabildo selected the friars who were to be nominated, nor does he make any reference to the custodian, the ranking Franciscan prelate in New Mexico, as to whether the governor was to consult him in making the final choice. In 1804,[56] Real Alencaster advised the commandant that as governor he had removed the friar of Jémez from his post, and in 1810[57] that

52. Governor Mendinueta to the Viceroy, January 20, 1768, SANM, doc. 634. The patronato in the jurisdiction of the Audiencia of Mexico was exercised by the viceroy. Fray Juan Sanz de Lezaún, writing in 1760, noted that the New Mexican governors had usurped some powers related to the vice-patronage which at that time they did not legally possess. Hackett, *Historical Documents,* III, 476. On the claim of Don Mateo Antonio de Mendoza to powers under the vice-patronage at this same time, see Eleanor B. Adams, ed., *Bishop Tamarón's Visitation of New Mexico,* 1760 (Hist. Soc. of N. M. Publs. in History, Albuquerque, 1954), p. 32n.

53. Haring, *The Spanish Empire in America,* p. 187.

54. Since New Mexico formed part of the diocese of the Bishop of Durango, the governor exercised authority over temporal Church affairs under this bishop's direction. See, e.g., Instructions from the Bishop to the Governor of New Mexico, Durango, January 9, 1806, SANM, doc. 1944.

55. SANM, doc. 866.

56. Real Alencaster to Salcedo, Santa Fe, March 28, 1804, SANM, doc. 1714.

57. Salcedo to Manrrique, Chihuahua, December 21, 1810, SANM, doc. 2387.

he was transferring the priest from Santa Clara Pueblo to the vacant curacy of Zuñi. In both cases the action was taken with approval of the custodian. This, no doubt, was merely a courtesy which the governor extended to the prelate, there being no legal impediment which would have hindered him from acting without the friar's sanction. Surprising, indeed, it would have been had not the governor consulted with the custodian of mission affairs as a matter of course.[58]

With regard to the manner in which the bishop or cathedral chapter of Durango obtained the names which it submitted as nominations to the governor of New Mexico, it may be assumed that the Provincial of the Franciscan Order in Mexico City submitted suitable candidates to Durango for the posts to be filled in the northern provinces. In 1806 five mission stations in New Mexico were without the services of a priest. Under the circumstances the governor besought the commandant general to prevail upon the viceroy to request that the Provincial in Mexico provide proper replacements.[59] This tack by the governor must be regarded as somewhat unusual. At the time, however, the question of the governor's patronage had become embroiled in controversy, and that officer was confused about the authority which actually belonged to him. In 1800, the Audiencia of Guadalajara had challenged the right of the New Mexican governor to exercise the vice-patronato, but upon what legal basis this stand was taken is not clear. Seemingly, the Audiencia, at least in part, was expressing its resentment over having lost the patronato at the time of the creation of the commandancy.

58. In 1802, the governor and custodian were on unfriendly terms. The prelate had on his own authority ordered the transference of the friar at Isleta Pueblo to the village of Nambé. This was clearly an invasion of the governor's prerogative and he moved to prevent the carrying out of this action. The custodian, thereupon, initiated litigation, the *instancias* from which were delivered to the legal adviser of the commandancy who ruled against the churchman. Chacón to Salcedo, Santa Fe, November 19, 1802, SANM, doc. 1629. In reality, there was a long history of friction between the governors and the missionary friars dating back to the seventeenth century.

59. Fray Angélico Chávez notes that the Custody in New Mexico faded away fast in the early nineteenth century through the deaths or departures of old friars and lack of replacements. *Archives of the Archdiocese of Santa Fe* (Washington, 1958), p. 4.

In all events, contention and discord between the court and the governor rapidly developed.[60]

In summary it may be stated that the governors soon after 1776 began to be granted the vice-patronage of the Church upon assumption of office. The powers inherent in this privilege, which had been spelled out in previous colonial legislation and in Article 4 of the Croix instructions, permitted them to appoint the curates whose names had been advanced by the episcopacy in Durango and to transfer or remove friars from their posts in New Mexico. They were required to submit every two years a complete statement of the condition of New Mexican missions.[61] Although the rights regarding appointment and removal appear to have been in abeyance for a brief period after the turn of the nineteenth century, they were returned to the governor at least by 1810 and were probably held thereafter until the end of the colonial period.[62]

Economic Development. It was the duty of the governor to foster the economic stability and prosperity of New Mexico in all fields. The occupations outside of government service open to native citizens were limited, for the most part, to agriculture, stock raising, and commerce, since manufacturing, logging, mining, and similar enterprises showed little development. The lack of local capital, or in its place government support, the dearth of readily accessible mineral resources, the relative scarcity of hard money, and most of all, the disastrous raiding and pillaging of the countryside by enemy Indians all retarded economic growth.

60. Chacón to Salcedo, Santa Fe, March 28, 1804, SANM, doc. 1714; Chacón to Salcedo, Santa Fe, July 26, 1804, SANM, doc. 1746; Real Alencaster to Salcedo, Santa Fe, October 2, 1805, SANM, doc. 1900; Real Alencaster to Salcedo, Santa Fe, May 28, 1806, SANM, doc. 1988. For the Bishop's low opinion of the friars of New Mexico in this period, see Olivares y Benito to Real Alencaster, Durango, January 9, 1806, SANM, doc. 1806.

61. The document was to include a census of the pueblos apart from the yearly tabulation compiled for the entire province. Salcedo to the Governor of New Mexico, Chihuahua, January 18, 1806, SANM, doc. 1957.

62. On the nonexistence of the vice-patronato in New Mexico in 1806, see Real Alencaster to Salcedo, Santa Fe, April 1, 1805, SANM, doc. 1979(10). The text of a law of 1609 on the filling of parish vacancies is given by J. Lloyd Mecham, *Church and State in Latin America* (rev. ed.; Chapel Hill, 1966).

With his multitude of burdensome duties, the governor customarily had little time left to devote to expansion of the provincial economy, although there is record of at least one such official in the late eighteenth century journeying to Mexico with the object of obtaining funds for the promotion of mining.[63] There is considerable evidence to indicate that after the turn of the nineteenth century, the government began to display increasing concern for the economic backwardness not only of New Mexico but of all the Provincias Internas.

In 1804 the *consulado* or merchant's guild in Veracruz submitted to the commandant general a request for specific information on the agriculture, industries, and public works in the internal provinces. The following year the government arranged a contract with the master weaver Ignacio Bazán and his assistants to go to New Mexico and teach their trade. This action resulted in the improvement of local weaving and the production of a higher grade of cotton cloth.[64] In the summer of that year, the governor called a special junta which met in the palace and was composed of leading men of the province to consider the best measures for development of New Mexico.[65] At about the same time, the commandant general notified the governor that a new publication entitled *Semanario de agricultura y artes* was soon to be circulated and that it would contain pertinent data on new techniques and discoveries to aid economic advancement.[66]

It is doubtful that these or similar measures produced any significant improvement in New Mexico's economic system. Pedro Bautista Pino, writing in 1812, presented an altogether dismal picture of conditions in his province. Especially detrimental was the trade deficit with Chihuahua which, he declared, amounted to 52,000 pesos annually. Specie was extremely scarce, the salaries of the soldiers being one of the few sources of money in circulation. All

63. Benjamin M. Read, *Illustrated History of New Mexico* (Santa Fe, 1912), p. 345.

64. Weaver's Contract, Mexico, September 3, 1805, SANM, doc. 1885.

65. Economic Junta Report, Santa Fe, June 17, 1805, SANM, doc. 1844.

66. Salcedo to Real Alencaster, Chihuahua, August 8, 1805, SANM, doc. 1872.

areas of economic endeavor, Pino noted, were in need of encouragement and development.[67]

Public works and their maintenance included the construction and care of roads, bridges, and perhaps a few public inns. The camino real or king's highway, beginning in Mexico City, led by way of Durango and Chihuahua to El Paso del Norte and Santa Fe, ending in Taos.[68] That portion of the road within the boundaries of New Mexico was maintained by the provincial government using citizen or convict labor. Since no fund or municipal fee could be applied to this project, the citizens donated their services in the public interest. Prisoners from the local jails worked under the guard of a corporal or carbineer from the Santa Fe garrison, and were sustained with the aid of small fines levied against other delinquents.[69] Bridges across the Rio Grande were constructed in the late colonial period at El Paso, Belén, and perhaps other points. Continual repair of these was required since the spring floods caused heavy damage.[70]

For procurement of goods produced outside the province, New Mexico was almost wholly dependent upon the annual trading fair held each winter in the city of Chihuahua. A caravan (*cordon*) was formed, usually in November, to attend this event, and merchants and stock raisers to the number of several hundred gathered to take advantage of the safety afforded by a military escort.[71]

In 1805 the viceroy decreed that the annual fair should be held in

67. *Eposición,* pp. 21-22. Pino and several other contemporary writers refer to the absence of hard money in New Mexico. Government reports of the period, however, indicate that more specie circulated than Pino would have us believe, suggesting that his account may be exaggerated in this particular. Further reference to this subject is made in the following chapter.

68. After independence, the camino real became the camino constitucional.

69. Concha, "Advice on Governing New Mexico," p. 250. On a petition for road improvements by residents of San José de los Ranchos in the partido of Pajarito in the jurisdiction of Albuquerque in 1813, see SANM, doc. 2505.

70. Lansing B. Bloom, "Early Bridges in New Mexico," *El Palacio,* XVIII (1925), 163-82.

71. Referring to the caravan, Bishop Tamarón defined it as "the annual departure to Vizcaya for the purposes of trade and usually comprising five or six hundred men." Adams, *Bishop Tamaron's Visitation,* p. 92.

the Valle de San Bartolomé (today Valle de Allende) far to the south of the city of Chihuahua.[72] Possibly as a result of this action, New Mexico's governor, in the same year and in accord with the wishes of leading men of the province, urged establishment of an annual fair at the city of El Paso to stimulate the regional economy.[73] The commandant general referred the matter to Mexico City for consideration by the governing council of the royal treasury.[74] Whether this fair was inaugurated before the end of the Spanish regime is uncertain, but that it existed in the Mexican period is evidenced by one observer who credited the fair of Nuestra Señora de Guadalupe at El Paso with surpassing that of San Bartolomé in size and interest.[75]

The Regulation of Settlements. From the first days of the founding of the province of New Mexico, it was recognized that strength lay in the clinging together of colonists for mutual protection. The natural tendency of the citizens, however, was to disperse over the countryside in pursuit of the few economic activities which were open to them. Viceroy Luis de Velasco observed as early as 1609, "I have been informed that the small population of that country [New Mexico] is very scattered over it so that they are destitute of administration because very few reside in each place and they also are too far apart to be helped and protected."[76] This situation remained an abiding problem to the end of the colonial period, although special efforts were made in the second half of the eighteenth century to concentrate the people in easily defended settlements.

The governors were empowered to select sites for new settlements, to make arrangements for and certify their establishment, and to

72. Orders and Decrees, II, p. 115 (SANM, doc. 1935). The dates of this fair were set as the 18th to the 23rd of December. Salcedo to the Governor of New Mexico, Chihuahua, March 5, 1806, SANM, doc. 1972.

73. Real Alencaster to Salcedo, Santa Fe, October 2, 1805, SANM, doc. 1900(9).

74. Salcedo to Real Alencaster, Chihuahua, November 14, 1805, SANM, doc. 1919.

75. Rómulo Escobar, "La feria de Paso del Norte," *BSCEH,* II (1939), 131-33.

76. Bloom, "Instrucción a Peralta por vi-rey," p. 182.

provide the support needed in their earliest stage of development.[77] Related to this authority, the governors were obliged to see that no settlers abandoned their communities, or, for that matter, left the province without his expressed permission.[78] Spanish law was explicit in this latter regard. A person who left his place of residence without the proper license might forfeit any offices he held in addition to his house, lands, and other possessions.[79] The prohibition against traveling without a permit was reiterated specifically for New Mexico in a royal order of 1784 and was proclaimed throughout the area by the alcaldes mayores acting under orders of Governor Anza.[80]

Increasing Indian pressure upon the Spanish settlements in the eighteenth century accentuated the need for assembling the people of New Mexico to better resist the enemy. Governor Mendinueta, in 1772, bewailed the fact that among "the Spaniards there is no united settlement, so that to the dispersion of their houses the name of ranches or houses of the field is properly given and not that of villas or villages."[81] Antonio de Bonilla, four years later, echoed the governor's complaint and warned of impending ruin, for "the force of settlers is divided, and they can neither protect themselves nor contribute to the general defense of the country." By contrast he extolled the merits of the Indian pueblos which "are defensible because of their excellent and unified formation." In addition, he supported an earlier proposal by Governor Mendinueta which would

77. A certificate of the founding of Albuquerque and Galisteo by Governor Cuervo y Valdez in 1706, for example, may be viewed in translation in Hackett, *Historical Documents,* III, 379.

78. Scholes, "Civil Government in New Mexico," p. 76.

79. *Recopilación,* lib. v, tit. 1, ley 17.

80. Order on Public Travel, Santa Fe, April 24, 1784, SANM, doc. 891. Permits were occasionally issued by the governor through the alcaldes mayores for individuals to venture out onto the plains to trade with the nomadic Indians or hunt the buffalo. Instances of persons making such journeys illegally were frequent. See, e.g., Sanchez Vergara to Governor Manrrique, Jémez, January 16, 1811, SANM, doc. 2391.

81. Alfred B. Thomas, "Governor Mendinueta's Proposals for the Defense of New Mexico, 1772-1778," *NMHR,* VI (1931), 27.

have forced the New Mexicans to congregate in well-organized settlements.[82]

Fray Juan Agustín de Morfi, writing sometime in the 1780's, enumerated the injuries to government and society resulting from the people's careless habits of settlement. Some of these appear as follows: citizens, because of the isolation of their homes, felt free to act with independence and insolence in a manner which they would not have dared in the presence of the authorities; for the same reason, great crimes were committed since the wrongdoers held little fear of being punished; settlers were deprived of the benefits of the sacraments since the few priests could not reach those in the outlying areas; the men lived so far apart that when the government sounded the call to arms, the enemy had ample time to escape before the militia could assemble to give chase; and since many lived without neighbors to observe them, they were not ashamed to go about nude so that lewdness was seen here more than in the brutes, and the peaceful Indians were scandalized.

Morfi decried the fact that not a single Spanish town was well organized for defense. In particular he singled out the Villa of Albuquerque, complaining that its inhabitants were distributed for a dozen leagues along the banks of the river. If the people were brought together, a large town would be the result, common defense would be promoted, and abundant lands for cultivation and pasturage could be had by all.[83]

The arrangement of the Villa of Santa Fe appears to have been in similar disarray during the entire colonial period. As early as 1620, there was official concern expressed over the poor defensive qualities of the current site, and a proposal was advanced to move the capital to a more favorable location.[84] The sacking of the outlying districts of the Villa in the several days preceding its total abandonment by the Spanish during the Pueblo revolt emphasized the weaknesses

82. Thomas, "Antonio de Bonilla, Notes," pp. 196-200.

83. Fr. Juan Agustín de Morfi, Desórdenes que se advierten en el Nuevo México, AGN, Historia, 25.

84. Lansing B. Bloom, "A Glimpse of New Mexico in 1620," *NMHR,* III (1928), 369.

inherent in the haphazard growth hitherto permitted in the Santa Fe municipality. Notwithstanding, the capital was subsequently reconstructed on its former site, and disorderly sprawling over the surrounding countryside was resumed by the colonists.

The sad spectacle of the Santa Fe defensive position again became a subject of concern in the second half of the eighteenth century. Criticism of the capital's condition was implied in the remarks by Mendinueta and Bonilla. It was during the administration of governor Anza, however, that overt action on the question appeared imminent. Involved was not only an active proposal to reorganize Santa Fe, but the remaining towns of the province as well. Indian incursions had devastated large areas, so that Miera y Pacheco's map of New Mexico for the year 1780 showed more abandoned settlements than occupied ones.[85]

Anza received instructions from the commandant general to devote himself to the task of implementing the ideas originated by his predecessor, Governor Mendinueta, with regard to reform of the settlement patterns adopted by the New Mexicans. Although he set about enthusiastically to fulfill his charge, Anza was able to achieve results which were only partially successful. Albuquerque and Santa Cruz de la Cañada were apparently reduced to some order,[86] but the citizens of Santa Fe remained adamant in refusing to meet the demands of the governor who was seeking the transfer of the Villa to the south side of the river. Twenty-four of these fled the province without his permission and presented themselves before the commandant general in Arizpe to state their grievances. This bold action won an order restraining the governor from moving the capital until all complaints could be judiciously heard,[87] and in the final outcome, Santa Fe remained on its original site.

85. Cleve Hallenbeck, *Land of the Conquistadores* (Caldwell, Idaho, 1950), p. 243.

86. Thomas, *Forgotten Frontiers,* p. 379.

87. Fr. Juan Agustín de Morfi, Descripción geográfica del Nuevo Mexico, 1782, AGN, Historia, 25 (also translated in Thomas, *Forgotten Frontiers,* pp. 87-114). In addition to the provision noted above, the commandant general decreed that any citizen who wished to make an appeal to the superior government should not be prevented from leaving the province. This meant the governor could not deny travel permits to those who might want to make representations against his policies or actions.

In 1788 the commandant general approved a project by Governor Concha to reform the Villa of Santa Fe, but this concerned more the construction of a *cuartel* or presidial barracks than an attempt to concentrate the populace. A proposal current at this time, however, did advocate the shifting of the capital to a site near Santo Domingo Pueblo, but the hostile attitude of the citizens of the Villa, not to mention that of the Indians, caused the idea to be hastily abandoned. At this time two thousand pesos was assigned for work on the barracks to provide badly needed improvements.[88]

Land Grants. The Spanish king was proprietor of all territories conquered in his name and was at liberty to dispose of them as he chose. They were distributed in several ways. Lands were conceded to the support of new towns and their citizens, for Indian pueblos, and to vassals who had served in the conquest of a new territory. Certain property was retained by the crown under the title of "vacant or royal lands." It was these last which were made as grants to individuals, but with the understanding that final title was retained by the king. Grants were made for occupation and use, the subject taking the rents and profits, and normally a time limit was specified. The amount of land given varied according to the needs of the individual.[89]

The governor of New Mexico was empowered to make both Spanish and Indian land grants in the name of the king. Spaniards who desired lands presented a formal petition to the governor who then instituted an investigation to determine if the land requested would produce a conflict with other claims. The alcaldes mayores were actually in charge of examining applications which fell within their respective jurisdictions and they placed grantees in possession after the governor had drawn up the appropriate title.[90]

A common occurrence in the New Mexico province was the fre-

88. Bancroft, *Arizona and New Mexico,* p. 281. Further information on the cuartel is contained in Chapter 7 of the present study.

89. Frank W. Blackmar, *Spanish Institutions of the Southwest* (Baltimore, 1891), p. 319.

90. Details of Spanish land grant procedure in New Mexico are set forth by Myra Ellen Jenkins, "The Baltazar Baca 'Grant': History of an Encroachment," reprinted from *El Palacio,* LXI (1961), p. 50.

quent abandonment of settlements and lands under pressure from hostile Indians. Such removal was often hastily taken by terrified colonists without the official sanction required from the governor, who was hard pressed sometimes to force the people to return to their homes. Governor Vélez Cachupín, for example, declared in February of 1766, that the lands in the region of Ojo Caliente which had recently been abandoned because of the Indian menace had reverted to the crown, and were available to other subjects of the king who might apply for them.[91]

Pedro Bautista Pino mentions his part in a case involving land distribution.

> During the administration of Señor Chacón, I was commissioned to found two settlements and to distribute lands to more than 200 families at Pecos ford. After I concluded this operation, and upon taking leave of them . . . my heart was filled with joy. Parents and little children surrounded me and thanked me with tears in their eyes for the land I had given them for their subsistence.[92]

Related to the governor's land grant powers was his obligation to protect Indian properties from trespass and encroachment by Europeans. Carefully wrought legislation was designed to safequard all native land which was actually used or occupied. Unfortunately, as one authority has noted, the laws were honored more in the breach than in the observance.[93] With increased European population, the eighteenth century was a time of stress for the Indian communities, as the governors and alcaldes mayores at best ignored the laws while whites impinged upon pueblo lands, and at worst connived openly to exploit the natives.[94]

In 1705 Governor Francisco Cuervo y Valdés had proclaimed an order prohibiting all Spanish citizens from residing in Indian pueblos or even entering them without express permission of the gov-

91. E. Boyd, "Troubles at Ojo Caliente, A Frontier Post," *El Palacio,* LXIV (1957), 349-50.

92. *Exposición,* p. 5.

93. Jenkins, "The Baltazar Baca 'Grant,' " p. 53.

94. Charges against the civil officials in this regard were leveled by the Franciscan friars. See Hackett, *Historical Documents,* III, *passim,* and Morfi's Desórdenes cited above.

ernor.[95] This was merely a restatement of the law that had long prevailed in New Spain and though it was reiterated on subsequent occasions in New Mexico, it did little to stem the tide of white encroachment. The aggrieved pueblos might formally petition the governor or they might send representative delegations to appear before him with their complaints, but in the end it was the personal feeling of the governor rather than Spanish law which decided the issue in any given case.[96]

Registry of Brands. Governor Juan Bautista de Anza besought the commandant general to prescribe regulations which should prevail in New Mexico regarding the registering of cattle brands, as he had no orders to guide him in the matter.[97] Croix responded with a set of instructions setting forth the procedure to be followed in future cases.

Cattle owners and raisers were to be allowed to select their own brands. These were to be described in petitions submitted to the governor who would issue the appropriate permits. For this service, cattlemen were to be charged no more than one peso for paper and clerical expenses.[98] The governor was to delegate these same powers of issuance to his alcaldes mayores, and he, as well as the local justices, were to record all brands and permits in a special book for that purpose.[99]

Paper work. The clerical work attached to the fulfillment of the governor's official duties often approached enormous proportions. This task weighed heavily upon his time, particularly when he was without the services of a secretary or clerk. When Governor Chacón

95. Twitchell, *The Spanish Archives of New Mexico,* I, 397.

96. It should be observed here that the natives had recourse to an official known as "the protector of the Indians." The function of this individual will be outlined in a later chapter on the alcaldes.

97. Bando, Santa Fe, March 13, 1784, SANM, doc. 884.

98. The usual fee in New Spain for such service was thirty pesos.

99. Croix to Anza, Arizpe, January 15, 1783, SANM, doc. 850. In New Spain proper the sale of branding licenses was in the hands of the treasury officials. The practice for brand registry in early eighteenth-century New Mexico, as suggested by a *registro de hierro* for Santa Cruz de la Cañada in 1716, SANM, doc. 278, would seem to have been similar to that ordered by Croix in 1783. For some unexplained reason in the fifty or so years which followed, the manner of recording brands appears to have been forgotten.

surrendered his office to his successor in 1805, he passed on an inventory of the many reports, statements, and accounts which had to be prepared periodically for the superior government. This surviving document presents a vivid illustration of the bulk of paper work which consumed the energies of the governor and diverted his attention from more pressing matters.[100]

Copies of documents were made in duplicate or triplicate and sent to the commandant general, while the originals remained in the provincial archives. For a time, the governor, in a separate statement, notified the commandant of each document sent or received by him. Since this procedure overworked the officials concerned, the commandant general, in 1803, authorized substitution of cumulative indexes which listed the corresponding papers over a specified period.[101]

The Lieutenant Governor. The character of the office of lieutenant governor during the seventeenth century has been described briefly by France V. Scholes.[102] Lieutenant governors were designated from time to time to perform special duties, such as an inspection of the province in the name of the governor, to administer the province during the absence of the governor, or to assume control over some portion of the New Mexican area. There was little regularization of the official's functions until about 1660 when it became customary to divide the province into two major subdivisions or administrative districts known as the Rio Arriba and the Rio Abajo. The governor commanded the former since it contained the capital of Santa Fe, while the lieutenant governor, acting under his orders, administered the Rio Abajo.

Examination of documents has disclosed no mention of a lieutenant governor in the early eighteenth century, and the office may well have fallen into disuse during this period. In all events, the formal

100. Record of the Transfer of the Governor's Office, Santa Fe, March 27, 1805, SANM, doc. 1800. The actual nature of this paper work is discussed later in relation to other facets of administration.

101. Salcedo to the Governor of New Mexico, Chihuahua, February 11, 1803, SANM, doc. 1642.

102. "Civil Government in New Mexico," p. 91.

creation of the office of lieutenant governor was decreed anew by the presidial Reglamento of 1772.

By this document a lieutenant governor was to be appointed by the viceroy, he was to be an officer of the army whose conduct was of good repute, and he was to receive an annual salary of one thousand pesos.[103] The official was to be stationed in El Paso where his principal duty would be that of organizing the militia, protecting the settlers and mission establishments, and providing for caravan escorts as far north as the *paraje* of Robledo.[104] A company of regular troops under a captain had been occupying El Paso. The Reglamento, however, ordered it to Carrizal in the south to act as a guard on the Chihuahua road. The crown deemed the El Paso militia under the direction of the new lieutenant governor sufficiently strong to patrol and protect the stretch of the Rio Grande Valley in that vicinity.[105]

The official nature of the lieutenant governorship, as spelled out by the Reglamento, was limited to the points noted, but some changes occurred later. Appointment of the lieutenant governor, as stated, was originally in the hands of the viceroy. His selection was, of course, subject to royal confirmation. Rather quickly, with the separation of the Provincias Internas, the appointive power devolved upon the new commandant general who selected the lieutenant governor and delivered his commission of office which was approved by the king.[106]

With administrative alterations within the Provincias Internas, the authority to select the El Paso official may have shifted back from time to time to the viceroy. Upon reassertion of the independence of the internal provinces after 1792, this power of a certainty reverted

103. Pino, in 1812, noted that the salary of the lieutenant governor was two thousand duros. This would be the one thousand assigned to the lieutenant governor by the Reglamento of 1772, plus an additional one thousand which represented his salary as a lieutenant in the Santa Fe presidial garrison. Carroll and Haggard, *Three New Mexico Chronicles,* p. 44n.

104. Parajes were official campsites on the Chihuahua trail. They were selected, if possible, where wood, water, and feed for the animals were available.

105. Thomas, "Antonio de Bonilla, Notes," pp. 198-99.

106. Ysidro Rey to Real Alancaster, El Paso, September 26, 1805, SANM, doc. 1893.

to the commandant general and was held by him at least until 1810 and probably until the final reduction of commandancy power in the following decade.[107]

The lieutenant governors were selected as a rule from among the officers of the commandancy who were serving with the presidial garrisons or with the several mobile units.[108] Occasionally the first or second lieutenant attached to the Santa Fe presidio received the El Paso appointment. The lieutenants originally had advanced to their rank through nomination by the governor, as previously described, but the governor had no hand in selection of these or other persons as lieutenant governor since this was expressly forbidden by Spanish law.[109]

The lieutenant governor at El Paso was, in many respects, independent of Santa Fe. If the governor found it necessary to be absent from New Mexico, which, in fact, occurred on several occasions, the lieutenant did not assume control in his stead, but rather the governor designated an officer in Santa Fe who enjoyed his confidence to rule ad interim. Similarly, if the lieutenant governor was called out of his jurisdiction, he left in charge some worthy citizen, often the miltia commander (*capitán de milicia*) of El Paso.[110]

The independence of the lieutenant governor was based on expediency rather than upon any well-defined statement of his authority. Since El Paso lay midway between Santa Fe and the commandancy capital at Chihuahua, it was only natural that the lieutenant governor should seek to communicate directly with the commandant general instead of going through his nominal superior, the gover-

107. Carroll and Haggard, *Three New Mexico Chronicles*. p. 44n. José Agustín de Escudero wrote in 1834 that the lieutenant governor (*teniente de gobernador*) at El Paso in the Spanish period had been regularly named by the viceroy. Referring to the general situation, this is in error, as the evidence just offered indicates. The viceroy, it seems, did select the lieutenant governor in the two or three years immediately prior to independence when the authority of the commandancy had been reduced to a shadow of its former self. *Noticias estadistícas del estado de Chihuahua* (Mexico, 1834), p. 23.

108. See, e.g., the appointment of Ysidro Rey referred to in Real Alencaster to Salcedo, Santa Fe, November 20, 1805, SANM, doc. 1925(14).

109. Ots Capdequí, *Instituciónes*, p. 469.

110. Uranga to Chacón, Chihuahua, May 18, 1791, SANM, doc. 1121.

nor, who resided many leagues to the north. The commandant, for his part, found it convenient to summon the lieutenant governor now and again to Chihuahua to confer on matters of urgency involving the El Paso district.[111] At least one governor, Real Alencaster, became surly because the lieutenant governor was not following proper channels in communicating with the commandancy offices. He admonished his subordinate to report to him in the proper manner all matters which belonged within the jurisdiction of the governor and not to trouble the commandant general with affairs outside his sphere.[112]

The lieutenant governor within his own district was charged with both military and civil administration. Although the first demanded his greatest attention, much time was passed in the care of civil affairs. In this respect, his functions were similar to the governor's, especially regarding the minor matters of his office. The lieutenant governor formed legal cases (*causas* or *sumarias*) in the same manner as the alcaldes mayores with whom he was co-equal in judicial concerns. Proceedings were submitted to the governor and from him they followed the normal course of all legal cases. The lieutenant governor issued passports, compiled a census, made economic surveys, and attended to all the numerous details of public administration.

Secretary of Government, Assessor, and Clerks. These officials must be mentioned for their conspicuous absence in the late eighteenth and early nineteenth centuries. The secretary of government and war, as attested by Scholes, was a prominent figure in the seventeenth century.[113] He combined in his person the authority of notary and the function of active adviser to the governor. In the former capacity, he certified all official documents and papers issued in the governor's name. In his advisory role, he kept the chief executive informed of administrative details and served as something of a spokesman for colonists who wished to make their wishes known

111. Ysidro Rey to Real Alencaster, El Paso, April 17, 1807, SANM, doc. 2047.
112. Real Alencaster to Ysidro Rey, Santa Fe, July 4, 1805, SANM, doc. 1850.
113. "Civil Government in New Mexico," p. 91.

to the governor. The post of secretary often went to a member of one of the older families or some well-known soldier-citizen.

The practice of appointing a secretary continued into the eighteenth century, for we have as evidence the notarization of an official document of 1708 by Gaspár de los Ríos, Secretary of Government and War. At the same time, documents indicate that the cabildo of Santa Fe possessed its own notary (*escribano*).[114] The situation, thereafter, remains hazy. Within a few decades, New Mexico was without the services of a secretary or, for that matter, anyone who had sufficient legal training to serve as assessor or legal adviser to the governor and alcaldes mayores. This development adds weight to the view that there was a general decline in governmental efficiency and that in the first three quarters of the eighteenth century, the administrative machinery was progressively simplified.

During the second half of the eighteenth and continuing into the nineteenth century, there was difficulty in observing legal forms, owing to the lack of persons trained in law. One of the strongest statements in this respect was made by Governor Fernando de Chacón to the Audiencia of Guadalajara in 1802. He declared,

> All my predecessors and I have made known to the audiencia on repeated occasions that in this Province of New Mexico there are no, nor have there ever been, asesores, lawyers, or notaries who can prepare and direct a legal case in the proper manner. . . .[115]

While Chacón's complaint is somewhat exaggerated, it does demonstrate that New Mexico had been deprived of servants of the law for as far back as men in the governor's day could recall.[116] This circumstance was regarded as highly prejudicial to the correct dis-

114. Twitchell, *Spanish Archives of New Mexico,* II, 143. Generally there were two types of escribanos—ordinary notaries (*escribanos públicos*) and those attached to the cabildos, government councils, and tribunals (the *escribanos de concejo*).

115. Chacón to the Audiencia, Santa Fe, March 28, 1802, SANM, doc. 1593.

116. This writer finds a single reference to a *notario procurador* (notary attorney) in Santa Fe in 1764. Further information on this individual has not been discovered. Case Against Juan José Moreno, Santa Fe, January 19, 1764, SANM, doc. 577. A case as early as 1744 refers to the "well known lack of a royal public clerk, there being none in this kingdom of New Mexico." Hackett, *Historical Documents,* III, 413.

pensing of justice. In the absence of notaries to certify official papers and court proceedings, the governors were in the habit of naming some reliable citizen who, albeit deficient in official qualifications, could go through the motions of maintaining legality. The papers in a number of legal cases reveal that documents were customarily signed by two persons, in addition to the judge, who were listed as *testigos de asistencia* (witnesses in attendance). These presumably functioned in the absence of an official notary and served without salary or other remuneration.

When Pino composed his significant report in 1812, he cited the fact that the governor still did not have an assessor nor even a clerk since neither was available in the entire province.[117] This situation probably prevailed until the close of the Spanish period, for the first reference to an assessor appears under Mexican administration.[118]

Since the governor did not have a lawyer to advise him in his own office, he often submitted questions to the legal adviser of the commandancy and, in some cases, it seems, even to the adviser of the Intendancy of Durango.[119] These men trained in law responded with official opinions prescribing the lawful procedure the governor or his subordinates should observe. Such a process, merely to secure proper advisement, was unwieldy and time-consuming, hence the repeated requests to the superior authorities for qualified persons to fill the offices of notary and legal adviser.

In lieu of trained legal and clerical assistants, the governor turned increasingly to the officers and in some cases the men of the Santa Fe presidial garrison. As one example, the case of Second Lieutenant Antonio de Arce may be cited. In 1797 he was named by the governor as extraordinary magistrate (*juez comisionado*) in a case involv-

117. *Exposición,* p. 6.

118. Carroll and Haggard, *Three New Mexico Chronicles,* p. xx.

119. For examples of the governor's recourse to the assessor of Durango, see: Ysidro Rey to Real Alencaster, El Paso, July 21, 1805, SANM, doc. 1862; and Real Alencaster to the Audiencia, Santa Fe, November 20, 1806, SANM, doc. 2029.

ing the Indian officials of the Pueblo of Sandia.[120] We also have the assertion by Pino that a corporal of the company served as the governor's personal secretary for ten years.[121] The alcalde mayor of Santa Fe also assumed many of the tasks which the governor perforce was required to delegate to a subordinate.

120. Trial Record, August 13-23, 1797, SANM, doc. 1394. The term *juez comisionado* will be defined fully in a later chapter on the alcalde system.
121. *Exposición,* p. 16.

Chapter VII

COLONIAL ADMINISTRATION OF FINANCES

New Mexico never possessed a treasury office of its own during the colonial period. Aside from an administrator of tobacco and other monopolies, who began to function in the late eighteenth century, and a presidial supplymaster, there were no regular fiscal officers. Instead, what financial concerns existed fell to the care of the governor. It must be admitted that the bulk of these were military in character so they rightfully belonged under his jurisdiction.

The provinces within the commandancy general remained a financial liability to the royal treasury until the end of the colonial period. New Mexico, in particular, forced a heavy drain on the crown's coffers because of the large number of friars who ministered to the Pueblo Indians and of the substantial expenditures necessary for military defense. For maintaining the province during the period 1776 to 1781, the king paid out in salaries for the missionaries alone 51,264 pesos.[1] All expenses taken together, New Mexico was costing the Spanish government about 55,000 pesos annually in the first years of the nineteenth century.[2] Pino suggested in 1812 that more enlightened policies might be adopted regarding fiscal administration in New Mexico—he specifically urged the abolition of monopolies—which would result in a rise of prosperity and a concomitant decrease in the outlay forced upon the treasury.[3]

Fiscal affairs in New Mexico fell into three categories—military, civil, and ecclesiastical. The governor was directly responsible for superintendence of all three, his superior in each case being the com-

1. Thomas, "Antonio de Bonilla, Notes," p. 202n.
2. Economic Report, 1803, Santa Fe, SANM, doc. 1670a.
3. *Exposición,* p. 17.

mandant general. Under the heading of military, financial direction centered on disbursements for regular troops, which encompassed salaries, pensions, rewards, etc.; the *fondo de aliados*, or extraordinary expense fund; and the gunpowder fund of the Santa Fe presidial company which for a while was administered as a separate account. These will be described in a subsequent chapter on the military structure. Some reference has already been made to the civil and ecclesiastical finances in the commandancy general. The discussion below will elaborate on the fiscal procedure in these spheres as it applied specifically to New Mexico.

Concerning administrative details of the financial regimen as a whole, the governor was assigned the role of general supervisor. Besides the supplymaster, the administrator of monopolies and, while they were active, the friars who collected tithes were subject to his direction and intervention. Hard cash was deposited for safekeeping in a chest with three keys (*la caja de tres llaves*). One key was held by the governor, another by the supplymaster, and the third by the officer of highest rank who was resident in Santa Fe. All three thus had to be present when the treasury box was opened.[4]

Yearly requests for operating expenses were submitted to the commandant general by the governor. The commandant referred these itemized statements to his auditor and assessor who studied them and made recommendations. After final approval, the commandant ordered the director of the treasury office to release the prescribed amounts to the supplymaster, who traveled with the annual caravan from Santa Fe. With regard to taxes and the state of finances generally in his province, the governor of New Mexico occasionally had dealings with the governing council of the royal treasury (*junta superior de real hacienda*) which, as noted earlier, exercised broad supervisory power throughout New Spain. As a rule, the infrequent communications between the two involved matters of general policy

4. Real Alencaster to Salcedo, Santa Fe, March 31, 1805, SANM, doc. 1804. It should be noted that the supplymaster of the Santa Fe presidio, under the watchful eye of the governor, not only administered the accounts of the royal troops, but, in lieu of an officer of the general treasury, fulfilled certain fiscal functions for the civil and ecclesiastical systems whose monies were customarily deposited in his charge.

established by the fiscal authorities in Spain. Ordinarily, however, such correspondence passed through the office of the commandancy general.

Owing to the prevailing poverty in New Mexico, collection of the usual government taxes was often suspended, or special exemptions were introduced which relieved the citizens of a number of burdens imposed upon their countrymen to the south. The present writer has discovered sufficient information to permit some kind of authoritative comment on the following revenues only: the alcabala, the voluntary tax (*donativo*), and the government monopolies of tobacco, playing cards, gunpowder, and stamped paper. The media anata, a tax collected on the governor's salary, has already been mentioned. *Penas de cámaras,* or judicial fines, in significant amounts seem to have been received, but each was handled individually according to its own case and by an alcalde who pocketed the revenue, so that no general statement is possible at this time.

The Alcabala. There has been some question as to whether the alcabala, or sales tax, was ever collected in New Mexico during the colonial period.[5] Oñate's contract specifically exempted the province for a period of twenty years and recommended that the privilege be extended for another fifty.[6] The exemption seems to have been renewed without interruption well into the eighteenth century, applying to goods sold within New Mexico as well as those bartered by local merchants who traveled yearly to Chihuahua.

Early in 1775, the government required the merchandise purchased in Chihuahua and destined for New Mexico be subject to a two per cent excise tax.[7] The citizens of New Mexico, supported by their governor, Fermín de Mendinueta, petitioned the commandant general for relief from this measure. Collection, they argued, should be suspended for the following reasons: men of the province per-

5. The alcabala was definitely levied by the Mexican government after independence on goods brought over the Santa Fe Trail. Carroll and Haggard, *Three New Mexico Chronicles,* pp. 64, 109.

6. Hammond and Rey, *Don Juan de Oñate,* I, 54.

7. As stated previously, the usual rate of the alcabala in the poorer northern provinces of New Spain was two per cent, while it was somewhat higher further south.

formed military service without pay; the local economy was retarded, especially agriculture and cattle raising, because of Indian depredations; the only real commercial business was transacted once a year when New Mexicans journeyed to Chihuahua City to market their produce and purchase necessary clothing and horses; and, until the recent directive, goods had always been free of the imposts of the alcabala.

The assessor of the commandancy received the petition, appended his opinion in support of the citizens, and submitted it to the commandant general. In his written statement, he noted that the merchants, upon selling their wares in Chihuahua, merely added the amount of the alcabala to their final sale price, thereby placing the burden of the tax upon the consumer. This bore heavily upon the New Mexicans because of the difficulties at home which they had summarized in their petition.[8] The commandant reviewed the situation and subsequently notified Governor Mendinueta that in conformity with the judgment of the assessor, the tax, as it applied to New Mexico commerce, was being suspended.[9]

In February of 1787, Francisco de Guizarnótegui, a private merchant, was awarded a contract to supply the presidios of Nueva Vizcaya and that of New Mexico in Santa Fe.[10] His goods were assembled in Chihuahua, excise taxes were levied against them, and thence they were distributed to the various military establishments. Two years later it was suddenly realized that the merchandise dispatched to New Mexican troops was being illegally taxed since it was not subject to the alcabala. As a result, the commandant general ordered that the individuals of the Santa Fe presidial company be reimbursed for the tax sums which had been withheld from their salaries for the years 1788 and 1789.[11]

In the Santa Fe Archives, there is a copy of a royal order of October 12, 1795, which freed the products of New Mexico from the

8. Dictamen of Pedro Galindo Navarro, Durango, September 27, 1777, SANM, doc. 706.

9. Croix to Mendinueta, Durango, September 30, 1777, SANM, doc. 706a.

10. The question of presidio supply will be discussed at length in the chapter on the military system.

11. Diego de Borica to Governor Concha, March 31, 1789, SANM, doc. 1043a.

alcabala for a period of ten years.[12] Apparently, similar documents had been issued throughout the eighteenth century, but these no longer remain in the state archives. Governor Fernando de Chacón, in an economic report prepared in 1803, noted that New Mexico had made no contribution to the royal treasury from the time of the reconquest since the alcabala was not collected.[13] This supports the conclusion that the tax was not applied within the province during the colonial period.[14]

The Donativo. Although the populace of New Mexico was exempt from all but a few specialized taxes, nevertheless, it was subject to not-infrequent levies for so-called voluntary contributions or donativos.[15] Such demands often originated with the king who was in need of funds for some extraordinary exigency such as that occasioned by war at home or abroad. Religious houses in Spain were accustomed to seek donativos from colonials through regular government channels, and records remain of the modest contributions which New Mexicans provided for convents, nunneries, and similar establishments in the mother country.

The people of New Mexico were also assessed from time to time by the provincial governor in Santa Fe for voluntary contributions, usually in kind, to be applied to special purposes of mercy. Specifically, this often involved support in the form of food and clothing to Indian pueblos or Spanish hamlets where the threat of war, famine, or other disaster wrought human misery. The Zuñis, beleaguered by enemies, decimated by smallpox, and faced with starvation in the late eighteenth century, no doubt were spared from extinction by the

12. Orders and Decrees, I, 99, SANM, doc. 1344a.

13. Chacón Report to the Consulado of Vera Cruz, Santa Fe, August 28, 1803, SANM, doc. 1070a. In the same year the *junta superior de real hacienda* requested Governor Chacón to prepare a report setting forth the advantages his province derived as a result of its exemption from the alcabala. Salcedo to Chacón, Chihuahua, January 6, 1804, SANM, doc. 1698.

14. For a general summary of the alcabala, see Carroll and Haggard, *Three New Mexico Chronicles,* p. 183.

15. José María Ots Capdequí acknowledges that some *donativos* were genuinely voluntarily given, while others were that in name only. *Instituciones* (Barcelona, 1959), p. 495.

timely aid provided by such contributions. Money in the form of alms was collected also for the purpose of ransoming captives held by enemy Indians.

A royal cedula of August 17, 1780, is illustrative of the conditions which surrounded a crown assessment for a war fund. It was stipulated that all vassals in the Indies, that is, all adult men who were free, would be required to subscribe to the contribution. Spaniards, including nobles, were to pay two pesos, and Indians and mixed-bloods, one. The commandant general in a communication with the governor of New Mexico specifically relieved the men of the presidial troop from this obligation. He concluded that the soldiers' small salary could not be expected to cover extra expenses such as this.[16]

With the political turmoil in Spain beginning in 1808, the government found itself in continual need of funds. The demand for donativos was greatly increased and abundant evidence indicates that New Mexicans were expected to contribute their share. A rather extensive list of donativos from the jurisdiction of Alameda in 1809 shows that several hundred citizens contributed in cash and kind 117 pesos, 218 serapes, 149 fanegas of maíz, 49 beeves, 52 tanned skins, 18 ristras of chile and 32 of garlic, among other items. Eusevio Real of Alameda, for example, donated a serape and nine reales in coin. Juan Felipe, an Indian of San Felipe Pueblo, gave one buffalo hide and one peso in coin. And José Segura of Peña Blanca offered a half fanega of maíz and two reales.[17]

Other requests for donativos followed, but apparently the results could not satisfy the pressing needs of the government. In 1813 an edict was issued which levied an extraordinary direct contribution on the incomes of all citizens of the realm. Only persons earning less than three hundred pesos a year were exempt, while those earning more were ordered to pay sums in accordance with a fixed

16. Croix to Anza, Arizpe, August 12, 1781, SANM, doc. 827; and Croix to Anza, Arizpe, August 12, 1781, SANM, doc. 828.

17. List of Contributions, San Carlos de la Alameda, April 29, 1809, SANM, doc. 2226.

schedule. Collection of the "tax" was placed in the hands of local municipal councils or alcaldes.[18]

On March 15, 1815, the governor of New Mexico convoked a junta in Santa Fe to consider various financial matters which had arisen, including that of donativos destined for Spain. With the governor himself presiding, the junta composed a set of instructions to guide the town councils and alcaldes mayores in transacting current fiscal affairs. All Spanish citizens and Indians were enjoined to pay their due which was to be collected in the head town (*cabecera*) of each district. The money and goods were then to be transported to Santa Fe, the cost of removal to be borne by the donativo itself, and turned over to the supplymaster of the presidial company.

Another matter considered at this time was a request by the royal treasury for a loan of five thousand pesos. The junta assigned various amounts to thirty-six wealthy men of the province, each of whom provided sums ranging from fifteen to one thousand pesos to make the total sought by the exchequer. Further action by this fiscal body resulted in a levy on certain citizens for grain to supply the presidial troops, with payment for the produce to be made by the treasury in Chihuahua. Also considered was an official edict which imposed a five per cent tax on agriculture and stock raising for a two-year period.[19]

The Tobacco Monopoly. The tobacco monopoly (*estanco de tabaco*), established in 1764 in New Spain under the direction of José de Gálvez, was a separate branch of the fiscal government. In New Mexico collection of tobacco revenues was in the hands of an official called the *fiel administrador*. His activities were directed by a superior, an *administrador de rentas* in Chihuahua, who in turn was subject after 1786 to the intendant of Durango. The commandant general acted in a supervisory capacity as superintendent of the tobacco office in his district.

The tobacco in its various forms was received in an annual ship-

18. Bando and Reglamento, Mexico, December 15, 1813, in Orders and Decrees, II, 175, SANM, doc. 2522.

19. Instruction of the Fiscal Junta, Santa Fe, March 5, 1815, SANM, doc. 2583.

ment at Santa Fe and was lodged in a storehouse (*almacén*) at the home of the administrator from whence sale or disbursement was made.[20] The fiel administrador served as inspector charged with the task of seeking out those who violated the prohibition against local production of the plant. Revenues derived from the sale of government tobacco were lodged for safe keeping in the warehouse or with the supplymaster's office of the presidial company. The supplymaster who accompanied the annual caravan southward conveyed these funds, after release from the administrator, to the offices of the monopoly at Chihuahua.

The officer in charge of the royal tobacco monopoly in New Mexico also had within his jurisdiction the administration of the lesser monopolies of gunpowder and playing cards, and after 1786 that of stamped paper. Although in theory he was allowed to act independently within the confines of the provincial government, he seems, nevertheless, to have been subject to certain supervision by the governor. The exact nature of this supervision was apparently spelled out by Viceroy Antonio Bucareli in a set of instructions dated January 1, 1773. All that is known of their contents, however, is that the governor was enjoined to assist the tobacco administrator whenever the occasion should demand it.

The administrator in Santa Fe was nominated for his office by the administrador de rentas in Chihuahua while final selection was made by the commandant general.[21] All officers of the monopoly enjoyed a special fuero which entitled them to be tried by their own superiors for crimes involving misuse of their position.[22] All employees at the provincial level were exempt from payment of the media anata.[23]

20. The local offices of the tobacco monopoly were variously referred to as *estanquillos* or *fielatos*.

21. Chacón to Nava, Santa Fe, March 29, 1801, SANM, doc. 1533.

22. The administrator in New Mexico, Santiago Abréu, claimed exemption under his fuero from certain enforced contributions levied on him by the governor in 1802. SANM, doc. 1584.

23. Fabián de Fonseca and Carlos de Urritia, *Historia general de real hacienda* (5 vols.; Mexico, 1845-1853), II, 394; and Fisher, *The Intendant System*, p. 158.

The entire question involving growth and sale of tobacco after creation of the monopoly was a perplexing one for the Spanish government, no less in New Mexico than in the remainder of New Spain. At the onset, a great public clamor resulted over the taking away of the privilege of everyone to roll his cigars and cigarettes in the manner which seemed to him best.[24] The problem in New Mexico was compounded by the fact that the people were in the habit of raising for their own consumption a poor grade of tobacco known as *punche*.[25]

Instructions for establishment of the tobacco monopoly in New Mexico reached Governor Vélez Cachupín in November of 1765, together with a proclamation forbidding all tobacco planting thereafter. The astute Governor demurred in acting, realizing that the measure would upset the local economy and affect relations with the neighboring nomadic Indians who were accustomed to obtain their tobacco from the crop grown by the New Mexicans. In January of the following year, he prepared a report for the viceroy outlining the detrimental effects which would result from the new regulation. In spite of his feeling, the Governor made public the proclamation in the spring and, as expected, a shortage of tobacco developed, arousing discontent among the settlers and Indians. Moreover, the royal treasury benefited little because the people had insufficient funds to buy tobacco from the government and, lacking punche, they turned to the use of *mata* and other wild plants.[26]

The documented details surrounding operation of the tobacco monopoly in New Mexico in the last quarter of the eighteenth century are scant.[27] A letter from Governor Chacón to the commandant general, authored on November 16, 1798, demonstrates that in spite

24. Smith, *The Viceroy of New Spain*, p. 151.

25. An inquiry into the significance of the term "punche" is made by Leslie A. White, "Punche Tobacco in New Mexico History," *NMHR*, (1943), 386-93.

26. The foregoing paragraph is based largely on Lawrence Kinnaird, "The Spanish Tobacco Monopoly in New Mexico, 1766-1767," *NMHR*, XXI (1946), 328-30. See also Marqués de Croix to Mendinueta, Mexico, September 3, 1767, SANM, doc. 622. The use of *oja de mata* is referred to in Neve to Anza, Arizpe, March 15, 1784, SANM, doc. 884a.

27. Bolton, in his *Guide*, p. 191, cited previously, records the existence of several hundred volumes in the AGN of a section entitled "Tabaco." Among other things these volumes in-

of numerous difficulties, the monopoly was continuing in operation.[28]

In the first decade of the nineteenth century a number of references to tobacco appear in the documents. An economic report drawn up by Governor Chacón in 1803 maintains that "tobacco is grown locally, is widely used even by the padres, and is an article of trade with the Indians."[29] In this document the governor acknowledges receipt of instructions from his superior which disclosed the procedure to be followed in prosecuting cases of tobacco fraud. He notes that the commandant general specifically exempted from the regulations those areas of the province which raised tobacco for barter with the gentiles or nomadic Indians. As the governor points out, this takes in his entire jurisdiction, as all districts must produce tobacco to meet the need of some nearby tribe.[30]

The situation, then, by 1803 is that punche or native tobacco was grown legally throughout the province. Its use was intended exclusively for the Indian trade, but the poorer classes consumed it since their only alternative was to do without. The tobacco of superior quality imported from Mexico was purchased by the rico class and by the presidial soldiers, and it was the revenue from these sales which made up the funds administered by the official of the monopoly in Santa Fe.

Several documents reveal the importance of the sums which were derived by the sale of tobacco. The only specific figure which has thus far come to light is that of eight thousand pesos of silver which the administrator deposited with the supplymaster of the presidial company for the year 1806.[31] This seems a surprisingly large amount considering the professed poverty of New Mexico. The figure is probably accurate, however, as related sources suggest that substantial sums were collected in other years. A set of judicial proceedings

clude reports of the factors of the different provinces and accounts of cost of freight on tobacco carried from the local factories. A survey of the material would probably reveal data pertinent to the monopoly in New Mexico.

28. SANM, doc. 1429.

29. SANM, doc. 1670a. See also White, "Punche Tobacco," p. 391n.

30. SANM, doc. 1592.

31. Real Alencaster to Salcedo, Santa Fe, November 20, 1806, SANM, doc. 2030.

for the year 1809 relates how a local citizen robbed the storehouse at the home of the tobacco administrator of two thousand pesos. This figure merely adds further proof that large amounts were being collected, but there is no way of knowing the length of the period which the two thousand pesos represents in tobacco receipts.[32]

A curious note relating to the tobacco funds is available for the year 1807. Governor Real Alencaster at that time became hard-pressed for money to meet the immediate expenses of the Santa Fe company, the predicament having arisen because of his manipulation of presidial funds. To extricate himself from the tight situation, Alencaster imposed a levy on Santiago Abréu for the tobacco revenues in the latter's charge which further involved the governor in financial difficulties. The point is, however, that he turned to the tobacco monopoly as a ready source of funds when the pressing need arose.

Throughout all of New Spain persons were engaged in defrauding the monopoly of its rents. This assumed the form of illegal production, of smuggling, and of counterfeiting the stamps placed on all items sold. A governmental instruction issued in 1777 against such practices apparently had little effect. Subsequent decrees on the same subject were equally impotent, and the crown to the end of the colonial period continued to be deprived of vast amounts of revenue.[33]

Gunpowder and Playing Card Monopolies. The administrator of tobacco in New Mexico included under his jurisdiction the monopolies of gunpowder and playing cards.[34] The revenues from these were probably never large, but the exact amounts cannot be determined since no separate records for the accounts have appeared.[35]

Gunpowder was manufactured in Mexico under close crown

32. Case Against José Ramón Villanueba, Santa Fe, November 7-13, 1809, SANM, doc. 2262.

33. Bando on the Tobacco Excise, Mexico, November 15, 1813, Orders and Decrees, II, 174, SANM, doc. 2520.

34. In New Spain neither of these revenues possessed its own ramo, or branch, the receipts of each being deposited in the tobacco treasury. Priestley, *José de Gálvez,* p. 375.

35. Pino, in 1812, was highly critical of the management of all government monopolies in New Mexico, *Exposición,* p. 17.

supervision. It came in several grades, including fine, which sold in Mexico City for eight reales a pound, and superfine, which sold for ten reales.[36] The price in New Mexico must have been substantially more when the cost of transportation and handling was added to the above prices.

The powder monopoly involved sale only for civilian use. Gunpowder for military purposes was provided to the troops through special supply channels. In 1777 the soldiers of the Santa Fe garrison were charged with wasting their powder ration and using it for hunting, which was not considered in the service of the king. They were warned that powder consumed unnecessarily would have to be replaced at their own expense.[37]

Purchases by citizens were usually destined for use in firearms or fireworks. The rural folk of New Mexico were generally without firearms, relying for their defense on bows and arrows or lances in the manner of the Indians. The upper classes, however, probably purchased enough powder to bring in a sizable revenue to the monopoly.

Regarding the sale of playing cards in New Mexico under the government monopoly, little is known. The commandant general in 1807 transmitted an edict to the governor announcing a royal order of October 17, 1804, which reduced the price of playing cards from eight to four reales.[38] If figures are ever discovered, it would be interesting to learn what New Mexicans were expending yearly on this diversion.

Stamped Paper. The crown of Spain derived revenue from the sale of paper bearing the royal coat of arms. The use of such paper in all legal transactions became obligatory in the seventeenth century.[39] By the Order of Intendants of 1786, the sale of stamped paper at the local level was removed from the hands of the governors and alcaldes mayores, who had been responsible directly to the treasury

36. Fonseca and Urrutia, *Historia general de real hacienda,* II, 247.
37. Rubio to Mendinueta, Chihuahua, December 21, 1777, SANM, doc. 709.
38. Salcedo to Real Alencaster, Chihuahua, January 28, 1807, SANM, doc. 2040.
39. Fonseca and Urrutia, *Historia general de real hacienda,* III, 24-31.

officials, and was placed under control of the administrator of the tobacco rents. For this added duty the official received four per cent of the proceeds.[40]

By 1786, then, a single functionary in New Mexico had charge of the four monopolies: tobacco, powder, playing cards, and stamped paper. Notwithstanding, at the close of each year he had to render and submit entirely separate accounts for each product. The accounts of the first three went to the respective director of each monopoly via the administrador de rentas in Chihuahua. Handling of the stamped paper revenues at the superior level, however, remained subject to the regular treasury officers, and accounts of this branch passed from Santa Fe to the treasury office in Chihuahua. Ultimately, summaries of the accounts of all four reached the accounting office (tribunal de cuentas) in Mexico for final auditing.[41]

Stamped paper was always scarce in the provinces of New Spain. This was particularly true in New Mexico where a chronic shortage seemed to exist. Paper came in four grades, selling at three pesos, six reales, one real, and one *cuartilla* (one and one-quarter cents) per *pliego* (double sheet), depending upon the quality.[42] The cheaper denominations were employed in New Mexico when available, and when lacking, the governor was required to see that the fees were collected anyway and deposited with the treasury though unmarked paper was used.[43]

Postal System. The postal service in New Spain was administered, at least after 1766, as a branch of the royal treasury with its own specially appointed officers subject directly to a superintendent general of posts (*superintendente general de correos, postas, y caminos*)

40. Fisher, *The Order of Intendants,* p. 208.

41. *Ibid.,* p. 279.

42. Priestley, *Jóse de Gálvez,* p. 334n.

43. Croix to Anza, Chihuahua, January 13, 1783, SANM, doc. 850. The use of unstamped paper is illustrated by a document prepared by Francisco Ortiz of Santa Fe who affixed the following notation as a heading: "Valga por el Sello 3° cuio valor de dos reales resivi y hare buenos a Real Hacienda en la cuenta de este Ramo año de 1813." SANM, doc. 2505.

in Spain.[44] Before a royal order of 1763, service in the Mexican area had been in the hands of a private contractor (*correo mayor*) who purchased his office from the crown. Each of his lieutenants had collected the *portes,* or postage revenues, from the total of which they remitted part to the correo mayor and kept part for their own salary. Under the new system, the royal postal service (*real renta de correos*) was transformed into a department of the royal treasury and the correo mayor and subordinate administrators became royal appointees with a fixed salary.[45]

The activities of the government postal service were not extended beyond Durango until the time of Teodoro de Croix. On January 10, 1779, the commandant general issued an edict from Chihuahua creating a system of east-west mail delivery which would serve to tie together his vast jurisdiction.[46] On the following February 15, he composed a set of instructions governing the establishment and operation of the new service.[47] Although New Mexico was excluded from consideration by virtue of its position far to the north of the proposed route, nevertheless, the provisions of Croix's instructions fix a pattern that was extended in part to New Mexico in the following decade.

Post offices (*estafetas* or *cajas*) for the handling of ordinary mail had been in operation in Durango, Saltillo, Chihuahua, and the Real de San Antonio de la Huerta[48] prior to formation of the Croix plan. In the first named, there existed a postmaster general (*administrador general*); in each of the remainder an official called the *administra-*

44. A rudimentary mail system had existed from the time of the conquest. It was dependent to a large degree upon the condition of the king's highways or *caminos reales,* which within a short time formed a network throughout the viceroyalty. Transportation of the mails was generally referred to as the *real servicio.* After independence it became the *servicio nacional.* Pino to Arce, Laguna, March 5, 1819, SANM, doc. 2798.

45. Walter B. L. Bose, "Orígenes del correo terrestre en Mexico," *Revista de historia de América,* XXIII (1947), 94-95. General regulations concerning the establishment and operation of the postal system may be found in Rodríguez de S. Miguel, *Pandectas,* I, 685-717.

46. Fernando B. Sandoval, "El correo en las Provincias Internas," *Boletín del archivo general de la nación,* XVIII (1948), 334.

47. Order of the Caballero de Croix, SANM, doc. 752.

48. A *real* or *real de minas* was a mining camp or town.

dor principal (chief postmaster). The new postal route which provided monthly service was to extend from the Bahía de Espiritu Santo on the Texas coast to the commandant's capital at Arizpe. Along this way branch offices were set up at the leading towns under subordinate postmasters (*administradores subalternos*). These were located at such places as San Antonio, Monclova, Parras, Mapimi, Gallo, and Horcasitas. In addition, the supplymasters of the presidios at intervening points were commissioned to act as postal clerks in the reception, distribution, and dispatching of the mails. They were required to open the mail pouches (*balijas*) in the presence of the couriers and the captain or other officers of the presidio, or in the absence of the latter before the chaplain of the garrison. The chief postmasters were instructed to inform their subordinates and the supplymasters of the presidios within their jurisdiction of the general regulations prescribed for the conduct of postal business.

Each post office possessed its own mail pouch and a postal seal (*sello de francatura*) which was affixed to letters and *pliegos*.[49] Under certain circumstances the postal fees might be paid by the receiver instead of the sender. The commandant general provided, for example, that letters to his office from his own administrative staff, from the commandant inspector, his assistants (the ayudantes), the provincial governors, and from the commandants and officers of the presidios, mobile companies, and militia units should all be stamped upon receipt to spare his subordinates this burden of expense.[50] Rates in the Provincias Internas were the same as those prevailing throughout New Spain. A document penned in the late colonial period indicates that New Mexico soldiers were paying three reales per letter which was probably the standard rate charged all citizens.[51]

The mails, as Croix organized them, were carried by soldiers of

49. A *pliego* was a parcel of letters enclosed in a single cover. The term was also used to mean a single sheet of paper folded once to form a two-page writing folder which was the unit sold as stamped paper.

50. Until 1777 royal officials were exempt from paying postage on government correspondence. As late as 1783, officers in the Provincias Internas were continuing with this privilege, although it had been abolished elsewhere.

51. Mail List, Santa Fe, September 17, 1819, SANM, doc. 2847.

the regular army. Expenses incurred by these couriers were met by the post office, as were those costs deriving from the general operation of the service. Any surplus made by the department was remitted to Spain through a postmaster general in Mexico City.[52]

Mail carriers were strictly forbidden to convey letters outside the mailbags and to carry written messages which had not been registered at a post office even if these had been handed to them by a governor or by local magistrates. However, the couriers were permitted to accept mail along the road at haciendas and other points so long as it was delivered over to the first postmaster encountered for processing. Upon arriving at a town, the couriers were obliged to proceed directly to the post office and there relinquish the pouches. Until this had been accomplished, they were not to report to the governor or military commander who might be resident in the town, nor were they to linger on the streets giving news to the citizens.

After implementation of the Croix plan, the internal provinces were closely linked to the postal system of the viceroyalty of New Spain. This service was improved further after 1789 by Viceroy Revilla Gigedo II, who established regular weekly deliveries between Mexico City and the intendancy capitals.[53]

New Mexico Postal Service. The special mail route laid out by Croix in 1779 was modified in the following decade so that El Paso was included in the system.[54] Santa Fe, however, remained outside this service and continued dependent upon the annual caravan each autumn for carrying both ordinary and official mail. Although the governors occasionally used special messengers to convey important dispatches, this method was costly and far from satisfactory or efficient.

The superior authorities tolerated this situation until 1783. In that year the commandant general addressed a letter to Governor Anza outlining steps to be taken in establishing regular mail delivery be-

52. This official in the Croix postal instructions of 1779 is referred to as the *administrador general de la renta de correos de Nueva España.*

53. Cayetano Alcázar Molino, *Los virreinatos en el siglo XVIII* (Barcelona, 1945), p. 96.

54. Sandoval, "El correo en las Provincias Internas," pp. 335-39.

tween Santa Fe and El Paso, linking the provincial capital with the postal service of the interior provinces.[55] The remoteness of the Villa of Santa Fe and the dangers prevalent on the long road north of El Paso were given as the reasons which had precluded extension of the mail service in the past. The commandant general observed that news of happenings in New Mexico often reached his attention a year late. Conversely, he could not keep the governor properly informed of developments growing out of new orders of the king which related to the general regimen of war and government.

Governor Anza was directed to investigate the means for inaugurating a regularly scheduled mail service between his capital and El Paso. While the final decision as to mode of organization was left to him, the commandant general tendered the following suggestions: every two, three, or four months a detachment composed of soldiers from the Santa Fe presidio and of private citizens might escort the mail as far as El Paso; alternately, it might prove more feasible to have the task performed by two or three men who would raise no dust on the trail nor leave tracks, and who could more easily hide from the enemy; whatever form the mail escort assumed, the governor should designate the exact route to be followed and prescribe the method to be used in the nightly marches and the precautions to be taken; no definite times should be set for dispatching of the mail lest the hostile Indians divine the pattern and lie in ambush for the escort; and advantage should be taken of troop detachments which passed between Santa Fe and El Paso periodically on other business to carry extraordinary posts outside the regular system. Beyond the presentation of these points for consideration, the commandant general explicitly ordered that neither cattle nor merchants with their wares were to be permitted to travel with the mail escort as this would hinder the march and serve to arouse the enemy.

The suggestions enumerated above were apparently incorporated into the system set up by Anza. The new mail service provided closer connection not only with the commandancy but also with the

55. Neve to Anza, Arizpe, December 18, 1783, SANM, doc. 873.

southern extremity of the New Mexico jurisdiction around El Paso. The lieutenant governor at that town appears to have been responsible for supervision of postal business and an *estanquillo,* or branch office, was maintained. Postal affairs were also conducted at the mail station of San Eleceario a few miles downstream.[56] The lieutenant governor was advised by the governor to make regular reports on affairs of administration, sending them to Santa Fe by the official postal couriers.[57]

Documentation is scant on the functioning of the courier system after its organization in New Mexico in 1783. Whether the supplymaster of the Santa Fe presidial company acted as postmaster or whether a regular administrator was appointed immediately is not known. By 1788, however, it is recorded that one Miguel Ortiz was serving as postmaster in the provincial capital.[58] The appointment of this official was made by the chief postmaster in Chihuahua, acting upon recommendation of the New Mexico governor.[59] A document of 1819 indicates that the Santa Fe postmaster put up a bond before assuming his duties.[60]

In 1804 this official informed the commandant general that it had become the practice for him to open the mail pouch in the house of the governor. The commandant responded with an order prohibiting this procedure since his legal adviser had declared that it was contrary to Articles 15 and 16 of the general ordinance governing the post office department. Presumably the mail should have been

56. San Eleceario was set up as a presidio (originally under the name of Guajoquilla) by the presidial Reglamento of 1772. It was sometimes located on the north side of the Rio Grande, sometimes on the south side, and occasionally on an island in the middle, depending upon the erratic course of the river at that point. Although territorially within the jurisdiction of New Mexico, the presidio was attached for administrative purposes to the province of Nueva Vizcaya. If the garrison possessed a supplymaster, which is not altogether certain, he probably handled the local postal business. The regular troops there usually averaged only fifteen men, although for a time a mobile company from Nueva Vizcaya was stationed at this small outpost.

57. Real Alencaster to Ysidro Rey, Santa Fe, July 1, 1805, SANM, doc. 1850.

58. Chacón to Nava, Santa Fe, November 18, 1799, SANM, doc. 1471.

59. Salcedo to Chacón, Chihuahua, September 19, 1804, SANM, doc. 1757.

60. Oniego to Melgares, Chihuahua, May 6, 1819, SANM, doc. 2813.

opened in the post office under surveillance of the proper witnesses.[61]

By 1805, the mail service was operating on a fairly regular schedule. Governor Chacón in that year listed the postal departures as follows: the first of April; the first of July; the first of September; and in November with the annual caravan.[62] A later description shows the manner in which the couriers were functioning. A mail escort composed of a lieutenant and ten men of the regular troops, together with two militia captains commanding a detachment of twenty citizens from the jurisdictions of Albuquerque and Alameda, transported the mail pouches as far as the campsite of Fray Cristobal. At that point a contingent from San Eleceario was waiting, the bags were exchanged, and the party from up river returned to deliver the mail from the south.[63] In addition to the regular service, however, the use of extraordinary couriers to carry urgent news continued.

During the summer of 1815, the acting governor, Alberto Maynez, announced to the alcaldes of his jurisdiction that, under orders of the commandant general, a monthly postal service would be organized to carry both public and official mail to El Paso. The first departure would be from Santa Fe at ten o'clock in the morning on the following September 18. The alcaldes were advised to inform their citizens of the new arrangement so that all who wished might take advantage of the improved service.[64] This suggests that there existed some form of intraprovincial postal delivery, a supposition which is supported by a letter from the alcalde of Laguna to Teniente José María de Arce at Santa Fe in 1819 which was folded into

61. Order of Nemesio Salcedo, Chihuahua, November 13, 1804, SANM, doc. 1770(3).

62. Instructions to Real Alencaster, Santa Fe, March 27, 1805, SANM, doc. 1800.

63. Manrrique to Salcedo, Santa Fe, March 31, 1810, SANM, doc. 2311. This particular mail delivery is cited by Max L. Moorhead, *New Mexico's Royal Road* (Norman, Okla., 1958), p. 46. Ordinarily, as noted, the mail was conveyed by the New Mexican dispatch riders to El Paso, so that this transfer of pouches at Fray Cristobal may have been an unusual circumstance. In the early Mexican period, this transfer was usually made at the Rancho del Bracito twenty-eight miles north of El Paso.

64. Maynez to the Alcalde of Abiquiu, Santa Fe, July 11, 1815, SANM, doc. 2605. Also, Charles F. Coan, *A Shorter History of New Mexico* (2 parts; Ann Arbor, Mich., 1928), I, 145.

a small packet, addressed on the cover, and labeled *real servicio.*[65] Further details on such service, however, are lacking.

Ecclesiastical Order of Finances. The intimate association of Church and state inextricably tied the financial administration of the ecclesiastical establishment to the colonial exchequer. New Mexico's religious affairs in the first years were controlled by the Franciscan friars who received an allowance annually from the royal treasury. In the eighteenth century this amounted to 330 pesos per religious a year.[66] The treasury office of Chihuahua in 1788 recorded that it was paying out 9,800 pesos each year in allowances for the thirty friars in New Mexico.[67]

There were three types of charges met by citizens on behalf of the Church. These were tithes (*diezmos*), obventions (*obvenciones*), and first fruits (*primicias*). Regarding collection of tithes in New Mexico in the eighteenth century, scholars recognize that the matter is not entirely clear.[68] As a general rule, the tithe amounted to a ten per cent income tax collected at the source on agricultural and pastoral industries.[69] In theory, the money obtained in this manner belonged to the crown, but since the sovereign was responsible for financial support of the Church, the funds were directed almost wholly to that end. Moreover, the royal treasury made up the difference when the tithes were insufficient to cover ecclesiastical operating expenses.

Collection in the first part of the eighteenth century was in the hands of clerics who functioned under government lease. The in-

65. Pino to Arce, Laguna, March 5, 1819, SANM, doc. 2798. A number of other pieces of correspondence in the archives display this same characteristic. Under orders of the governor, the alcaldes mayores and the tenientes named persons in their districts to serve as mail carriers. Manuel Rubí to Maynez, Pajarito, April 14, 1815, SANM, doc. 2588.

66. Bancroft, *Arizona and New Mexico,* p. 271n. These stipends were considered to belong to the priests individually and not to the mission or province. Bucareli to the Governor of New Mexico, Mexico, June 8, 1774, SANM, doc. 676.

67. Report of the Real Caja of Chihuahua, October 10, 1788, AGN, Prov. Int. 46.

68. Fr. Francisco Atanasio Domínguez, *The Missions of New Mexico,* 1776, tr. by Eleanor B. Adams and Fr. Angélico Chavez (Albuquerque, 1956), p. 29.

69. Haring, *The Spanish Empire in America,* p. 190.

efficiency of this system prompted the crown to issue a royal cedula on October 19, 1772, which took from the churchmen in the colonies the collection of tithes and reserved to itself the faculty of nominating collectors of this revenue.[70] Some time elapsed, however, before this measure went into effect in the farthest parts of the realm.

In 1760, Fray Juan Sanz de Lezaún observed that for thirty years the governors of New Mexico had collected the tithes. He complained that the Indians brought their contributions all the way from their pueblos to Santa Fe.[71] This statement is exceedingly confusing because as noted above, collection should have been in the charge of a clerical lessee rather than the governor, the Indians were usually exempt from tithes, and it was customary for persons to carry their tithes to the place of payment. The friar had no just complaint on this point.

This priest obviously held a partisan view and was endeavoring by all means possible, as the remainder of his report indicates, to discredit the civil authorities. It may be that the Indians were bringing to Santa Fe their first fruits, though they seldom paid these, or some other special contribution. Fray Domínguez, who visited New Mexico in 1776, mentioned that collection of tithes was in the custody of a religious.[72] Since this was the prevailing practice in New Spain up to approximately this time, it may be assumed that this had been the situation all along.

Shortly afterward, however, the governor of New Mexico did take charge of tithe collection everywhere but in El Paso under lease from the three *jueces acreedores* in Durango.[73] At least by 1788 he held this function, and possibly earlier.[74] A cedula of October 17, 1800, provided that the citizens of the Villa of Santa Fe should

70. Priestley, *José de Gálvez,* p. 353. In seventeenth-century New Mexico, the custodian of the Franciscan Order collected the tithes. France V. Scholes, "Problems in the Early Ecclesiastical History of New Mexico," reprinted from *NMHR,* VII, (1932), 43. For the system of tithe payment in that century, see Hackett, *Historical Documents,* III, 112-13.

71. Hackett, *Historical Documents,* III, 470.

72. *The Missions of New Mexico,* p. 296.

73. *Jueces acreedores* were officials who administered the funds pertaining to a bishopric. In the documents, the term occasionally appears as *jueces hacedores.*

74. Concha to the Jueces Acreedores, Santa Fe, May 6, 1794, SANM, doc. 1287.

be exempt from the levies of tithes and first fruits.[75] The remainder of the province, nevertheless, continued subject to such payments.

The governor did not long remain a *diezmero,* or tithe collector, for other qualified solicitors submitted yearly bids to the jueces acreedores of the cathedral of Durango and won the right to collect and convert the tithes of New Mexico. Usually the lessees sent southward about two thirds of the tithes which were owed by the province of New Mexico. The remaining third they kept to meet their own expenses and as profit. The hazards and difficulties attached to collection coupled with the fact that all losses had to be borne by the lessee meant that results were apt to be uncertain for the speculator who assumed the job.[76] The collector on occasion called upon the civil authorities to force reluctant citizens to pay their tithes. There is recorded at least one instance in which the governor ordered out a detachment of militia to arrest a certain individual who had been remiss in meeting his obligations.[77]

The rate of collection in New Mexico, as elsewhere, was ten per cent of all harvests and of the annual increase in livestock.[78] Customarily the collector accepted the tax in kind, converting it to cash and dispatching the predetermined sum to Durango. Citizens paid in such products as grain, garden produce, wool, native tobacco (punche), chickens, and livestock.

The total amount collected yearly in New Mexico tended to vary, but the sum was always substantial, considering that the province was not regarded as particularly wealthy. Pino wrote in 1812 that New Mexico paid from nine to ten thousand duros annually in tithes.[79] Earlier, Father Morfi recorded that 11,285 pesos had been collected for a single year in the 1780's.[80] These figures apparently excluded the El Paso district since settlements in that area were sub-

75. Real Alencaster to Salecdo, Santa Fe, January 4, 1806, SANM, doc. 1942(3).

76. Carroll and Haggard, *Three New Mexico Chronicles,* pp. 39-40.

77. Proceedings in the Case of Francisco Chávez, Santa Fe, June 4-10, 1820, SANM, doc. 2892.

78. Melgares to the Alcalde of Las Truchas, Santa Fe, May 21, 1821, SANM, doc. 2980.

79. Carroll and Haggard, *Three New Mexico Chronicles,* p. 3.

80. Desórdenes, no. 25.

ject to a different contractor. In the 1770's, it was reported that El Paso was producing 1,600 pesos in tithes, but there was some confusion in the method of collection. Morfi observed later that there had been no tax gatherer there for two years and urged that the employment be given over to the captain of the San Eleceario presidio downriver.[81]

Obventions and first fruits are the two remaining church revenues. The first constituted the fees for baptisms, marriages, funerals, etc., levied in accordance with a fixed schedule, with one at a lower rate for the Indians. The first fruits were an offering from the first produce of the harvests and herds, which the Indians seldom paid. Bishop Tamarón in 1760 discovered that the missionaries were collecting obvenciones and primicias from the Spanish citizens in their parishes and were enjoying them in addition to the annual amount granted by the crown for support of each friar.[82]

Pino more than fifty years later declared that all the missionaries and the priests (there were two secular priests, one at Santa Fe and another in the El Paso district) received an income from the treasury, excepting those of the villas of Albuquerque, Santa Cruz de la Cañada, and the capital, who had no income other than the offerings at the altar.[83]

In 1793 a special tax of half a fanega of corn, or its equivalent of twelve reales, was ordered levied annually on each adult Pueblo Indian male under the age of fifty. The grain or money was to be delivered to the Indian's priest (*puesta en su casa*) for his use. No other tax was to be made upon these people by the religious under any pretext.[84] Demands for personal services were prohibited in accordance with old and established laws on the subject.[85]

Regarding the sale of indulgences (*bulas de santa cruzada*) in New Mexico, evidence is scarce. An edict ordering publication of a Bull of the Crusade reached New Mexico in 1785 and was circulated

81. *Ibid.*, no. 23.
82. Adams, *Bishop Tamarón's Visitation of New Mexico*, p. 28.
83. *Exposición*, p. 7.
84. SANM, doc. 1457.
85. Nava to Concha, Chihuahua, October 19, 1793, SANM, doc. 1263.

among the superior alcaldes of the jurisdiction.[86] Stray reports in the papers of the Ramo de Provincias Internas indicate that New Mexico made a yearly remittance to the office of indulgences (*ramo de bulas*), but this writer has discovered no specific figures on these returns.[87]

What has been set forth in this chapter will convey some notion of the scope of colonial financial affairs. Many of the topics, presented here only in their broader outlines, are worthy of intensive investigation, and as increased understanding of this facet of government is achieved, new light, doubtless, will be shed on the subjects of economic and social history.

86. SANM, doc. 918.

87. Priestley asserts that sale of the dispensations or indulgences in the later colonial period was in the hands of the local tobacco administrator. *José de Gálvez,* p. 379. If this was indeed the case, it was contrary to the earlier practice whereby local business of the cruzada was in the hands of subdelegates and lay treasurers.

Chapter VIII

MILITARY ORGANIZATION

New Mexico from its first settlement to the end of Spanish domination, was under a strict military rule. In the seventeenth century, the formal military establishment was small and loosely organized, there being no regular presidio, or paid garrison. Defense of the province was entrusted to a handful of *encomenderos*, about thirty-five in number, who served as citizen-soldiers without salary. They performed escort duty, acted as guards in their own towns, and in times of emergency assumed command of citizen levies called out for campaigns against the enemy. The governor, as chief military officer, exercised direct control and planned offensive and defensive strategy. He also appointed officers among the encommenderos, many of whom received the rank of captain or higher.[1]

The general uprising of 1680 underscored the need for a permanent military establishment. With the reconquest, defense was placed upon a firmer footing by the creation of two regular presidios—one at El Paso in 1683 and the other at Santa Fe in 1693. While the presence of these posts served to shore up New Mexico's capacity to resist Indian onslaughts, the presidios provided no real solution for effecting a final peace. Military personnel were never sufficient in number or adequately equipped to deal properly with the Indians in the field or to garrison additional presidios. In the late 1720's, the Santa Fe troop numbered eighty men and that of El Paso only fifty. On repeated occasions governors called for soldier reinforcements and new outposts to distribute the burden of defense. Unfortunately for the tranquility of the province, their pleas went largely unanswered.

1. Scholes, "Civil Government in New Mexico," pp. 78-79.

Attention has already been directed to the effort on the part of the crown in the second half of the eighteenth century to stabilize the northern frontier of New Spain. This increasing concern for military affairs was reflected in a wealth of new legislation—the Reglamento of 1772 and the subsequent creation of the commandancy general standing as only the most conspicuous examples. Reports and memorials from local officers defined the problems, which were answered by cedulas and decrees from the central authorities.

In this sphere of government as in others, then, the last half-century of Spanish rule witnessed an expansion of existing programs, an elaboration of the administrative machinery, and a proliferation of new laws affecting all phases of the military organization. How these developments applied to the situation in New Mexico is the subject of this chapter.

The King's Presidios and Soldiers

The Santa Fe presidio, known officially as "El Real Presidio de Nuestra Señora de los Remedios y la Exaltación de la Santa Cruz," loomed as the province's principal bulwark against Indian invaders. By the Reglamento of 1772, the old El Paso presidio was abandoned and its garrison moved south to the village of Carrizal in the jurisdiction of Nueva Vizcaya. This transfer was undertaken so that the new post would conform to the presidial line erected by the Reglamento, and because the five thousand or so inhabitants of the El Paso district were deemed capable of defending themselves. The new military code provided for a presidio at Robledo on the southern end of the Jornada del Muerto, but for various reasons it was never established.[2]

The need for additional presidios called forth much comment. Settlers drafted into service for extended campaigns, merchants with caravans needing escorts, and the heavily burdened troops in Santa

2. This matter is discussed in Croix to Anza, Chihuahua, March 20, 1779, SANM, doc. 756. See also Paige W. Christiansen, "The Myth of Robledo," *El Palacio,* LXXI (1964), 30-34.

Fe all desired an increase in the number of outposts and presidial soldiers.[3] Governor Mendinueta in 1777 recommended new posts at the old pueblo of Socorro in the south and at Taos in the north.[4] In 1796 Governor Chacón again argued for a presidio at Socorro, and for another at a site on the Pecos River, but nothing was done.[5] Pino in 1812 presented an elaborate plan to the Spanish Cortes calling for five new presidios in New Mexico and outlining how these might be financed without injury to the treasury.[6] Notwithstanding, these and other representations from private citizens and government officials alike went unheeded by the central authorities, and the colonial years closed with New Mexico in possession of only the single presidio in Santa Fe.

This presidio in the first half of the colonial period formed part of the royal quadrangle, or provincial government buildings, with the governor's palace on the south side facing the main plaza. From an early eighteenth-century description, we learn that the quadrangle itself included an inner plaza enclosed by buildings several stories high and containing quarters for one hundred soldiers and their families.[7]

Through neglect, some governors allowed the buildings to fall into ruin, so that from time to time in the eighteenth century efforts had to be exerted to repair and remodel them.[8] In 1780 the king authorized construction of a new cuartel, or presidio, for the Santa Fe company, with two thousand pesos being assigned for the work.[9] The following year construction was begun using paid citizen labor

3. Warner, "The Career of Martínez de Torrelaguna," p. 11.

4. Thomas, "Governor Mendinueta's Proposals," pp. 30-36. On the reasons for the failure to establish the Taos post, see Thomas, "Antonio de Bonilla, Notes," p. 206.

5. Coan, *Shorter History of New Mexico,* I, 125. The commandant general in 1797 notified the governor that the royal treasury could not stand the expense of the two presidios requested. Nava to Chacón, Chihuahua, January 7, 1797, SANM, doc. 1375a.

6. *Exposición,* p. 21.

7. Twitchell, *Spanish Archives of New Mexico,* II, 117-21.

8. Twitchell, *Old Santa Fe,* p. 55.

9. Bancroft, *Arizona and New Mexico,* p. 281. The barracks were the main military buildings. There was really no fortress as such, according to Tamarón, in 1760. Adams, *Bishop Tamarón's Visitation,* p. 47.

which had been recruited throughout the province.[10] Funds were soon exhausted and a temporary loan from the mustering-out reserve (*fondo de retención*) had to be made. In the end the governor and officers of the company made a donation of 538 pesos of their own so that the work could be completed in 1791.[11]

Although the presidial garrison in El Paso was removed after 1772, references to the cuartel there continue to appear. This indicates that the barracks at least were maintained to serve the militia when it was active and to house regular troops when they passed through on campaigns, courier missions, and so forth.

As mentioned, the number of troops comprising the Santa Fe garrison was eighty. The Reglamento listed them with their corresponding annual salaries as follows: two lieutenants, 700 pesos each; one sub-lieutenant (alférez), 500 pesos; two sergeants, 350 pesos each; six corporals, 300 pesos each; sixty-eight soldiers, 290 pesos each. Not figured among these eighty was the governor who served as captain of the presidio at a combined salary of four thousand pesos. Also there was an army chaplain who received 480 pesos yearly. In addition, one thousand pesos were earmarked in the military budget for the lieutenant governor serving at El Paso. Since this individual was often the first lieutenant of the Santa Fe company, he received the salaries of both his political and military offices.

The pay scale did not remain constant. A record of the accounts of the Santa Fe company in 1794 shows that an adjustment had been made in the salaries of most of the men. In this document, too, provision is made for the extra pay of an armorer (*armero*), a drummer, (*tambor*), and six *carabineros,* all of whom were drawn from among the enlisted men of the garrison.[12]

The governor customarily possessed the title of *teniente coronel graduado,* or brevet lieutenant colonel, though the actual rank for which he received pay was that of captain. Similarly, the first lieu-

10. Bando of Governor Concha, Santa Fe, March 27, 1789, SANM, doc. 1042.

11. Nava to Concha, Chihuahua, December 11, 1791, SANM, doc. 1174.

12. Santa Fe Company Accounts in the Royal Treasury, Chihuahua, April 22, 1794, SANM, doc. 1283.

tenant (*teniente primero*) often had the breveted title of captain.[13] Beyond the *graduados,* other special classifications might include the *cadetes, distinguidos,* and the *reformados.* Cadetes were young men, usually sons of officers, who received their appointment directly from the viceroy or commandant general. Though serving in the ranks, they did not live with the soldiers, but associated with the officers. Receiving only soldier's pay, they were obliged to have an independent income to permit them to live and dress fashionably, and promotion for them was directly to the rank of alférez. Service records disclose that many officers serving in Santa Fe began their careers as cadets.[14]

A *soldado distinguido* was mustered into the service in the same manner as other soldiers. On demonstrating evidence of genteel birth, however, he was enrolled as a distinguido and permitted to add the prefix *Don* to his Christian name. He lived in the barracks and did military duty but was exempt from all menial tasks. *Reformados* were men who, though not on active duty, received salary as regular presidial soldiers. These might be serving as alcalde mayor in some district, or in another capacity close to the governor. Also this term referred to officers retired with half pay as a capitán or teniente reformado.[15]

In November of 1777, the New Mexican governor petitioned his superior in Chihuahua for a troop increase in Santa Fe. The commandant general responded by raising the garrison strength to a total of 120 men. The new soldiers were designated as *tropas ligeras* (light troops) and included a second alférez, a second sergeant, and thirty-eight enlisted men.[16] The number of men fluctuated some-

13. Santa Fe Company Records, Santa Fe, January 1, 1800, SANM, doc. 1476a.

14. Nava to Chacón, Chihuahua, April 5, 1802, SANM, doc. 1596; and Bancroft, *California Pastoral,* p. 395.

15. Warner, "The Career of Martínez de Torrelaguna," p. 171. The rank of Spanish officers in descending order was as follows: captain general; lieutenant general; *mariscal de campo* (major general or field marshal); colonel; lieutenant colonel; *sargento mayor* (major); captain; ayudante (adjutant); lieutenant; and alférez (sub-lieutenant).

16. Croix to Mendinueta, Valle de Santa Rosa, February 10, 1778, SANM, doc. 719. Apparently the governor had sought an increase of 150 men. Thomas, *The Plains Indians and New Mexico,* p. 212.

what, thereafter—the company muster rolls in 1815 showed 126—but the total never ranged far above or below the 120 mark.[17]

The men of the presidial company were designated as *tropas veteranas* (the veteran troops) to distinguish them from the militia. Within the company a division was made between the *tropa de cuera* (leather-jacketed troops) and the *tropa ligera* or light troops mentioned above.[18] The former wore stout skin jackets; carried shields; had six horses, a colt, and a mule for each man; and received the salaries previously indicated.[19] The light troop had no leather armor or shields, was assigned only three horses and a pack mule per man, and received lesser pay. The men of this classification, however, were exempt from some duties as, for example, guarding the company horseherd.[20] Croix indicates the following salary index for light troops; second alférez, 450 pesos; second sergeant, 320 pesos; and soldiers, 216 pesos.[21] Officers of the Santa Fe company were termed *oficiales,* while the enlisted men, including sergeants, were referred to as *plazas.*

Promotions to the rank of lieutenant or alférez were initiated by the governor. He proposed three individuals for the vacant office to the commandant general, submitting his recommendations and the service record (*hoja de servicio*) of each man in triplicate. He might draw upon the names of meritorious personnel of his own troop or those of other presidios, militia companies, and mobile companies within the Provincias Internas. The commandant general considered the nominations, selected one to fill the vacant post, and informed the king or viceroy, depending upon to which of these he was im-

17. SANM, doc. 2638.

18. Muster Rolls, Santa Fe, October 1, 1779, SANM, doc. 780a; and Thomas, *Teodoro de Croix,* p. 119.

19. *Reglamento para los presidios,* tit. 4.

20. Teodoro de Croix criticized the use of the heavy, long, four or six-ply coats used to fend off Indian arrows. He claimed that as protection they were ineffectual and served only to hinder the soldier's movements. He favored instead the light troop because of its superior mobility. Thomas, *Teodoro de Croix,* pp. 56-57. Later the light troops seem to have been used exclusively, but this practice must have come more as an economizing move since they received less pay than the *tropa de cuera.*

21. Croix to Mendinueta, Valle de Santa Rosa, February 10, 1778, SANM, doc. 719.

mediately subordinate, so that final royal confirmation might be obtained (via a *real despacho*).

Sergeants were to be chosen in a similar manner, and every effort was to be made to select persons for this category who could read and write. Corporals were named by the governor on his own initiative.[22] According to the instructions issued by Viceroy Bernardo de Gálvez in 1786, neither dark color nor circumstances of birth were to stand as obstacles to advancement for sergeants or officers who had merit, courage, wisdom, experience, aptitude for warfare, and the ability to take command.[23]

Most of the soldiers made the army a lifelong career, but since enlistments were for a specific period, they could seek a discharge at the end of their term by applying to the commandant general through the governor.[24] Every effort was made, however, to encourage re-enlistment. Commandant General Salcedo, for example, authorized presidial captains to offer special inducements, as one- and two-month furloughs, to men who would re-enlist.[25] The crown itself endeavored to make military service more attractive by granting special rewards (*premios*) and creating welfare funds to benefit soldiers and their families. The privileged military fuero, highly esteemed by the men and mentioned in an earlier chapter, also contributed to this end.

Service Awards. On October 4, 1766, the king through his Secretaría de Estado y del Despacho de la Guerra issued a *real ordenanza* on the presentation of *cédulas de premios* or service awards to deserving soldiers.[26] According to the original decree, infantrymen who completed three periods (*tiempos*) of enlistment of five years

22. Nava to Chacón, Chihuahua, July 29, 1801, SANM, doc. 1553; Chacón to Salcedo, Santa Fe, March 30, 1803, SANM, doc. 1651; and *Reglamento para los presidios,* tit. 8.

23. Worcester, *Instructions for Governing the Interior Provinces,* p. 54.

24. Real Alencaster to Salcedo, Santa Fe, June 10, 1807, SANM, doc. 2054.

25. Salcedo to Real Alencaster, Chihuahua, February 14, 1806, SANM, doc. 1969.

26. The commandant general in 1795 dispatched the decree on premios to the governor of New Mexico with instructions to file it in the provincial archives. It is this copy which is quoted here. Nava to the Governor, Chihuahua, January 22, 1795, SANM, doc. 1307.

each and cavalrymen or dragoons who served for three periods of six years each were to be awarded an increase in salary of six reales per month.[27] Whoever completed four periods was to receive nine reales, and those completing five might retire with the rank of sergeant (*sargento graduado*) and with a stipend of ninety reals per month. Those who completed thirty-five years, at least five of which had been served with the rank of sergeant, could retire as an alférez with a monthly pension award of 135 pesos.

Only enlisted men (the decree lists sergeants, corporals, privates, and drummers) were entitled to receive these service awards. To qualify, soldiers had to serve the required number of periods continuously and honorably. Recipients of premios, beyond their monetary rewards, were to be exempted from menial tasks, such as wood and water hauling, and were to receive preferential assignments on campaign duty. Persons on the retired or disabled list received their extra premiums in addition to their regular pensions.[28] After the initial legislation on this subject was issued in 1766, successive royal decrees modified some features of the program, but only to a minor degree.[29]

In Santa Fe, the governor as commander of the presidial garrison made premium recommendations for deserving soldiers. These were submitted in triplicate to the commandant general's office with the governor's yearly military report.[30] In Chihuahua the recommendations passed to the auditor for a legal opinion and then to the commandant general for approval or disallowance. Final confirmation rested with the king whose secretary authorized the issuance of the service award. With this, the commandant general ordered the royal

27. The original document states *seis reales de vellón.*

28. Real Ordenanza, San Ildefonso, October 4, 1766, SANM, doc. 1307.

29. Reales órdenes on premios, for example, were proclaimed on August 20, 1773, and December 3, 1804. Bancroft notes that veterans who had rendered honorable service from 30 to 40 years as privates and corporals, on their retirement, were granted the honorary rank of alférez for 30, and lieutenant for 40, years—besides their regular pensions. They could wear the uniform of such rank. *California Pastoral,* p. 295.

30. Chacón Documents, Santa Fe, March 27, 1805, SANM, doc. 1800.

treasurer in Chihuahua to release the appropriate funds to the supplymaster of the Santa Fe company, and the governor was advised to inform the fortunate individual of his award.[31]

A standing privilege enjoyed by regular army men and their dependents and which further contributed to making service more attractive was the system of *preeminencias.* These were immunities reserved exclusively for the military. Soldiers could not be forced to assume municipal offices, they were exempt from *servicios* (money aids to the crown), and they could not be imprisoned for debt. Moreover, those who retired honorably from the service received *cédulas de preeminencias* entitling them to such privileges for life and to the military fuero with certain limitations.[32] These cedulas in the internal provinces were issued by the commandant general.[33]

Pensions. Before the last quarter of the eighteenth century, retired and disabled soldiers were of only minor concern to the government they served. In late 1772, however, the viceroy of New Spain prepared a Reglamento de inválidos designed to provide for infirm and old veterans and based upon a similar practice instituted in Spain in 1761.[34] The king approved this measure by a royal order of June 13, 1773, but it apparently did not become effective until 1775.[35]

According to the new measure, a *cuerpo de inválidos* (retired and disabled list) was created and included officers and men of the regular troops. A deduction of eight *maravedís de plata* was made from the monthly pay and extra allowances of all soldiers in actual service and constituted the *fondo de inválidos* (retired and disabled fund) from which the pensions were drawn. The pension scale as established by the Reglamento stood as follows: officers upon retirement

31. Order of the Secretario de Estado, San Ildefonso, August 13, 1800, SANM, doc. 1568; and Report of Governor Allande, Santa Fe, September 30, 1813, AGN, Prov. Int. 253. An excellent chart for the enlisted men of the Santa Fe company, May 12, 1795, showing the time credited to each toward premios, is found in SANM, doc. 1235.

32. McAlister, *The "Fuero Militar,"* p. 8.

33. AGN, Prov. Int. 129, p. 6.

34. Croix to Mendinueta, Chihuahua, March 30, 1778, SANM, doc. 759. It should be noted that as early as 1717 the law provided a modest stipend for retired officers.

35. SANM, doc. 759; and Bancroft, *History of Mexico,* III, 423.

were to receive two-thirds of the salary enjoyed while on active duty; sergeants were to be paid ten pesos per month, and corporals, soldiers, and drummers, eight.[36] Bobb declares that before these amounts were delivered, deductions were made for food and clothing. In this way the veteran's maintenance was assured, and he was not given the opportunity to spend his entire allotment on riotous living.[37] This practice may have been employed initially in Santa Fe, but in 1805 the adjutant inspector directed that inválidos attached to the company be paid their salaries and premios in cash (*reales efectivos*) on the first of each month and be permitted to make purchases at the presidial warehouse.[38] To receive his retirement pay, a soldier was required to maintain his residence in the same jurisdiction as the presidio last served, since his records continued to be kept by the company supplymaster.[39]

Persons disabled in the line of duty were also eligible for awards under the *Reglamento de inválidos*. Those receiving permanent injury to their health were retired with the appropriate pensions noted above, while those regarded as temporarily disabled (*inválidos interinos*) were granted inválido certificates and were expected to return to active service as speedily as possible.

Inválido certificates were issued by the same procedure as previously described for the premio awards. A document of 1799 demonstrates that on occasion the commandant general could initiate action in inválido cases. In this instance, he observed that two New Mexican soldiers who had arrived in Chihuahua as part of an escort for the annual caravan were in ill health and should be transferred from the active to the retired list. This command was conveyed to the governor in Santa Fe for his attention.[40] When the office of the commandant general came to be located in Durango for a brief per-

36. *Ibid.*
37. *The Viceregency of Bucareli,* p. 103.
38. Instruction on Supply Distribution, Santa Fe, April 17, 1805, SANM, doc. 1812.
39. Bonavia to Maynez, Durango, December 27, 1815, SANM, doc. 2632.
40. Nava to Chacón, Chihuahua, January 16, 1799, SANM, doc. 1441.

iod after 1814, all certificates passed through the hands of the adjutant inspector who remained in Chihuahua.[41]

Commandant General Teodoro de Croix concluded in 1778 that the pension scale fixed by the Reglamento was insufficient to meet the needs of soldiers in the interior provinces since the cost of living here was much higher than in New Spain generally. Accordingly, he recommended substantial increases in monthly payments, although it is not certain if any immediate action was taken.[42] Subsequent legislation added further provisions to or modified practices of the pension plan,[43] and in 1816 a *Reglamento de sueldos* established a uniform schedule for all of Spain's new world colonies.[44]

Another important fund was the *fondo de retención*. This was formed by a sum retained from each private soldier of the Santa Fe company. The total of such retention, at first of fifty pesos, and later of one hundred pesos, was preserved by the presidial supplymaster and did not go into the royal treasury. Instead the above amount was reimbursed to the soldier as mustering-out pay at the completion of his term of service.[45]

Finally, a pension fund for the widows and orphans of officers dying in the service known as the *monte-pio militar* was introduced into New Spain in 1765.[46] This fund was supported by the *mesada* or a month's pay retained once, and 2½ per cent withheld thereafter from the running pay, and by an annual subsidy of two thousand pesos. On the death of an officer, his widow or children, under normal circumstances, received annually one-fourth of the salary he had

41. Alejo García Conde to the Governor of New Mexico, December 19, 1817, SANM, doc. 2689.

42. Croix to Mendinueta, Chihuahua, March 30, 1778, SANM, doc. 759.

43. A royal order of June 8, 1813, for example, stipulated that only soldiers disabled in the line of duty were entitled to inválido certificates. Other royal ordinances pertaining to this subject were issued on the following dates: September 17, 1788; December 12, 1789; November 22, 1799; June 8, 1803; and October 30, 1816. Accounts of the Santa Fe Company, January 1, 1821, SANM, doc. 2952.

44. *Reglamento de sueldos para los oficiales y demas clases del ejército de América que se retiran del servicio* (Mexico, 1817). Copy from the Bancroft Library.

45. Bancroft, *California Pastoral,* p. 298; and *Reglamento para los presidios,* tit. 5.

46. There was also a separate monte-pio for certain civil officers.

at the time of his demise.[47] A number of regulations and royal orders governing administration of the monte-pio appeared after 1765 and were filed by the governor in the Santa Fe archives.[48]

It should be borne in mind that officers and soldiers could not marry without first obtaining the consent of the king. Such license was not given to anyone below the rank of captain, unless he could produce evidence of having an income of his own separate from his pay.[49] This explains, in part perhaps, why no fund equivalent to the monte-pio was provided for enlisted men.

Troop Duties. The *Reglamento para los presidios* of 1772 set forth in general terms the powers and functions of the men of a presidial company, but the documents themselves permit us to see precise examples of the way in which the soldiers fulfilled their duties.

The prime function of the Santa Fe garrison, of course, was to provide for the military defense of the province through military campaigns, regular patrols, and the guarding of selected strategic sites. In reality protracted campaigns were infrequent and when they did occur it was usually during the four months of summer. At other periods the official duties of the men tended to be rather light, leaving them a measure of spare time to devote to their personal affairs.

Governor Concha in 1794 noted that the presidials should be kept occupied in useful tasks to prevent them from living in ennervating idleness. The guarding of the company horse herd (*caballada*) he foresaw as the chief activity engaging the men in winter.[50] An earlier proposal by Teodoro de Croix to stable and feed the company mounts for security reasons had never beem implemented in New

47. Revilla Gigedo, *Instrucción reservada,* art. 734; and Bancroft, *History of Mexico,* III, 422-23.

48. See, e.g., Governor of New Mexico to Nava, Santa Fe, May 14, 1798, SANM, doc. 1419(6); and Correspondence of Salcedo to the Governor in SANM, docs. 1725, 1726, and 1770.

49. Bancroft, *California Pastoral,* p. 298. The measure also was designed to curb the practice of many men to marry women of inferior status. Military governors issued marriage licenses in the name of the king.

50. Concha, "Advice on Governing New Mexico," p. 253.

Mexico, and protection of the horses and mules held on pasturage remained of continuing concern.[51]

The caballada of the Santa Fe company often numbered upward of a thousand horses and mules. Under certain conditions, citizens might pasture their mounts with this herd to take advantage of the added protection, but this significantly increased the burdens of the guard.[52] Moreover, all other livestock maintained by the company as a food source—cattle and sheep—were customarily herded adjacent to the caballada, and the guards were held responsible for the loss of any animals. Since the total number of all these might exceed two thousand, the need for finding adequate pasturage posed a serious problem. The stock was occasionally driven north to the area around Cuyamungue and Pojoaque, but more commonly the Galisteo Basin and the valley of the Pecos River provided the needed grass.

As a rule the horse guard numbered thirty men. Most of these, however, were armed citizens who had been drafted to serve a specific number of days.[53] Commanding the detachment was a sergeant —the three sergeants of the garrison served alternately—and assisting him directly were several corporals and privates.[54] Whoever served in charge of the guard was addressed as comandante.[55]

Another duty consuming the soldier's time was the frequent patrol and reconnaissance missions called for by the superior authorities. The governor, whenever possible, led these parties personally, but more frequently they were conducted by subordinate officers, sergeants, or even corporals, each of whom, when in command of a detachment, bore the title of comandante. The commandant general demanded that all frontier zones subject to Indian incursions be

51. Thomas, *Teodoro de Croix,* p. 55.

52. Instructions from the Ayudante Inspector to the Governor of New Mexico, Santa Fe, April 15, 1805, SANM, doc. 1812, art. 11. Mares under no circumstances were to be pastured with the military horses.

53. Full details of these citizen levies will be presented below.

54. Concha, "Advice on Governing New Mexico," p. 253.

55. Instructions issued to a comandante of the caballada by the governor on November 1, 1807 are contained in SANM, doc. 2085.

kept under constant surveillance by patrols except during periods of excessive rain or snow.[56] The person in command received from the governor before departure a set of instructions which cited the objective of the mission, outlined the route to be followed, and enjoined the exercising of vigilance and prudence. Routine patrols were to be composed of only the number of men deemed necessary to insure safety of the unit.[57] At the conclusion of the reconnaissance, the commander submitted a full day-by-day report (*diario de novedades*) to his superior.

The garrisoning of temporary outposts formed an additional task engaging the Santa Fe troops. This work, likewise, was confined largely to the summer months. A report of 1808 shows a detachment (*destacamento*) of eight soldiers at Sevilleta and contingents of three each at the following places: Carnue and Abó, San Pedro, Galisteo, Pecos del Bado, Laguna, and Zuñi. Most of these were under the charge of a corporal and included, in addition to the troops named, citizen-levies drawn from throughout the province.[58]

Other places from time to time also enjoyed the protection of similar military detachments. Among these were the highly vulnerable villages of Ojo Caliente and Taos in the north. Governor Concha in 1794 mentioned the existence of a unit composed of fifteen Queres Indians, a resident of Vallecito or of la Cañada who alternated, and a carbineer of the Santa Fe presidial company who commanded the whole group. This body patrolled along the foot of the Sierra de San Pedro (Jémez Mountains?) to cover the entrance of the Apaches into the territory. Unfortunately, as Concha noted, this effort was largely ineffective.[59]

It will be recalled that Taos had been recommended more than once as a possible site for a new presidio. While this was never realized, the inroads of hostile Indians in that vicinity and the presence

56. Nava to Chacón, Chihuahua, March 23, 1795, SANM, doc. 1318.

57. Instruction on Patrols and Campaigns Against the Enemy, Pedro de Nava, Chihuahua, November 24, 1791, SANM, doc. 1171.

58. Governor Maynez to the Alcaldes Mayores, Santa Fe, June 14, 1808, SANM, doc. 2114.

59. Concha, "Advice on Governing New Mexico," p. 245.

of an annual trading fair in the summer months often forced the governor to assign a sizeable detachment to the several villages making up the larger Taos community. In 1810 the military body there was composed of twenty troops from Santa Fe commanded by the company's second lieutenant. A daily report submitted by this officer to the governor for the month of August reveals that the men of the detachment were performing these duties: guarding the horse herd (guards were relieved every four days), participating in weekly patrols under a corporal comandante, and acting as couriers to carry important news whenever it arose and to bring a copy of the daily report every month to the capital. Moreover, the men underwent an arms and clothing inspection once a week.[60]

The forming of an effective guard for the annual trading caravan to Chihuahua served as an additional function of the Santa Fe troop. In the fall of the year, the merchants and ranchers of New Mexico assembled at the campsite of Sevilleta with their goods and livestock. Here they awaited the arrival of the protective military detachment or escort (*escolta de cordón*) from Santa Fe and the citizen-guards who were to reinforce it.[61] In 1817 the soldiers numbered twenty and were led by a lieutenant who was in charge of organizing the order of march and the necessary precautionary measures.[62] The officer in command acted under explicit instructions supplied him by the governor.[63]

Other duties of the soldiers included serving as mail couriers, escorting important persons or extraordinary caravans along the camino real, and standing guard over the military buildings in Santa Fe. In addition, they maintained and cleaned their barracks and

60. Record of Events, Taos, August 1810, SANM, doc. 2345. Upon receipt of this document, the governor ordered his lieutenant not to reduce his strength by using soldiers as couriers, but to employ Indians instead. Manrrique to Gonzales, Santa Fe, August 2, 1810, SANM, doc. 2346.

61. Twitchell, *Old Santa Fe,* p. 158.

62. The details of caravan organization are succinctly outlined by Moorhead, *New Mexico's Royal Road,* pp. 45-48. He states that escorts on occasion number upward of forty troops.

63. Instructions on the Forming of the Cordón, Santa Fe, November 20, 1817, SANM, doc. 2703.

hauled wood and water for their own needs. After all these tasks had been performed, the men were allowed the use of whatever free time remained.

There were a number of individuals employed in specialized work who should receive separate mention; to wit, the armorer, the surgeon, the military chaplain, and the Indian interpreters and scouts. The post of armorer had existed as early as the seventeenth century when he was the only paid military functionary besides the governor. The Reglamento of 1772 provided that one soldier in each presidial garrison should serve in this capacity and that he should be freed of all other duties except in time of war.[64] The armorer's job consisted of maintaining and repairing the weapons of his company.[65]

The treasury made no provision for the salary of a surgeon at Santa Fe and when one was employed he was supported by the soldiers themselves. There existed no other doctor in the province, so citizens sought out the services of the presidial surgeon when he was available.[66] This physician was in charge of periodic vaccination programs ordered by the commandant general after 1804, and for this service he received one real for each person vaccinated.[67] By and large, New Mexicans depended upon their own skill in treating sickness with the many medicinal herbs abounding in the province.

Whenever the Santa Fe presidio was lacking a doctor, wounded or ailing soldiers were forced to journey to Chihuahua for treatment. Ordinarily they accompanied the annual caravan which afforded the most comfortable means of travel. In the spring of 1790, construction on a *hospital militar* was begun in the city of Chihuahua.[68] For upkeep of this establishment, a deduction was made against the soldiers' salaries in Nueva Vizcaya. Men of the New Mex-

64. Tit. 4.

65. Nava to Chacón, Chihuahua, January 7, 1797, SANM, doc. 1375a.

66. Pino, *Exposición,* p. 19.

67. Record of Vaccinations in the Province of New Mexico, May 24, 1805, SANM, doc. 1833. See also Lansing B. Bloom, "Early Vaccinations in New Mexico," *Hist. Soc. of New Mexico, Publ.* 27 (1924), 4.

68. Revilla Gigedo II, *Instrucción reservada,* art. 684.

ico troop might seek medical care at this hospital, but they were charged for all services and the bills were entered against their future salaries by the treasury officials. If there was no prospect of a recovery sufficient to permit a return to active duty, the Santa Fe soldier might request a discharge (*licencia absoluta*) directly from the commandant general.[69]

If the crown displayed only minor concern for the physical welfare of its soldiers, it endeavored to compensate by careful attention to their spiritual state. From the earliest days a military chapel was maintained in the southeast tower of the governor's palace. Perhaps by 1717, services for the troops were transferred across the plaza to a new military church commonly called the *castrense*. Later this edifice was completely rebuilt and dedicated anew in May of 1761.[70]

By the Reglamento of 1772, a chaplain with an annual salary of 480 pesos paid by the royal treasury was provided for frontier garrisons.[71] He was to be nominated for his curacy by the governor and selected by the same procedure as specified for officers.[72] His obligations as outlined by the royal regulations were extensive. He administered the sacraments, consoled the sick and wounded among the officers and men, and offered reprimands to those who mistreated their families. The policing of the troop's morals also fell to the chaplain, and he reported all instances of illicit or scandalous conduct to the garrison commander.

In possession of this priest was a company register (*libro de registro*) in which were recorded all baptisms, confirmations, marriages, and deaths, not only of the soldiers but of all civilians attached to the presidio who came under his jurisdiction. In addition, he issued birth, marriage, and death certificates to the individuals or families

69. Allande to Arce, Santa Fe, November 20, 1817, SANM, doc. 2703. Also see Report of Expenses of the Intendant of Durango, 1791, AGN, Prov. Int., 12. As late as 1797 only a single doctor was reported for Chihuahua and another for Durango. Navarro García, *José de Gálvez,* p. 510.

70. A. von Wuthenau, "The Spanish Military Chapels in Santa Fe and the Reredos of Our Lady of Light," *NMHR,* X (1935), 176, 181, 189.

71. Tit, 2.

72. *Ibid.,* tit. 8.

concerned.[73] The possessions of soldiers dying without families and wills were disposed of by the chaplain. He accompanied military expeditions whenever required by the commander and ministered to troops in the field.[74]

Requiring special explanation is the *jurisdicción* (or fuero) *eclesiástica castrense* or the military-ecclesiastical privilege. As the principal feature of this jurisdiction, the vicar general of the armies (*vicario general de los ejércitos*), who was also patriarch of the Indies residing at court in Spain, took cognizance of civil and criminal cases under the ecclesiastical fuero in which persons were involved who came under the military fuero. Further, this special jurisdiction held the exclusive power to administer and promote the temporal and spiritual welfare of all military forces throughout the empire. This privilege was deemed necessary to insure uniform treatment in ecclesiastical matters to all troops and their dependents wherever they might be serving.[75]

According to the practice established by the fuero, special dispensations from certain ecclesiastical obligations were arranged for the king's soldiers, their families, employees, or servants, owing to the peculiar hardships the men were forced to undergo in defense of the realm. In one particular instance on the frontier of New Spain, permission was given soldiers to eat meat on those days when the Church ordinarily prohibited it.[76] The Bishop of Durango in an edict directed to the Santa Fe garrison decreed that disabled and retired soldiers were not to be included within the military-ecclesiastical jurisdiction except for any brief periods when they might return

73. Examples of death certificates for the Santa Fe company may be seen in Report of Anza, Santa Fe, December 11, 1785, SANM, doc. 927.

74. *Reglamento para los presidios,* tit. 13.

75. Bancroft, *History of Mexico,* III, 423-24. The legal basis for the jurisdicción eclesiástica castrense resided in an apostolic brief of Pope Clement XIII issued in 1762. Further papal briefs were forthcoming in 1803 and 1807, and an edict of the patriarch was proclaimed in February of 1779 on this subject. See Joaquin Escriche, *Diccionario razonado de legislación y jurisprudencia* (Paris [1834]), pp. 1123-24.

76. Order of the Vicario General, certified copy, Chihuahua, February 20, 1785, fragment from the Janos Archives. Photograph copy in the Schroeder Collection, State Records Center and Archives, Santa Fe.

to active duty as guarding of the company horse herds, joining campaigns against the enemy, or garrisoning of plazas.[77]

The bishop in this case was acting in his capacity as *teniente vicario general* or subdelegate of the patriarch. He exercised jurisdiction over the chaplain of the Santa Fe company (the *cura castrense*), but in matters involving the military-ecclesiastical fuero he communicated with him through the offices of the commandant general and the governor.

The final group of persons to be accorded special mention here are the Indian scouts (*indios exploradores*) and the interpreters. The Reglamento provided that frontier garrisons should possess the services of scouts who were to be paid one real per day and were to receive rations to sustain themselves and their families.[78] Moreover, they were entitled to the use of a pistol, shield, and lance in addition to their own bows and arrows and were to be furnished saddle horses and pack mules.[79]

Governor Fernando de la Concha in his report of 1794 informs us of the number and activities of the Indian interpreters. Four of these for the Comanche tribe were salaried by the king. One resided in Taos, and two more in Santa Fe, and the fourth lived among the Indians "in order to observe them and to give an account of their movements." For the Navajos, two interpreters were supported by the crown, and they alternated between the capital and residence with the tribe.[80] All six of these men were formally attached to the presidial company, received their salaries from the supplymaster, and were allotted seven horses and a pack mule each, the same number as enlisted men.[81] For the other Indian groups, Concha noted that private individuals served as interpreters and were rewarded with fifty pesos annually from the province's extraordinary fund. Gení-

77. Order of Bishop Olivares y Benito, Durango, January 7, 1799, SANM, doc. 1440.

78. Teodore de Croix determined that the exploradores attached to the mobile companies of Nueva Vizcaya should be paid three reales per day. Instructive Paper, Croix to Oconor, July 22, 1777, Biblioteca Nacional, MSS, legajo 57, expediente xv.

79. *Reglamento para los presidios,* tits. 4-5.

80. Concha, "Advice on Governing New Mexico," p. 240.

81. Accounts of the Santa Fe Company, 1804, SANM, doc. 1808.

zaros were employed in this fashion to translate for the Utes and the several Apache tribes, except the Jicarillas who possessed a fair knowledge of Spanish.[82]

Reference at this point might be made to a schoolmaster who seems to have been hired by the presidial garrison. As early as 1721, according to one writer, the crown directed that "free schools" be established in the New Mexican settlements.[83] The lack of funds, however, precluded organization of such institutions, and Pino observed in 1812 that only children whose parents could contribute to the salary of a teacher were receiving a primary education.[84] This statement is open to question, for records reveal that in the city of El Paso, 584 children were attending school in 1806 and 460 in 1807.[85] Further, in a letter of 1808 the commandant general commended the governor of New Mexico for his action in the care and development of public schools.[86]

Whatever the general conditions, it is certain that in the nineteenth century a primary school was attached to the Santa Fe presidio, for attendance rolls are included among the garrison records. In this period, Ramos de Arizpe refers to schools in the eastern interior provinces, and the conditions there were, doubtless, similar to those prevailing in New Mexico. He declared:

> The military posts and larger towns with donations from the garrisons and voluntary contributions support some inept persons of bad conduct who bear the title of teachers. These teachers as a rule waste their time in teaching the Christian doctrine badly, for they are usually incapable of imparting the fundamentals of a common public education.[87]

82. Worcester, "Advice on Governing New Mexico," p. 241. The term genízaro will be discussed at some length below.

83. Hallenbeck, *Land of the Conquistadores,* p. 213.

84. *Exposición,* p. 18.

85. Bancroft, *Arizona and New Mexico,* p. 304n.

86. Salcedo to Maynez, Chihuahua, August 10, 1808, SANM, doc. 2144. An order of the audiencia of Guadalajara in 1818 to establish schools for the Pueblo Indians was apparently carried out. SANM, doc. 2896.

87. Nettie Lee Benson, tr., *Report that Dr. Miguel Ramos de Arizpe . . . Presents to the August Congress* (Austin, 1950), p. 18.

A summary for 1818 shows that in Santa Fe a schoolmaster was being maintained and that 76 children were receiving instruction. Fourteen of these were offspring of the soldiers while the remainder were of civilians. Subjects taught, in addition to religion, included writing, reading, and mathematics.[88]

Administration and Supply

As commandant of the Santa Fe presidio and subinspector of the New Mexican province, the governor had immediate charge of company administration and supply. In cases of his absence or illness, a junior officer of the garrison served as commandant ad interim, often with the title of adjutant (ayudante).[89]

General instructions for fostering the good government and welfare of the troops were frequently passed to the governor. He was required to familiarize himself thoroughly with the abilities and weaknesses of his officers and men; to keep a strict accounting of company funds; to review frequently the mounts, arms, and supplies on hand; and to promote efficient operation of the garrison as a whole. Since all these matters pertained to the Department of Inspection (ramo de inspección), the adjutant inspector of the commandancy assisted the governor whenever possible.[90] Other related affairs handled by the governor included the issuing of marriage permits to soldiers and the processing of cases under the military fuero, as, for example, instances regarding desertion.[91]

Monthly inspections were called for by the presidial Reglamento, and from the records it is clear that these were held in Santa Fe on

88. Santa Fe Presidial Records, August 1, 1818, SANM, doc. 2708.

89. See, e.g., Santa Fe Company Returns, 1821, SANM, doc 2952.

90. Instructive Paper, issued by Pedro de Nava, Chihuahua, November 24, 1791, SANM, doc. 1171; also Nava to the Governor, Chihuahua, March 10, 1795, SANM, doc. 1316.

91. Bolton, *Guide,* p. 189. The king often granted a general pardon to deserters on the occasion of a birth or marriage in the royal family. See, e.g., Real Orden, December 5, 1804, SANM, doc. 1864.

the first of each month with only slight variations from the form prescribed by law.[92] At the review, the governor surveyed the condition of officers and men, their arms and equipment, and the state of the garrison's horse herd. At such times the sick and disabled might be observed and placed on the inactive list.

At the conclusion of each review, the Reglamento stipulated the form to be followed in preparing the *extracto de revista* and the *lista de revista* (muster rolls). The names of all officers and men were to be entered and beside each should be inserted a P if he was present, the explanation of his whereabouts (*destino*) if on a mission, an A (*ausente*) if he was simply absent, and a V if the rank was vacant. Other brief statements were to be made regarding the number of men on the inactive list, the quantity of arms on hand, the status of the horse herd, the list of interpreters, promotions and demotions (*altas y bajas*) and so forth.[93] Two copies of a summary muster roll (the *extracto*) were dispatched to the commandant inspector who, as remarked earlier, was the commandant general after 1788, while the original, signed by the governor and his subordinate officers, remained in the provincial archives.[94]

According to the Reglamento, the two copies destined for the commandancy were to be sent monthly if possible. By 1805, however, the collected returns were being forwarded only every three months.[95] Beyond the thirty-day lists, an *extracto general de revista* was filed by the governor at the end of each year. This was a sum-

92. Tit. 9. Teodoro de Croix in 1781 mentions that he composed "methodical rules to bring out clearly in the reviews of inspection the actual condition of the presidio and companies for the purpose of finding ways to improve them. . ." Thomas, *Teodoro de Croix,* p. 117.

93. The term *alta* might also mean the returns of the effective men of a company, or alternately a certificate of discharge from a hospital. A *baja* could be a list of casualties in a muster roll or places vacant in a military company. In addition, altas and bajas frequently referred to additions and diminutions of company personnel strength.

94. A fine example of an extracto de revista for August 1, 1818, is found in SANM, doc. 2708. One of the two copies received by the commandant was conveyed to Spain. Salcedo to the Governor, Chihuahua, December 24, 1812, SANM, doc. 2470.

95. Chacón Documents, Santa Fe, April 27, 1805, SANM, doc. 1800.

mary of the twelve one-month reports and included further data on condition of the garrison.[96]

A number of other documents relating to presidial administration were prepared periodically by the governor. Quarterly a summary of events (*diario de novedades*) which listed all major actions as well as incidents of garrison life was submitted to the superior government. So, too, every six months was a report of the several company expense funds (*fondos*) to be discussed below. Once a year a description of each enlisted man—his physical description, native country, religion, marital state, past services, ability to read or write, etc.—was forwarded to the commandancy. This information was drawn from the company roster called the *libro de filiaciones*.[97] Similarly, service records of officers (*hojas de servicios*) were included in the yearly accounting.

Troop Supply. The financing of the frontier presidios was carried out through the military department (*ramo de guerra*), a branch within the royal treasury. As illustrated in Part One of this study, funds destined for New Mexico were released by the royal exchequer in Chihuahua and averaged about 35,000 pesos yearly. This sum included, in addition to military expenditures, the salaries of the missionaries whose fiscal affairs were administered by the ramo de guerra.

Reference has been made as well to the difficulties relating to presidial supply in the early eighteenth century. As other writers have adequately covered this topic elsewhere, only summary mention need be included here.[98] Initially, the soldiers had been paid their entire salaries in cash, from which amounts they were obliged to provide for themselves and their families. Forced to buy from un-

96. Salcedo to the Governor, Chihuahua, May 21, 1801, SANM, doc. 1728.

97. The *filiaciones* are filed separately in the Spanish Archives at Santa Fe, being listed as Enlistment Papers, 1738-1820.

98. On presidial supply, consult the following: Warner, "The Career of Martínez de Torrelaguna," chap. 1; Max L. Moorhead, "The Private Contract System of Presidio Supply in Northern New Spain," *Hispanic American Historical Review,* XLI (1961), 31-54; and Max L. Moorhead, "The Presidio Supply Problem of New Mexico in the Eighteenth Century," *NMHR,* XXXVI (1961), 210-30.

scrupulous merchants, they found themselves continually in debt. Later the power to purchase supplies was centralized in the presidial captains who, it was felt, could bargain with the merchants more effectively than individual soldiers.[99] The nefarious practices of these supply officers created new scandals and did nothing to alleviate the precarious financial position of the troops. For a while, the salaries of the men were paid in provisions rather than cash (the *factoría* system), but in spite of fixed price ceilings, frauds continued.[100]

The viceroy in 1768 ordered that presidial soldiers once again should be paid in cash. The governor of New Mexico, however, appealed for exemption from this requirement on the ground that there was never sufficient specie in his province to meet the pay roll.[101] The viceroy was convinced and a dispensation was extended in the following year.[102]

As a result of the Marqués de Rubí's report, the Reglamento of 1772 was issued, as we have seen, to reorganize and stabilize the entire presidial system. A portion of this new instrument was dedicated to reforming the method of supply. Commanders of garrisons, under penalty of removal from office and denial of further employment in the royal service, were divorced entirely from the purchasing of provisions for their companies. This function, along with that of paying the troops was now vested in an officer, the *oficial habilitado,* or supplymaster, who was to obtain the goods needed and sell them to the soldiers at cost plus two per cent, an amount regarded as sufficient to cover his expenses.[103]

The regulations governing selection and operation of the supplymaster were precise. When it came time to choose him, the presidial commander ordered the corporals and privates to assemble in the

99. Moorhead, "The Presidio Supply Problem of New Mexico," p. 210.

100. Warner, "The Career of Martínez de Torrelaguna," p. 123.

101. Moorhead, "The Presidio Supply Problem of New Mexico," p. 214.

102. Apparently this shortage of coined money continued for some time. According to one source in 1790, the number of silver coins circulating in the internal provinces was small, and in New Mexico practically nil. Letter of Revilla Gigedo II, Mexico, March 27, 1790, translated in J. Villasana Haggard, *Handbook for Translators of Spanish Historical Documents* (Austin, 1941), pp. 88-94.

103. Moorhead, "The Private Contract System," pp. 33-34.

quarters of the sergeants for the purpose of naming a representative (*apoderado*) from among their number. As soon as this was accomplished, the governor speedily convoked in his own house a meeting attended by the officers, the chaplain, and the apoderado. This group named one of the junior officers (*subalterno*) as supplymaster to serve for a term of three years.

Owing to the small number of officers eligible to act as the supplymaster, re-election for an indefinite period was provided. If no one in the company appeared suitable for the post, the superior authorities reserved the right to appoint an individual from some other company and transfer him to the new assignment.[104] In any event, confirmation of the elected officer was made by the commandant inspector.[105]

The specific duties of the supplymaster were twofold: he served as the accounting officer of the company charged with the management of general fiscal affairs, and, with power of attorney conveyed by his election, he represented the officers and men of the garrison in Chihuahua where he drew their salaries (situados) against the treasury office and made purchases of needed supplies.

Estimates of the coming year's expenses were submitted by the governor to the commandant general who authorized the approved or adjusted amount to be released by the treasury officials. The supplymaster traveled to the treasury office in Chihuahua twice yearly to make his withdrawals.[106] One of his trips usually coincided with departure of the caravan in the fall, and he served as military commander of the protective unit. Often his buying tours on behalf of the Santa Fe company led him to Durango and other places, so that

104. *Reglamento para los presidios,* tit. 14. Governor Concha in 1794 warned his successor of the disordered activities of the then current supplymaster, but noted that no other officer was fit for the responsibility. Concha, "Advice on Governing New Mexico," p. 252.

105. "On this day of the 12 of November, a meeting of officers was called to elect a supplymaster for the coming year of 1807, and the first alférez Don Josef Tapia having been elected, I advise Your Excellency with the hope that he merits your approbation." Governor Real Alencaster to the Commandant General, Santa Fe, November 20, 1806, SANM, doc. 2030(1).

106. The treasury officials were authorized to release presidial funds in late December and on or about July 1. *Reglamento para los presidious,* tit. I.

he might be gone from his headquarters three to six months of the year. At least part of the time in the late colonial years, an assistant to the supplymaster (a cashier) functioned in Santa Fe to maintain the accounts until his return.[107]

The fact that the junior officers elected to the supplymaster's job had little or no experience in accounting caused considerable confusion in the keeping of financial records. Likewise, they were often ignorant of purchasing practices and fell victim to merchants who artificially advanced prices. Such problems were common to all presidios along the northern frontier.

As a result, beginning in the early 1780's a new system was instituted whereby private contractors were given the exclusive right to supply the presidios for a specified term. Francisco de Guizarnótegui, a member of the merchant guild of Chihuahua, received a contract covering the military establishments in Nueva Vizcaya and New Mexico. He was to transport all supplies directly to the presidios, except in the case of Santa Fe. The supplymaster of this post was to receive deliveries at Chihuahua as had been the custom in the past.[108] For several reasons operation of the private supply system was not successful, and later we find, at least in New Mexico, that the supplymaster returned to the earlier practice of purchasing directly from merchants who could offer the best prices.[109]

Although all but the simplest manufactured commodities had to be purchased in Chihuahua or other supply centers, there were many

107. Commandant General Croix in 1782 recommended creation of formal adjutant supplymasters, but it is doubtful if any action was taken by the government. Thomas, *Teodoro de Croix,* p. 58.

108. Moorhead, "The Presidio Supply Problem." pp. 218-19. See also related documents in AGN, Prov. Int. 13 which includes a copy of the contract between the commandant general and Guizarnótegui.

109. See, e.g., receipts of goods purchased by the supplymaster in Chihuahua, January-December, 1818, SANM, doc. 2708. Apparently on February 27, 1805, the commandant general issued an Instrucción which defined how the supplymaster's office of the Santa Fe Company should be managed. Unfortunately since this document does not remain in the archives, we cannot know if it contained provisions on the method of supply. A later reference mentions that Article 14 of the Instrucción forbade the supplymaster to lend out money in his keeping on promissory notes during the course of the year. Salcedo to Real Alencaster, October 7, 1807, SANM, doc. 2081.

items, particularly foodstuffs, which could be conveniently secured in New Mexico itself. Apparently these goods were paid for in specie, a practice which argues against the emphatic statement often repeated that little or no coin circulated in the late colonial period.[110] Grain, beans, and other agricultural products were bought from both the Spanish citizens and the Pueblo Indians.[111] Governor Mendinueta in 1773 called attention to the bounty of the Pueblo harvests which kept the storehouses full and noted that frequent purchases were made, at prices established throughout the province, to supply the royal troops with maize and other grains.[112]

Regarding distribution of salaries, the presidial Reglamento stipulated that corporals and privates should receive directly a *prest* (daily pay) of two reales to cover their own personal expenses and those of the their families. The remainder of their due was to be retained and administered by the supplymaster, and against it were to be charged their food, clothing, arms, and horses.[113] Individual discounts were also made for pension and retirement funds, hospital bills originating in Chihuahua, and for special charges as those made for salary advances.[114]

No mention of the method of salary distribution to officers and sergeants is made by the Reglamento, but in the early nineteenth century, they were paid in reales on the seventh of each month and were permitted to purchase their own necessities at the company supply depot.[115] Probably this system or a similar one had prevailed for some time.

Each soldier estimated his own needs in material goods and submitted it to the presidial commander for approval. The cost of provisions requested was not to exceed the man's income except by

110. See note 102 above.

111. Circular of Governor Maynez to the Alcaldes, Santa Fe, July 1, 1808, SANM, doc. 2132.

112. Pedro Fermín de Mendinueta, *Indian and Mission affairs in New Mexico, 1773,* trs. by Marc Simmons (Santa Fe, 1965), p. 16.

113. Tit. 5.

114. Fisher, *Order of Intendants,* p. 300.

115. Instruction on Economic Management, Ayudante Inspector Antonio García de Tejada, Santa Fe, April 17, 1805, SANM, doc. 1821.

special arrangement. After approval the list was then passed to the supplymaster who acted upon it in the course of his next buying tour.[116] In transacting the affairs of the individual troops, the supplymaster kept two records. One consisted of the soldier's accounts into which was entered the amount of his salary, the sums paid out, a list of debts, and the balance on hand.[117] The other was the account book (*cuaderno*) in which was set down the purchases made by the officers and men through the supplymaster.[118]

A schedule for the year 1805 shows that enlisted men drew their rations on the seventh and sixteenth of each month. The standard withdrawal for a married man included the following basic items and amounts: eight *almudes* of maize, one almud of beans, soap worth three reales, four reales' worth of smoking tobacco, and one real of salt. Bachelors received similar articles, but in smaller quantities.[119]

Soldiers were required to be uniformed and to wear the following articles: a short jacket (*chupa corta*) of wool shag (*tripe*) or blue cloth (*paño azul*) with a red collar (*collarín encarnado*), blue wool trousers (*calzon de tripe azul*), a blue cape, a cartridge pouch (*cartuchera*), a cross belt (*bandolera*) on which was to be embroidered the name of the presidio, a black tie, hat, shoes, and leggings (*botines*).[120] Various reports made after reviews of the Santa Fe company indicate that the troops here, as elsewhere on the frontier, conformed in some measure to this pattern of dress. The adherence to a common standard in attire, no doubt, increased troop morale and enhanced prestige of the company in the eyes of civilians.

The armament of the presidial soldiers was to consist of a wide sword, a lance, shield, musket, and a brace of pistols.[121] A list of weapons held by the men in Santa Fe for 1816 shows that they did

116. *Reglamento para los presidios,* tit. 6.

117. Santa Fe Company Accounts, June, 1816, SANM, doc. 2638.

118. A fine example of such a cuaderno for the year 1820 is contained in SANM, doc. 2902.

119. SANM, doc. 1812.

120. *Reglamento para los presidios,* tit. 3.

121. *Ibid.,* tit. 4.

not possess a full complement of arms since most of the enlisted men had only a single pistol and no sword.[122]

The supplymaster secured firearms, cartridges, powder, and flints from the commandancy headquarters in Chihuahua and deposited them in the company armory in Santa Fe. One hundred muskets and a like number of pistols were always to be held in reserve at the armory, but often this was not possible.[123] At times stores of weapons were maintained at strategic locations outside Santa Fe for use by the citizens in emergencies or during campaigns, but ordinarily it was the civilian rather than the military who bore the cost of these.[124] Consignments of firearms were also made from time to time by the supplymaster directly to militia captains or alcaldes.[125]

Gunpowder was administered through a separate account by the office of the supplymaster under the governor's supervision. The company's yearly allotment was stored in the powder magazine within the armory and was secured by a lock with two keys. One of these was in the possession of the governor and the other was held by the supplymaster. The presence of both was thus required for any removal, and jointly they maintained a record in a special account book of all withdrawals. By the Reglamento of 1772, each soldier was allotted three pounds of gunpowder yearly. An exception was made for recruits, who were issued six pounds, the extra amount to be used in practice. Indian scouts attached to the company received one pound annually.[126]

The manufacture of gunpowder was a monopoly reserved to the crown, and in the royal powder works (*reales fábricas*) of New

122. Report of the Santa Fe Presidial Company, SANM, doc. 2638.

123. A weapons report (*relación de armamento*) prepared by the governor at Santa Fe in 1804 showed, for example, that the company held only 64 muskets and 88 pistols in reserve. SANM, doc. 1789.

124. Governor Mendinueta declared in 1775 that "the resident population is not so bad off in regard to arms which number about 600 guns and 150 braces of pistols in fair condition in the whole kingdom." Frank D. Reeve, "Navajo-Spanish Diplomacy, 1770-1790," *NMHR,* XXXV (1960), 211. See also Nava to the Governor of New Mexico, Chihuahua, January 7, 1795, SANM, doc. 1375a.

125. List of Receipts for Weapons and Supplies, 1818, SANM, doc. 2708.

126. Tit. 7.

Spain several grades were produced. The two most common powders were designated as regular (*ordinaria*) and fine (*fina*). In 1777 the former grade was commonly used on the frontier, but since it was considered much inferior, occasioning great danger in time of war, a suggestion was made that a presidio's ration be half and half—the regular to be used for practice, the fine for campaigns.[127] A report on the powder fund prepared for the Santa Fe company in 1791 suggests that this procedure had been adopted, for part of the supply on hand is listed as fina and part as ordinaria.[128] In 1804, however, the records reveal that only the superior grade was being used.[129]

Gunpowder was consumed in practice exercises, in target shooting, and in war operations. Also it appears that considerable amounts were wasted. When artillery was added to the Santa Fe company, it, likewise, consumed its share of powder.[130] A certain quantity, in addition, was presented to allied Indians who seemed to have been well supplied with firearms. At first, powder given to peaceful tribes was charged to a gunpowder fund (*fondo de pólvora*), but this was ordered extinguished in 1805, and thereafter such expense was borne by the special company fund (*fondo de gratificación*).[131] The gunpowder fund had been formed by the governor in 1802 and represented the funds acquired through sale of powder to civilians.[132]

On the frontier with its formidable distances, the horses of the

127. Viceroy to Croix, Mexico, February 22, 1777, AGN, Prov. Int., 74.

128. Accounts of Gunpowder, Santa Fe, October 31, 1791, SANM, doc. 1162.

129. Accounts of Gunpowder, Santa Fe, December 31, 1804, SANM, doc. 1786.

130. A record of the accounts of the Santa Fe company shows that in 1815 gun carriages were made for the *cañones de artilleria*. Report of the Supplymaster, Santa Fe, November 18, 1816, SANM, doc. 2638(14). The cannons were four four-pounders (*cañones de a quatro*) and were stored in the company warehouse. Two years later the cannon numbered six pieces. Thomas, "Anonymous Description of New Mexico," p. 58. In the years just before independence, three artillerymen from Durango served in Santa Fe and acted as instructors for eight men of the local garrison. SANM, doc. 2782.

131. Salcedo to the Governor of New Mexico, Chihuahua, December 19, 1805, SANM, doc. 1936; and Real Alencaster to the Commandant General, Santa Fe, April 1, 1806, SANM, doc. 1979(14).

132. Salcedo to the Governor of New Mexico, Chihuahua, April 23, 1803, SANM, doc. 1653.

Santa Fe garrison were of extreme importance. In an earlier chapter, mention has been made of the frequent raids on presidial horse herds, and the concern over this matter expressed by Teodoro de Croix when he became commandant general. According to the Reglamento, each soldier was to possess seven horses and a pack mule, together with the appropriate saddle and pack equipage. One of the horses was to be picketed close by at all times and ready for instant use.[133] The eight animals belonging to individual soldiers were personal property purchased, Governor Concha notes in 1794, at an average cost of eight pesos apiece.[134] In addition to the private horses and mules, a certain number of animals were listed as belonging to the king and included replacement stock and a string (*atajo*) of mules for use in campaigns.

A chart showing the strength of the Santa Fe company herd for the year of 1816 indicates the following: the governor and first lieutenant each owned six horses and four mules, the remaining officers and the sergeants three horses and one mule each.[135] Earlier records note that the mounts held by the company frequently did not reach the total specified by the regulations, suggesting that depletion of the herds by raiding Indians was a continuing problem. Remounts were obtained within the province when possible by the supplymaster. At other times he procured them in Chihuahua, or, when this was difficult, the superior authorities would approve the commission of a sergeant or junior officer to go on a buying tour seeking replacements for the New Mexican presidio.[136]

Company Funds. To meet emergency expenses of the Santa Fe troop, there existed two general funds, one the officers' reserve or special fund (*fondo de gratificación*), and the other the common fund of the enlisted men (*fondo común*). The fondo de gratificación, by the Reglamento of 1772, amounted to 680 pesos annually

133. Tit. 4.

134. Concha, "Advice on Governing New Mexico," p. 251.

135. List of Livestock, Santa Fe, March 18, 1816, SANM, doc. 2638(5).

136. Salcedo to Sergeant Miguel Portillo, Instructions, copy made in Santa Fe, July 20, 1805, SANM, doc. 1860.

for Santa Fe,[137] but toward the end of the century it had been reduced to 450 pesos.[138] This was a catch-all fund to provide for any financial crises arising during the course of the year. Whatever sums were not spent were carried over to the following year, and the fund might grow rather large during prolonged periods when no major demands were made upon it. A summary of the fund prepared on November 18, 1816, reveals that in the year just ending, 2,576 pesos were in the account against which a total of only 135 pesos had been charged.[139] At other times, the fondo de gratificación might be exhausted as when extensive repairs were made on the company buildings. Beyond various incidental expenses, the fund sustained the cost of feeding prisoners and paying new recruits whose salaries had not been included in the year's estimate.

The fondo común of the enlisted men has been alluded to previously. This was the amount retained from each soldier's pay which served to supply, arm, and mount him. Articles purchased with this money were lodged in the company storehouse, or *almacén de la tropa,* over which a constant guard was maintained. To this fund were charged expenses common to the men as a whole, and also the cost of any animals lost or strayed from the company herd.

Every six months the governor submitted a record of these two accounts to the commandant general as the former was responsible for the correct investment of such finances. These and other funds pertaining to the military were deposited in a triple-locked chest with one key each in the possession of the governor, the first lieutenant, and the company supplymaster.

Another account which has never been fully explained is the *fondo de aliados,* called also the *fondo de paz y guerra,* or occasionally the *fondo extraordinario.* This was a special fund employed to supply gifts and rations to nomadic Indians who had made peace and to feed them whenever they appeared in Santa Fe for talks. Behind

137. Tit. 2.

138. Santa Fe Company Accounts, Royal Treasury, Chihuahua, January 20, 1798, SANM, doc. 1413a.

139. SANM, doc. 2836.

this seemingly simple presentation of goods to friendly tribes lay a devious motive which seems to have been part of Spanish thinking from the earliest days of conquest in the New World. When force of arms failed to overcome enemy Indians, a second more effective plan could be adopted. No less an exalted person than Viceroy Bernardo de Gálvez expressed it thus in the year 1786:

> The interest in commerce binds and narrows the desires of man; and it is my wish to establish trade with the Indians. . . . They should be made accustomed to the use of our foods, drinks, arms, and clothing, and they should become greedy for the possession of land. Even if in the beginning we are not successful in achieving these ends, as they require much time, this course will put us on the path to eventual success.[140]

By this strategem the Indians could be made economically dependent upon the Spaniards and would be forced to live in peace since war would cut off the supply of goods which for them had become a necessity. The first stage of this long-range plan as it was envisioned for New Mexico involved the delivery of gifts through the fondo de aliados to those tribesmen who sought to establish amiable relations. From the first, this was intended to be a temporary expedient. As the commandant general himself informed the New Mexican governor in 1788, "once the Indians become accustomed to the use of our goods and to living by our system we may reduce the gifts to them without risk until the practice has been entirely ended and the treasury relieved."[141] Given the immensity of the task, this observation was overly optimistic. The fondo de aliados remained in existence to 1821, was inherited by the Mexican government, and continued to function long after independence.

This fund possessed, too, other related objectives though of a briefer scope. When the Indians ventured into the settlements to receive their presents, it was felt they would observe the benefits of permanent residence enjoyed by the Spanish citizens and Pueblo In-

140. Worchester, *Instructions for Governing the Interior Provinces,* p. 42.

141. Ugarte y Loyola to Concha, Arizpe, January 23, 1788, SANM, doc. 994.

dians and would be more inclined to abandon their nomadic ways.[142] Moreover, the distribution of gifts was customarily accompanied by prodigious feasts. When the governor honored the leading men of the pagan tribes (*naciones gentiles*) at his banquet table and held them under the influence of good food and wine, he sought to ascertain their views on current affairs and to fathom the key to their peculiar way of thinking. The clever Spaniard thus pressed every advantage in an effort to gain mastery over the native inhabitants.[143]

Indians initially became recipients of Spanish goods upon signing a treaty of peace. Viceroy Gálvez in 1786 authorized a regular allotment of food rations to such peoples, the cost to be borne by whatever fund existed in the presidio concerned. Separate legal accounts of such business were to be kept so that a reimbursement of the company fund might be made by the royal treasury.[144] Rather quickly, however, a formal fondo de aliados came to be organized, at least in Santa Fe, to meet expenses of treating the Indians.

In the year 1788, we find that only the small sum of sixty pesos was directly set aside for Indian expenses in New Mexico.[145] At this time, however, supply of such goods was in the hands of the private contractor Guizarnótegui, and in his accounts were figured the manufactured articles destined for the natives in this province.[146] Within a brief time after this date, the contract was terminated, and in 1790 we find the king himself authorizing release of 4,000 pesos for extraordinary expenses for peace and war (*de paz y guerra*) in New Mexico. This meant that gifts were now to be procured directly by the presidial supplymaster.[147]

From this time onward, the fondo de aliados was administered as an individual branch of presidial financial affairs. Monthly lists were

142. Regarding the long-standing Spanish policy of instructing wild Indians by example, see Marc Simmons, "Tlascalans in the Spanish Borderlands," *NMHR,* XXXIX (1964), 101-110.

143. Chacón to Salcedo, Santa Fe, November 19, 1802, SANM, doc. 1629.

144. Worcester, *Instructions for Governing the Interior Provinces,* pp. 50-51.

145. Ugarte y Loyola to Concha, Arizpe, January 23, 1788, SANM, doc. 994.

146. Cueva to Concha, Chihuahua, February 23, 1788, SANM, doc. 1002a.

147. Ugarte y Loyola to Concha, Chihuahua, June 18, 1790, SANM, doc. 1084.

kept of the articles furnished the Indians, and these were included in a yearly *cuenta de aliados,* or summary of the branch, carried in duplicate from Santa Fe to the commandancy general. A final audit of these accounts was undertaken by the head accounting office in Mexico City.[148]

In the governor's annual financial report, he showed the sum credited or owed to the ramo de aliados and estimated the needs for the coming year.[149] The commandant general, whose action was subject to royal confirmationn, then instructed the treasurer in Chihuahua to release the approved amount to the Santa Fe supplymaster. Goods were purchased by the supplymaster in the same manner as those for supply of the presidial garrison. The accounts of these two, however, were maintained separately, and in Santa Fe the Indian provisions were lodged in a special warehouse, the *almacén de aliados.* Whenever possible, the products for the *indios gentiles,* especially the foodstuffs, were acquired in New Mexico, and since amounts ranging from two thousand to four thousand pesos annually were designated for this purpose, the conduct of such business must have served to stimulate the local economy.

Gifts were distributed at formal treaty conferences, and subsequently on all occasions when the Indians should appear in Santa Fe. On these later visits, the governor met them in a friendly manner, ordered the killing of a beef or sheep to provide an abundant feast, and supervised the presentation of gifts. The amount of ceremony in these instances was dependent upon the prestige of the tribe involved—the Comanches, for example, merited considerable attention, while the remnants of the Jicarilla Apaches who clung to the Spanish settlements for protection received little.[150]

Provisions given to the Indians included jerked meat, salt, metal wares, cloth, shoes, hats, jackets, lump sugar, gunpowder, tobacco,

148. Arce to the Treasurer, Santa Fe, June 18, 1799, SANM, doc. 1453a.

149. An excellent example of such a statement for the year 1804 may be found in SANM, doc. 1769.

150. Instructions from the Governor to Ysidro Rey, Santa Fe, May 31, 1810, SANM, doc. 2323, art. 13.

abalone, livestock, mirrors, buttons, and so forth. On occasion the Spanish citizens were called upon to make contributions toward the fondo de aliados, apparently when the funds or goods on hand ran excessively short.[151]

It should be emphasized that the fondo de gratificación and the fondo de aliados were entirely separate accounts, as they have been described in this chapter. There has been some tendency to confuse the two and regard them as a single fund, owing, it would seem, to the fact that the word gratificación (meaning gifts or rewards) was sometimes used in connection with the distribution of Indian presents through the fondo de aliados.

Citizen Soldiers of New Mexico

New Mexico's defense in the seventeenth century, as we have seen, was entrusted to citizens who were led by officers drawn from members of the encomendero class. Even after the formation of the Santa Fe presidio, citizen soldiers continued to support the official military establishment in protecting the province. The documentary evidence remaining to us on this subject is rather fragmentary, but it does suggest that able-bodied civilians were gathered into loose militia companies from a very early date.[152] In the later colonial years, a stricter organization was the rule with formal militia units operating under precise instructions from the superior government. In the nineteenth century, formal companies of Pueblo militia and a *tropa de genízaros* came into being in defiance of an earlier practice in New Spain which excluded Indians from such participation.

The interest of the crown in New Spain's government of the 1760's, manifested by the reform measures explained earlier, extended to the question of the citizen's militia. At the beginning of 1761, the Viceroy Marqués de Cruillas began to take measures to reorganize

151. In 1814, for example, the citizens of Albuquerque made significant contributions for this purpose. SANM, doc. 2545.

152. In 1716 militia companies existed at least in Santa Fe, Albuquerque, and Santa Cruz de la Cañada. Lansing B. Bloom, tr., "A Campaign Against the Moqui Pueblos," (collected documents), *NMHR,* VI (1931), 172-73.

the country's militia units since, according to him, they had fallen into a lamentable state.[153] Shortly afterward, José de Gálves looked into the same problem during the course of his general investigation of colonial affairs. When his reform program came to be implemented in the northern provinces, abundant consideration was given to renewal and expansion of the militia.

The condition of New Mexico's citizen soldiery at this period is not altogether clear. Nicolás Lafora, accompanying the Marqués de Rubi to the frontier in the years 1766 to 1768, noted that Albuquerque maintained a company of "eighty militiamen, well mounted and armed, with their corresponding officers."[154] The state of the militia elsewhere in the province may not have been as favorable, but Lafora fails to offer further information.

The reorganization of the El Paso militia was provided for by the Reglamento of 1772.[155] It will be recalled that by this instrument, the presidio there was ordered removed southward to Carrizal, and defense of the El Paso district was left in the hands of its citizenry. At first, six poorly armed companies totaling 857 men were organized under the direction of the new lieutenant governor. Later reorganization produced four companies of 53 men each, but as the central government insisted that the settlers outfit themselves, this militia proved ineffective owing to the shortage of weapons.[156]

In 1776 Antonio de Bonilla made some statements regarding the condition of the militia generally throughout New Mexico. He pointed out that all inhabitants of the province, both Spaniard and Indian, had an obligation to assist in general defense. The available manpower, however, was not utilized to best advantage because of the lack of organization and discipline and the scarcity of arms and horses. He advised a general enlistment of formal militia with selection of able colonists to serve as officers and instructors. This mea-

153. Carmen Velázquez, *El estado de guerra en Nueva España,* pp. 33-34.

154. Kinnaird, *The Frontires of New Spain,* p. 90.

155. Art. 11.

156. Thomas, "Antonio de Bonilla, Notes," p. 186.

sure might be financed through contributions or a modest tax on produce of the province.[157]

Bonilla's views on the poverty of the New Mexican militia coincide with those of Governor Mendinueta expressed four years earlier and reveal that the settlers were ill-prepared to resist Indian incursions.[158] The El Paso area, as a result of the withdrawal of the soldiers to Carrizal, was particularly hard-pressed. When Governor Anza visited there in 1788, he reduced the number of militia companies from four to two.[159] These were composed of both Spaniards and Indians; the presence of Indians indicated that the earlier government policy of excluding them from the militia had been altogether abandoned. Anza recommended that the government relieve the desperate situation at El Paso by equipping and paying the militia for three-to-four-month campaigns each year.[160]

The general enlistment of militia for New Mexico as urged by Bonilla in 1776 was ordered by Commandant General Croix in 1779 under royal sanction.[161] To what extent this measure was applied, however, is uncertain. It seems evident that informal companies functioned in the larger towns and in some of the smaller places as well. In 1786, for example, reference was made to the Third Company of the District of Abiquiu and Chama.[162] Even where no companies came into being, steps were taken to increase the ability of the settlers to repel invaders. Representative of this was an edict issued by the governor in 1782, directing all citizens to provide themselves with bows and arrows within two months.[163] Before the end of the

157. *Ibid.*, p. 203.

158. Thomas, "Governor Mendinueta's Proposals," p. 28.

159. Thomas, "Antonio de Bonilla, Notes," p. 187.

160. *Ibid.*

161. Croix to Anza, Chihuahua, September 23, 1779, SANM, doc. 768.

162. Order of Governor Anza, Abiquiu, April 26, 1786, SANM, doc. 934. A table appended to the report of an expedition against the Comanches in 1779 lists militiamen from such places as the alcaldías of the Queres and of San Carlos. Thomas, *Forgotten Frontiers,* p. 122. For the same year, militia companies are mentioned with captains, lieutenants, and other officers. Biblioteca Nacional de México, 10, pt. 3.

163. Bando of Governor Anza, Santa Fe, August 27, 1782, SANM, doc. 843.

1780's, a census was compiled listing all able-bodied men in New Mexico between the ages of eighteen and fifty-eight and classifying them according to infantry or cavalry.[164] This survey may have come as a result of a royal order of 1788 which authorized reorganization of the militia of New Spain according to a plan laid down by Inspector General Francisco Antonio Crespo.[165]

The general situation with regard to the militia in New Mexico at the end of the eighteenth century appears thus: all able men were enlisted in hometown units lead by their own officers, either captains, lieutenants, or alféreces who received their appointments from the governor. Militiamen ordinarily received no pay, furnished their own arms, and, if joined to a cavalry company, they provided the necessary horses and pack animals.[166] Periodically, they underwent inspections (revistas) at which time the unit's strength and armaments were listed. The militia was called out by the sound of a drum in times of emergency or whenever a campaign was to be undertaken. Service was distributed as fairly as possible among the citizens so no individual would be overburdened. Occasionally, in special instances, the government appropriated funds to pay militiamen who were called upon to perform extraordinary service outside their own districts.[167]

An order of the king in 1801 exempted merchants and farmers in

164. Ugarte y Loyola to Concha, San Bartolomé, January 27, 1789, SANM, doc. 1037. According to the *Reglamento de milicias* of 1767, militiamen were to be drawn by lot, but this procedure was not enforced and voluntary enlistment came to be the common practice. In New Mexico every man capable of bearing arms could be called upon to defend the province. *Notas de la legislación mexicana* (Mexico, 1854), p. 94.

165. Reales Cédulas, vol. 141, no. 106. This item is reproduced in Carmen Velázquez, *El estado de guerra en Nueva España,* pp. 243-45.

166. Viceroy Bernardo de Gálvez in 1786 stated that settlers participating in defensive sorties should provide themselves with the necessary firearms and munitions at cost, providing that these were available in the royal warehouses. Worcester, *"Instructions for Governing the Interior Provinces,"* p. 78. Earlier, however, the general practice seems to have been for the royal treasury to make small periodic outlays for the purchase of lead and powder for use by the local militia. Warner, "The Career of Martínez de Torrelaguna," p. 16.

167. Teodoro de Croix in 1779, for instance, ordered five hundred pesos released to pay salaries to El Paso militiamen who conducted a caballada to Santa Fe. Croix to Cordero, Arizpe, December 31, 1799, SANM, doc. 780.

the vicinity of Santa Fe from militia service. It is not known why this measure was taken or if it was enforced in New Mexico.[168] In the muster rolls, individuals were not divided according to occupation, but rather by race, the categories being Spanish citizen, Pueblo Indian, and genízaro.

The genízaros were Indians of the nomadic tribes who had been captured or ransomed by the Spaniards and educated as Christians. Initially most of these had served as domestic servants in the houses of the Spanish citizens; but as some received ill treatment in this station, they petitioned the governor for permission to congregate in their own towns on the frontier. Villages for them were subsequently founded at Tomé, Abiquiu, and San Miguel del Vado, and some of the people were settled in the old Barrio de Analco in Santa Fe. Because of their warlike nature, they proved formidable soldiers in battle and were useful as scouts and interpreters since they held little fear of the savage plains tribes.[169]

Before 1808 the genízaros served as other members of the militia, but in that year a body of them was organized as a separate unit commanded by a corporal from their own ranks.[170] Apparently this distinct military organization was maintained in Santa Fe, but membership was drawn from all the genízaro settlements.[171] Unfortunately little information survives regarding the operation of this unit.

Along with the order commanding establishment of the *trozo de genízaros* in 1808 came a similar directive for founding of three volunteer cavalry companies in the principal towns of Santa Fe, Santa Cruz de la Cañada, and Albuquerque. These were to be formal military organizations with a full complement of officers and men who were entitled to the fuero militar and preeminencias.[172]

168. The Governor to Nava, Santa Fe, July 13, 1802, SANM. doc. 1612(4).

169. Hackett, *Historical Documents,* III, 401; and Morfi's Desórdenes.

170. Salcedo to Maynez, Chihuahua, August 12, 1808, SANM, doc. 2146; and Maynez to Salcedo, Santa Fe, June 20, 1809, SANM, doc. 2234. In these documents the term *trozo de genízaros* is used. Trozo means a column which forms the advance or rear guard, but it is possible that the general significance of troop (*tropa*) was intended.

171. Twitchell, *Old Santa Fe,* p. 12.

172. The militia enjoyed the fuero only when on active duty. McAlister, The "*Fuero Militar,*" p. 67.

The total number of each company came to 69 men, according to Pino, including a captain, a lieutenant, two alféreces, two sergeants, four first corporals, four second corporals, and a drummer. The men were to be paid a modest salary (which was seldom forthcoming), were enlisted for a period of ten years, and were mustered into service in a manner similar to the regulars with a filiación or enlistment record being filed for each volunteer.[173]

Co-ordination and administration of the three units was in the hands of the governor. In Santa Fe he often drilled the militia company personally, while in the remaining towns this task was left to the captains.[174] These "crack" troops, who were termed *urbanos,* provided valuable support to the regular presidials—a more effective kind of support than could be obtained from the informal citizen's militia.[175] Prominent and active men of the rico class coveted the officers' positions in these companies, and those of lesser affluence filled the ranks.

By the time of independence the official records were still referring to the three veteran militia companies of New Mexico.[176] Be this as it may, fragmentary rosters indicate that the word "company" was being used at the same time to mean divisions within a militia squadron. A muster roll for the alcaldia of Albuquerque in the year 1819, for example, shows three companies of fifty men each, including officers, who together comprised the second squadron.[177] Presumably, the first squadron was the unit in Santa Fe and the third that of Santa Cruz de la Cañada.

As noted above, Pino in 1812 declared that the three militia or-

173. Pino, *Exposición,* p. 19; and Libro de Filiaciones, Volunteer Cavalry Company, Albuquerque, 1808, SANM, doc. 2159.

174. Thomas, "Anonymous Description of New Mexico," p. 59.

175. In New Spain urbanos were militiamen sponsored by a municipality, in contrast to the provincials who were organized and supported by the central government. But the term urbanos also seems to have been used to refer to militiamen in general. McAlister, The "*Fuero Militar,*" p. 6. On the several kinds of Mexican militia, see Smith, *The Viceroy of New Spain,* p. 206.

176. García Conde to the Governor of New Mexico, Durango, June 27, 1820, SANM, doc. 2899.

177. Militia Review, Albuquerque, November 1, 1819, SANM, doc. 2856.

ganizations numbered 69 men each. Since by 1819, at least the Albuquerque body had grown to 150 men, it is not surprising that a more elaborate administrative machinery had been introduced. The basis for reorganization may well have been the Spanish Constitution of 1812 and later decrees which provided for creation of a "national" militia and described the character which this was to assume.[178]

In the Spanish system, the smallest unit of the militia was a squad (*escuadra*) of ten to thirty men led by a sergeant and a first and second corporal. Above this was a company, and three to five companies formed a squadron (*escuadron*). Unlike the English system, these terms did not refer to a body of troops of a definite number. The word "company" in particular conveyed a variety of meanings, though most commonly it was employed in the general sense of organization or unit.[179]

While the volunteer militia companies of the three major towns were expanding their membership, the informal citizen's militia seems to have been growing along its own lines. A partial roster for Cochití in 1819 refers to three infantry companies in that pueblo in addition to the cavalry.[180] Available returns from the other districts unfortunately are too sketchy to permit an adequate view of this subject.

One facet of military service which should be noted in connection with the militia is the use by the Spanish of Indian auxiliaries other than the genízaros mentioned above. In the reconquest of New Mexico beginning in 1692, Pueblo warriors played a crucial role in the battles to re-establish European control.[181] Thereafter, they provided vital aid in the campaigns directed against the hostile nomads of the plains and desert.[182] A report published in 1748 ob-

178. Reglamento provisional de la milicia nacional, 1817, SANM, doc. 2885, and Manuel Dublan and José María Lozano, *Legislación mexicana* (2 vols.; Mexico, 1876), I, 378. In SANM, doc. 2634, there is reference to a Nuevo Reglamento de Milicias for 1815.

179. Smith, *The Viceroy of New Spain,* p. 204n.

180. Muster Roll, Cochití, November 5, 1819, SANM, doc. 2857.

181. Oakah L. Jones, Jr., "Pueblo Indian Auxiliaries and the Reconquest of New Mexico, 1692-1704," *Journal of the West,* II (1963), 257-80.

182. The Pueblo support of the Spanish government in the eighteenth century has been treated by Oakah L. Jones, Jr., *Pueblo Warriors and Spanish Conquest* (Norman, 1966).

serves that the defensive nature of the Pueblo Indian villages renders them a natural bulwark against the enemy tribes. The Pueblo people, it states, make themselves readily available whenever the government calls them out to fight the enemy. Since they are accustomed to supplying their own provisions, horses, and arms, the royal treasury is relieved of this burden.[183]

The Pueblo Indians in later years were not regarded as auxiliaries in the strictest sense of the word. As may be seen from the previous discussion of the militia, they were considered part of the citizenry and were expected to contribute toward provincial defense in the same manner as Spaniards. They were called forth when the governor made levies against the alcaldías mayores for citizens to garrison outposts or to serve on the presidial horse guard. Likewise, when a campaign was proposed, the villages in the areas involved were called upon to supply contingents of warriors.[184] During the tour of duty, however, the Pueblo soldiers formed their own units under their leaders or war chiefs who were subject directly to the field commander.

Beyond the Pueblos, the Spanish forces, particularly in the late colonial years, often were favored with the services of nomad warriors who joined in expeditions against unpacified groups of Indians. Apaches, Navajos, Utes, and Commanches all figured in this capacity on one occasion or another, and it was these whom the Spaniards regarded in the narrower sense as the auxiliary.[185]

The effectiveness of the auxiliary forces is open to question. If the campaign was against a traditional enemy, as the Navajos joining an expedition against the Gila Apaches, for example, the auxiliaries

183. Joseph Antonio de Villa-Señor y Sanchez, *Teatro americano* (Mexico, 1748), p. 412.

184. For garrison or guard duty, service was usually for a period of eight days. Maynez to Sanchez Vergara, Santa Fe, June 20, 1808, SANM, doc. 2126 (located on the back of doc. 2121). For a campaign, citizen-soldiers were expected to serve as long as necessary. Pino declares, however, that expeditions against the enemy averaged forty-five days, though sometimes they lasted as long as two or three months. *Exposición,* pp. 15-16.

185. The commandant general in 1791, for instance, referred to "auxiliary Indians (the gentiles) and our own Indians, i.e., the Pueblos or Christianized peoples." Campaign Instructions, Pedro de Nava, Chihuahua, November 24, 1791, SANM, doc. 1171, art. 2.

might arm themselves adequately and report for duty well mounted. At other times, Indians who were impoverished attached themselves to a Spanish force for the food provided and with the hope of stealing arms or horses which the government supplied. To indicate the possible opportunities for theft, for a single campaign in 1786, two hundred carbines, four hundred horses, and twenty mules were sent to New Mexico by the commandant in Chihuahua for use by allied and Pueblo warriors.[186] On the use of this kind of native soldier, the governor of the province candidly remarked in 1788, that in a recent campaign he took along a certain number of Comanches, Utes, and Jicarillas, less as auxiliaries than to present a united front to the other Apaches, and also to have these warriors where he could keep them under surveillance.[187]

As a final note on the subject of the military in New Mexico, reference should be made to the so-called mobile companies, or *compañías volantes*. These were well-armed light troops of the internal provinces which patrolled the highways and the areas remote from cities and towns. They were usually stationed in specific places, but they could be speedily transferred to other districts when the need arose. In this lay their chief difference from the presidials who were maintained in a permanently placed garrison. In other respects, the mobile companies seemed to have been organized, paid, and equipped in a fashion similar to the presidial companies.

Three mobile companies existed in the Provincias Internas as early as 1721.[188] When Teodoro de Croix took office as commandant general in the late 1770's, he found two such companies operating in Nueva Vizcaya; soon he added two more.[189] These units on their missions quite frequently penetrated southern New Mexico, and from the existing records it is clear that many officers and men stationed at the Santa Fe presidio were transfers from such companies.

186. Reeve, "Navajo-Spanish Diplomacy," p. 227.

187. Concha to Ugarte y Loyola, Santa Fe, June 24, 1788, AGN, Prov. Int. 65, part viii.

188. Bancroft, *History of Mexico,* III, 409.

189. Thomas, *Teodoro de Croix,* p. 116.

There is nothing in the documents, however, to substantiate the claim by many writers that New Mexico possessed her own mobile units. On the other hand, there is abundant evidence from contemporary sources to indicate that the province for defense relied solely upon the Santa Fe garrison, the militia, and the Indian auxiliaries.

PART THREE

Chapter IX

LOCAL GOVERNMENT IN NEW MEXICO

The subject of New Mexico's local government as it existed in the eighteenth and early nineteenth centuries is a confusing one. In this area as in others, a host of legislative orders, following upon the Gálvez visita and continuing almost until independence, altered in varying degrees the forms of municipal and district government in the province. Although Scholes has presented an adequate sketch of the Santa Fe cabildo and the system of alcaldías mayores for seventeenth-century New Mexico, his description is applicable in only a small degree to the later colonial period.[1]

Prior to destruction of the New Mexican province in 1680 by rebellious Pueblo Indians, a relatively simple system of local government had prevailed among the approximately 2,500 Spanish and *mestizo* inhabitants. The governor personally administered the northern portion of the colony, the Rio Arriba, while his lieutenant governor took charge of the Rio Abajo. Beyond this basic division, New Mexico was further separated into subordinate districts—varying in number from six to eight—known as *jurisdicciones,* each of which was administered by an alcalde mayor. This official combined within his office practically all functions relating to local government, the most important being judicial and police powers. He was appointed by and was answerable to the governor, and he served without salary.[2]

Only the Villa of Santa Fe and its immediate district were outside the jurisdiction of an alcalde mayor. In the provincial capital a reg-

1. "Civil Government in New Mexico," pp. 91-93.

2. The distinction between the office of alcalde mayor in New Mexico and that in New Spain has been set forth by Scholes, *ibid.,* p. 92n. This official within the viceroyalty proper was in effect a governor in all but name, while in New Mexico he remained a purely local officer subordinate to the provincial governor.

ular cabildo or municipal council functioned from the days of earliest settlement. The cabildo was composed of four *regidores,* or councilmen, who were elected annually by the citizens of the villa. This council chose two *alcaldes ordinarios,* or municipal magistrates, and selected, in addition, persons to serve as *alguacil* (bailiff), notary, and royal standard bearer (*alférez real*). All elections were subject to confirmation by the governor. The cabildo not only administered the affairs of the villa and its environs but also served as an advisory council to the governor and spokesman for all citizens of the province in representations to the royal government. Its role in New Mexico's political life, therefore, was an extremely broad and important one.

This comparatively uncomplicated system of district and municipal administration in the seventeenth century is readily comprehensible. It is when we view the picture a hundred years afterward that the issue of local government becomes clouded. A multiplicity of new terms appear—especially as they relate to the judicial sphere—as a result of the administrative reforms of Gálvez and others acting under royal stimulus. Since no general legal code appeared in this period to update in a comprehensive fashion the old *Recopilación,* it becomes difficult to determine in many instances what was the law and what were the powers held by certain local officers of government.[3]

The burdening complexity of this problem becomes obvious when the single example of the term "alcalde" is pursued in the documents of the period.[4] The following terms all make their appearance in New Mexico's colonial records: alcalde mayor, alcalde ordinario, teniente alcalde, alcalde constitucional, alcalde de barrio, and alcalde

3. Five reprintings of the *Recopilación* were issued in the eighteenth and nineteenth centuries, but no revised edition was ever published.

4. The word "alcalde" was an adaptation of the Moorish *al-cadi* or village judge. It has no precise English equivalent. Theodore Grivas, "Alcalde Rule: The Nature of Local Government in Spanish and Mexican California," California Historical Society *Quarterly,* XL (1961), 11. From this article, the wide divergence in local administrative practices between New Mexico and a nearby province may be noted.

de agua.[5] Each of these was a distinct expression of a different rank or function embodied in a separate official, and thus to speak simply of an alcalde, without a qualifying adjective, is to promote ambiguity. Moreover, certain of these officers were commonly addressed or referred to by other titles. The alcalde mayor was frequently called the *justicia mayor* while his assistant, the teniente alcalde, might be addressed either as *comisario de justicia,* as *teniente de justicia,* or as *teniente político.*[6] Expressions used in speaking of the alcaldes mayores and their tenientes together were *jueces* or *justicias territoriales* and *jueces reales.* The term "justicias" used alone could refer to them also, but it might likewise refer to Indian justices or the council of *principales* among the Pueblos.[7]

Some of the intricacies and, heretofore, little-understood aspects of the alcalde system in New Mexico may be comprehended by a detailed analysis of the two principal offices which carried the title—that of alcalde mayor and alcalde ordinario. By way of introduction, however, it will be well to elaborate upon the system of legal jurisdictions (fueros) that existed in New Mexico.[8]

Some attempt has been made in an earlier chapter to describe the division of justice throughout New Spain generally. It may be recalled that courts were designated as either ordinary or privileged—the justicia ordinario representing the regularly established tribunals, and the justicia privilegiado taking in the courts of special interest

5. Other types of alcaldes, as the *alcalde de indios* and *alcalde de crimen,* existed in New Spain but not in New Mexico.

6. The title of teniente político, no doubt, originated to distinguish from a teniente of the army or militia. On at least one occasion the governor referred to the lieutenant governor at El Paso as "un teniente de justicia mío." Real Alencaster to Salcedo, Santa Fe, November 20, 1805, SANM, doc. 1925.

7. Indian justicias were elected annually by the Pueblo and were confirmed in their offices by the provincial governor in Santa Fe where they received their *varas de justicia* or staffs of justice. In 1797 the justicias of Sandía Pueblo included the governor (*gobernadorcillo*), the war captain, and several other notable persons. Trial of Sandía Indians, Santa Fe, August 13-23, 1797, SANM, doc. 1394.

8. It should be noted that the Spanish word "fuero" may convey the general meaning of "jurisdiction" or it may, as is usually the case, refer specifically to the privileged courts, e.g., the fuero militar.

or fueros.[9] The only privileged bodies which exercised any significant jurisdiction in New Mexico were the military and the Church.[10]

The system of ordinary justice was itself divided into three classes based upon procedure and function. The judges of each were known respectively as ordinary, delegated, and arbitrary.[11] The jueces ordinarios proper were the regular presiding alcaldes mayores and alcaldes ordinarios who served as judges of first instance (jueces de primera instancia).

In contrast to these permanent magistrates was the delegated judge appointed from time to time by the governor to investigate and hear a particular case. Such a judge was known as a *juez comisionado, juez delegado,* or occasionally as a *juez receptor.* In assembling evidence, this juez and his assistants were said to act *por receptoría.*[12] In actuality, a juez comisionado appointed by a New Mexico governor had simply the power to examine, and thus resembled a fiscal or public attorney more than a judge. In any event, when the sumaria of the case was submitted to the governor, the juez's commission was ended.

9. Escriche, in his *Diccionario de legislación y jurisprudencia,* p. 945, notes that the phrase "justicia ordinaria" may be used in both a general and a particular sense. He says:

> Speaking in general, a juez ordinario is anyone judging or exercising jurisdiction in an official capacity, whether he be exercising the common royal jurisdiction or the special jurisdiction of the privileged courts. . . . But in a narrower sense only those magistrates are called jueces ordinarias who exercise the *real jurisdicción ordinaria o común* in contrast to those who operate within the privileged courts.

The term appears in both senses in New Mexican colonial documents. For example, *juez eclesiástico ordinario* occurs frequently in the records and represents an expression of the term "ordinario" in the general sense. Far more usual, however, is the simple use of juez ordinario with the more limited meaning of a judge of the common royal jurisdiction.

10. The liberal Spanish Cortes abolished all other fueros throughout the empire on October 9, 1812. Dublán and Lozano, *Legislación mexicana,* I, 393.

11. Joseph M. White, *A New Collection of Laws, Charters and Ordinances of the Governments of Great Britain, France, and Spain . . . together with the Laws of Mexico and Texas* (2 vols.; Philadelphia, 1839), I, 263.

12. "Receptoria" literally meant the power of a delegate judge. Under usual circumstances, a royal notary acted as juez receptor, but, in this later period, there were no escribanos in New Mexico. It should be noted that the juez comisionado in New Mexico was different from the official who held this same title in California. Florian Francis Guest, "Municipal Institutions in Spanish California, 1769-1821," (unpublished Ph.D. dissertation, University of Southern California, 1961).

There are a number of cases in the archives at Santa Fe in which a juez comisionado appears, so that it is possible to attain a fairly clear idea of his character and manner of action.[13] A special judge of this kind would be commissioned by the governor to conduct an inquiry into a case in which the alcalde mayor had submitted insufficient or confused evidence to the governor for review, the magistrates of an alcaldía mayor were the subject of accusations by their citizens, or a dispute between two or more alcaldes mayores was the issue.

The governor was in the habit of appointing the juez comisionado from among the officers of the Santa Fe presidial garrison and from the ranks of retired officers, both regular and militia. On occasion he might name an alcalde mayor to serve as juez comisionado in some special case, usually one involving other alcaldes. The examining judge was seldom concerned with his task for more than a few days or perhaps weeks. To assist him, the governor, and sometimes the judge himself, appointed an escribano to take down testimony and to notarize official documents. More often in place of a notary, the governor would select two *testigos de asistencia* (assisting witness), one of whom acted as secretary in the proceedings.[14]

Under orders of the governor, the juez comisionado, with his staff, proceeded to the town or pueblo which was to serve as his headquarters and opened a formal investigation. His first duty was to verify in person the fact of an offense having been committed. Testimony (*declaraciónes*) were then taken from witnesses who had received a summons (*auto de llamiento*) to appear before him. When the proceedings (*diligencias*) were completed and certified, the record was submitted to the governor, together with the recommendation of the juez comisionado. It was then the task of the governor to reach a decision in the matter, or to consult the assessor of the com-

13. Legislation governing the functioning of this judge may be found in the *Recopilación,* lib. xi, tit. 1, ley 3; and in Escriche, *Diccionario razonado de legislación y jurisprudencia,* p. 950. The printed literature commonly refers to this judge as a juez delegado, but the New Mexico documents of the period prefer the synonym, juez comisionado. This latter term is employed, therefore, in the present discussion.

14. A secretary attending a delegate judge was known as the *receptor.*

mandancy general, or to submit the case to the Audiencia of Guadalajara.

An interesting case arose in the summer of 1797 which necessitated appointment of a juez comisionado and provides a specific example of the way proceedings involving such a magistrate were handled. The Indian justicias of the Pueblo of Sandía had taken it upon themselves to punish one of their tribesmen for some petty crime. The accused had been placed in the stocks inside the *casa de comunidad* (council house for the village elders) and was beaten so severely that he died. Several witnesses to this deed voluntarily appeared before the alcalde mayor of the district and reported the details. The alcalde recorded their statements, and these, together with a brief of his own, were submitted to the governor.

The alcalde himself might have been authorized to conduct formal proceedings, but the governor expressed dissatisfaction with the preliminary reports—he declared they were not thorough or exact. Therefore, he appointed Antonio de Arce, lieutenant of cavalry in the Santa Fe presidial company, to act as juez comisionado. Arce was permitted to name his own escribano and he selected one of the soldier-interpreters of the garrison.

Transferring himself to Sandía, the juez comisionado ordered the local teniente alcalde to leave the area and proceed to the plaza of Bernalillo three leagues distant where he was to remain until termination of the investigation. Acre then began summoning witnesses and questioning them under oath. Each raised his right hand, swore to speak the truth, and made the sign of the cross. The individual's name, age, residence, and occupation were declared before he was examined. When they had finished testifying, witnesses were required to sign the written statement which had been taken down and this was duly certified by the notary. When all evidence was assembled, Arce concluded to order the arrest of those Indians named in the case and had them moved to Santa Fe where they were lodged in jail (the *carcel real*).[15] The juez comisionado re-

15. Whenever a person was charged with a serious offense, he was arrested and held until his trial was concluded.

turned to the capital bringing with him two witnesses who were also jailed for safekeeping.

Subsequently, each of the Indians was removed from confinement and questioned under oath. Then followed the *careo* or confrontation of the accused by the two witnesses, a common practice in Spanish court procedure. At this point the juez collected the record of charges, testimony, and results of the confrontation of witnesses and submitted all to the governor. Appended was a statement of his own which expressed the belief that sufficient information had been obtainned to permit a higher authority to render a definitive judgment. In this instance, the juez comisionado offered no opinion of his own, but deferred completely to the governor the task of determining further disposition of the case.[16]

The arbitrators (*árbitros*) or mediating judges, which are the third and final group falling within the ordinary jurisdiction, were magistrates chosen by contending parties to settle some matter in dispute between them. Customarily the arbitrator was an alcalde mayor or one of the teniente alcaldes since these men lent both authority and prestige to the weight of their decisions. There is scarcely any record remaining of individual cases since almost universally they were handled as *procesos verbales.*[17]

The Constitution of 1812 explicitly provided that Spaniards could not be deprived of the right to settle differences by means of jueces árbitros elected by both parties.[18] Further articles in this document refer to the procedure of these ad hoc courts. The sentence rendered by the judge was to be executed unless the parties had reserved the right of appeal. Ordinarily the juez árbitro should be the local alcalde to whom citizens with grievances could present themselves. The alcalde, with two reliable men who represented each party, heard the testimony of the complainant and the defendant. After

16. Trial of Sandía Indians, Sandía-Santa Fe, August 13-23, 1797, SANM, doc. 1394.

17. White, *A New Collection of . . . the Laws of Mexico,* p. 263; Jenkins, "The Baltasar Baca 'Grant,' " p. 53; and Bancroft, *California Pastoral,* pp. 574-76.

18. Art. 280 in Dublán and Lozano, *Legislación mexicana,* I, 372.

listening to the opinion of his two associates, he passed judgment (*la providencia*) ending the litigation.[19]

Local administration in the Spanish colonies was in the hands of municipal governments and district officers, the alcaldes mayores and their assistants. The line separating the jurisdiction of city or town governments from that of the districts was often difficult to determine since the crown seldom spelled out in exact terms the powers which each was to hold exclusively. Overlapping of authority was common and conflicts of jurisdiction frequently arose. Moreover, conditions tended to vary from one area to another so that it is often difficult to conclude from the general laws the precise situation in a given province.[20]

In New Spain, for example, the government of large cities was superintended by an alcalde mayor (unless the city was the residence of a governor) who presided over the local cabildo. The alcalde's authority extended throughout the district while that of the municipal council encompassed only the larger limits of the city.[21] Smaller towns without an alcalde mayor were subject solely to the direction of their own cabildos.[22] The situation in New Mexico, however, was somewhat different from that of New Spain proper.

Throughout most of the colonial period, available evidence confirms the existence of only a single cabildo in all of the New Mexican province—that of the municipality of Santa Fe. Even this body ceased to function some time after the close of the first quarter of the eighteenth century, and from at least the 1740's until the first decade

19. *Ibid.*, arts. 281-83. A detailed discussion of the juez árbitro may be found in Escriche, *Diccionario razonado de legislación y jurisprudencia*, pp. 205-15.

20. According to José María Ots Capdequí, "No están bien definidos en la legislación de la época las relaciones entre alcaldes mayores y los cabildos municipales de sus ciudades respectivas. . . . Los conflictos de jurisdicción entre unos y otros fueron frecuentes." *Manuel de historia del derecho español en las Indias* (Buenos Aires, 1945), p. 366.

21. Article 2 of the law of the Cortes of May 23, 1812, provided that an ayuntamiento's jurisdiction should extend into the countryside until it encountered the limits of adjacent municipal governments, and that small towns without a council should be subject to the nearest ayuntamiento as had been the custom in the past. It is not certain that this law was ever extended to New Spain. Dublán and Lozano, *Legislación mexicana*, I, 380.

22. Herbert Ingram Priestley, "Spanish Colonial Municipalities," *California Law Review*, VII (1919), 400-01.

of the nineteenth century, local government was almost exclusively the property of alcaldes mayores and their assistants. All alcaldías mayores were divided into *partidos,* or lesser units, each subject to a teniente alcalde.[23] There were no fixed boundaries between any of these territorial divisions, the people of outlying villages, hamlets, and ranches merely addressing themselves to the nearest official.

The alcalde mayor established his residence in the principal town of his district; the tenientes were located in the chief villages of their own jurisdictions.[24] This simple structure—the division of district administration between the alcalde mayor and the teniente alcalde—hitherto has not been clearly set forth in the historical literature.

The term "partido" as it appears in New Mexico's Spanish documents of the late colonial period precipitates considerable confusion because of the variety of meanings it assumed. In the Mexican period, partido referred to the larger divisions of the province, i.e., the groupings of several alcaldías, and in this sense it was far removed from the significance it possessed in the colonial years.

Generally, partido simply meant a district or territorial division and might refer to a kingdom, province, or any lesser jurisdictional unit.[25] In fact, the term was used with this significance not infrequently by colonial administrators in New Mexico. More particularly, the word was employed to denote a specific jurisdiction with prescribed limits, usually a judicial district.[26] The *Recopilación* provided that each province should be divided into partidos under an alcalde mayor and that within these districts the towns were to be subject to

23. Further south, the divisions of alcaldías mayores were called alcaldías menores, but this term does not appear in the New Mexico documents.

24. The town serving as the seat of government in each alcaldía mayor was often referred to as the *cabecera.* See Table of New Mexico Jurisdictions, Santa Fe, November 24, 1800, SANM, doc. 1518a.

25. Partido in a totally different sense may mean a contract or agreement. In colonial New Mexico it most often referred to a sheep contract. The feminine form of this noun, *partida,* occurs frequently in the documents and can signify a birth, marriage, or death certificate, or alternately a detachment of soldiers.

26. According to the *Diccionario universal de historia y de geografía* (7 vols.; Mexico, 1853-1855), VI, 267, "partidos judiciales son subdivisiones en que se distribuyen las provincias para la administración de justicia en primer grado."

tenientes alcaldes.[27] Over one hundred years later, the Order of Intendants of 1786 abolished the alcaldías mayores throughout most of New Spain and substituted for them districts called partidos served by officials known as subdelegates.[28]

As described in an earlier chapter, New Mexico remained, for the most part, outside the intendancy system so that its alcaldías mayores were not affected by the new ruling. The law regarding partidos as contained in the *Recopilación* apparently was not applied to New Mexico, or if it was, the original meaning of the provision was perverted, for in the eighteenth century, partido carried its own peculiar significance, at least as it was used in this province.

When surveying the Spanish documents in the New Mexican archives for any length of time, one is increasingly confronted with such terms as *teniente de partido, juez de partido,* and *justicia de partido*. It is obvious that these refer to a particular officer with clearly defined functions. The precise identification of this official emerges as a perplexing problem, since nowhere in the published historical literature on New Mexico is the subject treated.

Relating to this question in particular and casting important sidelights on local government in general is a report of Governor Pedro Fermín de Mendinueta addressed to the viceroy in 1773. Therein he states,

> In every two, three, or more pueblos the governor [of New Mexico] names an alcalde mayor who serves the Indians as well as the Spanish citizens of that district, with the aid of one or more tenientes according to the number of pueblos and settlements of Spaniards in order that all may easily have recourse to the law when cases arise.[29]

This statement clearly defines the jurisdictional division separating the alcalde mayor from his tenientes—a situation which has not been explained heretofore.

27. Lib. v, tit. 1, ley 1.

28. Fisher, *The Intendant System,* p. 28. Priestley notes that even after the Order of Intendants, the designation of local administrative units as alcaldías continued. *José de Gálvez,* p. 50.

29. *Indian and Mission Affairs,* p. 16.

With this in mind, we may refer now to an especially pertinent document of 1790. While concerned with the issue of passports for interior travel, mention of the term "partido" occurs and is followed by an illuminating interpolation. The document declares, ". . . and by this word partido is understood to mean the district limited to a lieutenant or commissary of justice."[30] In other words, the jurisdiction of a teniente [alcalde], known alternately as a *comisario de justicia,* is a partido, at least in New Mexico.

Other contemporary sources reveal that a partido consisted of a single town or Indian pueblo and the lands and settlers adjacent to it. For instance, the Pueblos of Santo Domingo and Cochití and the Spanish village of Peña Blanca were all listed as separate partidos within the alcaldía mayor of the Queres in 1808.[31] Not all partidos within the province possessed a teniente alcalde, however, because of the lack of qualified persons to fill these offices. Thus on occasion a single teniente appears ruling ad interim over vacant partidos adjacent to his own.[32]

In the absence of cabildos, the alcaldes mayores in the larger places and their tenientes in the smaller assumed by default the functions normally reserved to the municipal councils. The Order of Intendants required the governor of New Mexico to name alcaldes ordinarios for the larger towns where no cabildo was present to elect these as required by law. The governor procrastinated for many years, as will be explained below, and did not finally select alcaldes ordinarios until well into the nineteenth century.[33] Since he named the alcaldes mayores as well, there was very little real difference between these

30. The original Spanish reads, ". . . y por esta palabra partido se entiende el districto limitado de un teniente o comisario de justicia.' Concha to the Alcaldes of New Mexico, Santa Fe, September 17, 1790. This is re-enforced by a document of 1793 which refers to "tenientes o comisarios de sus partidos." Nava to Concha, Chihuahua, October 19, 1793, SANM, doc. 1263.

31. SANM, doc. 2154.

32. A similar situation developed now and then among the superior alcaldes for we find references to *alcaldes mayores interinos.*

33. From the rule of these alcaldes ordinarios over a municipality, Bloom may have derived his curious "half-ayuntamientos." See "New Mexico under Mexican Administration, 1821-1846," *Old Santa Fe,* I (1913), 45.

and the alcaldes ordinarios, and before any serious jurisdictional question could arise, both sets of officials were swept away by the new Spanish Constitution of 1812 which replaced them with alcaldes constitucionales. The new laws of the Cortes bearing on local government will be explored fully in the next chapter.

The Office of Alcalde Mayor

Aside from general comments by a few writers, relatively little attention has been focused on the official character of the office of alcalde mayor as it existed in colonial New Mexico.[34] As noted in this chapter, the nature of the office in this province was different from that of the alcalde mayor in New Spain. Hence, it becomes helpful in viewing the structure of local government to survey in some depth the many details which taken together define the attributes and functions of New Mexico's alcalde mayor. As an early document manifests, his larger role was that of overseer of the lives, actions, and customs of the inhabitants of his jurisdiction whatever their condition or station.[35]

Appointment, Removal, Term of Office. The power to appoint alcaldes mayores in New Mexico resided with the governor. The names of men selected were submitted to the commandant general for approval, and, in theory, final approbation rested with the king and Council of the Indies.[36] Persons desirous of offices often submitted petitions to the governor advancing their qualifications.[37] On occasion, they would circumvent his authority and dispatch their

34. The most extensive remarks on the alcalde mayor are contained in two works previously cited: Scholes, "Civil Government in New Mexico," pp. 91-93; and Jenkins, "The Baltasar Baca 'Grant,' " p. 53.

35. Neve to Anza, Arizpe, December 10, 1783, SANM, doc. 871.

36. In New Spain the more important alcaldes mayores were named directly by the king while minor ones were appointed by the viceroy and audiencia with the approbation of the Council of the Indies. Ots Capdequí. *Manuel de historia del derecho españal,* p. 366.

37. On August 16, 1805, Juan Andrés Tafoya, for example, petitioned Governor Real Alencaster for the post of alcalde mayor or teniente. The governor, who was somewhat haughty by nature, inserted the following terse comment in the margin: "Los que deven servir alcaldías los busca el que los provee." SANM, doc. 1875.

petitions to the commandant general or even the king.[38] In a celebrated case recounted by Twitchell, Don Eusebio Durán y Chaves journeyed from his hacienda near Albuquerque to Spain, where he secured a personal audience with the king and presented a petition asking that the position of alcalde mayor of the pueblos of San Felipe, Sandía, Santo Domingo, and Cochití be granted to him and to his son for life.[39] His entreaties were successful, for a later order signed by the viceroy of New Spain granted his request.[40]

The *Recopilación* indicates that alcaldes mayores were to serve a fixed term of three years, but this ruling was not extended to those officials in New Mexico who bore this title.[41] Alcaldes mayores in this province generally served for life unless forced to retire for ill health or removed from office for misconduct. Occasionally they were conceded the right to pass the office on to a second generation.[42] This writer has encountered no direct evidence that the post of alcalde mayor was ever sold in New Mexico, though such was the case in other areas of the colonial empire.

Removal of alcaldes mayores appears to have occurred only rarely, although harsh accusations were made against them regularly.[43] According to the friars and other citizens, corrupt officials were usually not removed because of collusion between the governor and his creatures, the alcaldes. In some instances when aggrieved persons produced complaints against their local magistrates, the governor did not feel competent to act without an assessor to advise him, and hence he would defer to the superior judgment of the commandant general. Such a case arose in 1799 when the commandant, in a rather complex

38. In 1800 Don Juan de Abrego besought the commandant general to intercede on his behalf with the New Mexican governor so that he might obtain the government of an alcaldía. Nava to the Governor of New Mexico, Chihuahua, July 29, 1800, SANM, doc. 1498. Upon being advised by the governor that Abrego was lacking in wisdom and was possessed by the vice of drunkenness, the commandant ordered his petition disallowed. Nava to Chacón, Chihuahua, October 6, 1800, SANM, doc. 1510.

39. Twitchell, *Spanish Archives of New Mexico,* II, 254-55.

40. Copy of Durán y Chaves Petition, April 18, 1774, SANM, doc. 675.

41. Lib. v, tit. 2.

42. On the inheritance of the office, see France V. Scholes, *Troublous Times in New Mexico* (Hist. Soc. of New Mexico, Publ. in History; Albuquerque, 1942), p. 40.

43. Allande to Manuel Rubí, Santa Fe, June 10, 1818, SANM, doc. 2725.

case, deprived the alcalde mayor of Santa Cruz de la Cañada and his teniente alcalde of their posts for a period of eight years for engaging in illegal procedure.[44]

Some alcaldes were removed from office merely because they incurred the displeasure of their superior in Santa Fe. In the church-state conflict of the middle 1700's, friars charged that alcaldes mayores were arbitrarily separated from their offices because they had displayed sympathy for the churchmen.[45] Cases of such action among governors, however, must have been relatively uncommon in the late colonial period for most were able to maintain a harmonious relationship with their subordinates.[46] Appointees of the governor would naturally be men who favored his cause and views. It must be remembered, however, that governors came and went every few years while the alcaldes mayores once in office lingered there often until death.

Qualifications. By law, officials of the stature of New Mexico's alcaldes mayores were required to be honorable men of ability and capable of reading and writing.[47] It was sometimes difficult to obtain persons for vacant posts with even these minimal qualifications. The governor of New Mexico in 1797, Fernando de Chacón, expressed this clearly in a message to the commandant general. He stated that shortly after assuming his post, two alcaldías mayores became vacant through the death of their occupants. Since he was new to the province, the governor consulted the alcalde of Santa Fe as well as the majority of the clergy regarding candidates for replacements. They replied immediately and as of one voice that no one was qualified to fill these positions.[48]

Upon investigation of local conditions, Chacón felt inclined to agree. Of members of the merchant class among whom one might expect to find suitable persons, he remonstrated:

44. Nava to Chacón, September 11, 1799, SANM, doc. 1462.

45. Hackett, *Historical Documents,* III, 473, 505.

46. Difficulties between the seventeenth-century governors and the alcaldes mayores are recounted by Scholes, *Troublous Times in New Mexico,* pp. 39-40.

47. *Recopilación,* lib. v, tit. 3, ley 4.

48. Chacón to Nava, Santa Fe, July 13, 1797, SANM, doc. 1451.

They are not merchants in the usual respected sense of the word, but rather itinerant vagabonds who go about the province peddling their wares four to six months out of the year. The rest of the time they spend working in their fields or in journeying to the capital. But if they did not arrange their affairs thus they could not subsist.[49]

Among those who classed themselves as hacendados, the governor noted the general lack of ability to read and write. In the past, he declared, when such persons had obtained an alcaldía mayor or a *tenencia* (the jurisdiction of a teniente) they had not been able to fulfill their obligations properly.[50] A similar view was expressed by his predecessor who in 1794 remarked:

In no country is it more difficult than in New Mexico to remove the alcaldes mayores, because of the impossibility of replacing them. There are few inhabitants who know how to write and inform, and even less to discharge a duty of such consideration, that few or none are useful.[51]

The Catholic clergy in the late colonial period was almost universally hostile in its regard for the district alcaldes. Bishop Tamarón in 1760 spoke disparagingly of their abilities as follows:

. . . some poor men whom the governors install as alcaldes mayores, individuals who have not prospered in other offices or who have been ruined in trade; or deserters from studies by which they did not profit, who become paper shufflers and swindlers. Such are usually the qualifications of these alcaldes mayores, a career aspired to by useless or ruined men.[52]

Father Morfi, at a later date, referred to the chief alcaldes as "unfortunates without education or breeding, mostly half-breeds with an occasional Spaniard."[53]

Governor Real Alencaster concurs in this criticism of the alcaldes.

49. *Ibid.*

50. *Ibid.* In addition to the hacendados, alcaldes mayores and tenientes alcaldes were frequently drawn from the ranks of disabled and retired soldiers (*inválidos y retirados*) of the Santa Fe presidial garrison.

51. Allande to Manuel Rubí, Santa Fe, June 10, 1818, SANM, doc. 2725.

52. Adams, *Bishop Tamarón's Visitation of New Mexico*, p. 111.

53. Desórdenes, art. 40. Also Bancroft, *Arizona and New Mexico*, p. 273.

He speaks of the stupidity and inability of all those who exercise any jurisdiction in New Mexico.[54] Again, he bewails the fact that to aid him in the administration of the province, he has only the assistance of the "alcaldes who are absolutely lacking in principles and who are incapable of acting efficiently or according to the law."[55]

While many of the complaints directed against the abilities of the alcaldes mayores no doubt were justified, there were mitigating circumstances. New Mexico was a poor province with only a rudimentary educational system. If blame is to be assigned for the almost universal ignorance prevailing among the citizenry, it must fall to the state and to the Church, neither of which felt capable of or interested in extending the full advantages of formal education to this remote area. If the alcaldes were deficient in knowledge of the law and in their capacity to read and write, they often compensated by demonstrating vigor and perseverance in performance of their military duties, as will be observed later in this chapter. All in all, given the place and the temper of the times, New Mexico probably could have expected little better in the way of public administrators.

Lack of Salary. The alcalde mayor in New Mexico received no salary.[56] He was allowed to collect certain small fees and judicial fines, but these never totaled a significant amount.[57] Citizens coveted the office because of the prestige it conveyed and the opportunity it offered to exploit the Indians. Discussion of this later consideration will be undertaken in reviewing the major abuses attributed to the alcaldes.

A royal decree dated February 1, 1796, exempted alcaldes from the media anata or tax on salary.[58] Although this order was proclaimed in New Mexico, it had no effect since the alcaldes had long been held to be appendages of the province's military government, and,

54. Real Alencaster to Salcedo, Santa Fe, November 20, 1805, SANM, doc. 1925, part 22.

55. Real Alencaster to the Real Audiencia of Guadalajara, Santa Fe, April 1, 1806, SANM, doc. 1977.

56. This is clearly stated by Pino in his *Exposición*, pp. 6-7.

57. Scholes, "Civil Government in New Mexico," p. 93.

58. Coan, *Shorter History of New Mexico*, I, 124.

therefore, not subject to the income tax.[59] The stressing of this point was unnecessary, of course, since the alcaldes mayores received no salary against which the government could make its levy.[60]

Residence of Alcaldes Mayores. By Spanish law, a person was forbidden to serve as alcalde mayor in the same district in which he had his residence or in which he held an *encomienda,* lands, mines, or other property.[61] This was intended to discourage the alcalde from advancing his private interests by taking advantage of his office. It is difficult to determine the extent to which this regulation was enforced in New Mexico. Appointments were usually given to persons living outside the jurisdiction in which they were to serve,[62] but as many officials filled their posts for the remainder of their lives, it is unrealistic to believe that they did not establish new residences within their chief towns.

As explained previously, the seat of an alcaldía mayor was its principal town or village. In most of the New Mexican jurisdictions, there existed a sizable Spanish settlement which offered a logical headquarters for the district alcalde. In some areas, however, as in the jurisdictions of Laguna-Acoma, Jémez, and Zuñi, there were no true Spanish towns, only Indian Pueblos. Since Spanish law forbade outsiders in Indian villages, the officials in such districts usually applied for a grant of unoccupied land near the chief population center and established themselves in their own haciendas. In such instances, the prohibition against property owning was clearly not observed. From these haciendas, the alcaldes mayores and their relatives were often charged with encroaching upon Pueblo Indian land.[63]

59. *Ibid.,* I, 106.

60. Curiously, however, the government of New Spain demanded for a time that alcaldes mayores there pay the media anata on salaries which they did not receive. Priestley, *José de Gálvez,* p. 225.

61. Ots Capdequí, *Manuel de historia del derecho español,* p. 366.

62. The alcalde mayor of Zuñi, in 1790, for example, had been a resident of the distant village of Chama before his appointment. Census Report, Zuñi, October 23, 1790, SANM, doc. 1092c.

63. A complete study of this problem in the alcaldía mayor of Laguna-Acoma is found in Jenkins, "The Baltazar Baca 'Grant,'" cited earlier.

We have reports of Fray Morfi and others who claim that alcaldes mayores were found residing in the Indian villages from time to time in the later colonial years.[64] This may have been true in some cases, but it should be borne in mind that many Indian establishments maintained a *casa de comunidad* or community house for accomodation of officials, merchants, travelers, or others who had reason to spend any time in the pueblo, and as a place in which to transact business with them.[65] Alcaldes residing temporarily in these, understandably, would have been breaching no law.

Judicial Powers. Some brief attention has been given previously to the judicial authority of the alcalde mayor as it related to the larger scheme of the administration of justice within the commandancy general. Unfortunately, determination of his precise powers in New Mexico is hindered by the fact that the provincial authorities themselves were often confused as to the manner in which justice was to be pursued.

In legal proceedings, little attention was paid to any code of laws since, in fact, the magistrates had no law books or written statutes to guide them. Many were perhaps unaware that such existed. Instructions as to how their inquiries and courts should be conducted came to them occasionally from the governor, the asesoría of the commandancy general, or the Audiencia of Guadalajara.[66] By and large, judgment of the alcaldes, when it was not corrupted by personal interest or sheer malicious obstinacy, conformed to the prevailing customs of the country.[67] A California governor once instructed an

64. Bancroft, *Arizona and New Mexico,* p. 269; and Thomas, "An Anonymous Description," p. 61.

65. Domínguez, *The Missions of New Mexico,* p. 353. Casas de comunidad were known also as *mesones* (inns) or occasionally as *casas reales.* Casa real was the term generally applied to the residence of the governor in Santa Fe. Regarding Indian community houses in colonial New Spain, Phillip Wayne Powell states that they were used as stopping places where food and lodging could be obtained from the natives. Indian officials had the duty of keeping these places supplied with food. *Soldiers, Indians, and Silver* (Berkeley, 1952), p. 22.

66. See, e.g., an opinion of the assessor general addressed to the commandant general prescribing proper legal procedure for the judicial process in New Mexico, SANM, doc. 1931.

67. Twitchell, *Leading Facts,* II, 13; Blackmar, *Spanish Institutions,* p. 291.

alcalde, who was ignorant of formal legal procedure, to administer the law in accordance with the principles of natural right and justice.[68] Such advice in reality could have formed the basis of New Mexican jurisprudence as well.

Notwithstanding the paucity of specific information, some general declaration of the judicial functions of the alcalde mayor may be made. The New Mexican magistrates determined civil cases of minor character and criminal matters where only reparation was to be made or a light punishment inflicted. That the lesser judicial officers of the area frequently exceeded their authority is indicated by an order from Chihuahua which reached New Mexico in 1809 prohibiting magistrates from assigning excessive punishment to the guilty and admonishing them to adhere strictly to formal judicial procedure, whatever that may have been.[69] In addition to functioning as judges in minor civil and criminal matters, the alcaldes mayores served upon demand as jueces árbitros in the manner described earlier in this chapter. In all of these cases, their judgment customarily was final.

In affairs of greater importance, the alcalde mayor initiated the *sumaria* (preparatory proceedings in a case) forming the *expediente* (collection of depositions) which included the charges, the testimony of witnesses, and the *declaración indagatoria* (statement made by the person arraigned). The case was then referred to the governor in Santa Fe who acted as judge of first instance within the justicia ordinaria. The governor was required to render a definitive judgment and permit appeals, thereafter, to the Audiencia of Guadalajara which sat as a court of second and successive instances.[70] In reaching his final decision, the governor might consult the asesoría of the commandancy as regards the meaning of the law, but he was not permitted to defer to it or to the commandant the responsibility

68. Bancroft, *California Pastoral,* p. 575.

69. Order of Nemesio Salcedo, Chihuahua, August 8, 1809, in SANM, Orders and Decrees, II, 129.

70. In case of extreme perplexity regarding the handling of a difficult matter, the governor was permitted to submit the appropriate papers to the audiencia, which then rendered judgment in the first instance.

of the verdict unless it was a case under the military fuero.[71] During thc course of all litigation, the accused was held in jail in Santa Fe.

In cases in which the defendant was found guilty and the verdict was upheld in successive appeals, execution of the sentence was in most cases referred to the alcalde mayor who had initiated proceedings and in whose district the guilty party resided. Thus in one case in which two persons received the death penalty as prescribed in the sentence (*real provisión*) of the audiencia, the alcalde mayor of Santa Cruz, to whose jurisdiction the condemned pertained, journeyed to Santa Fe where they were being held and personally saw to fulfillment of the superior tribunal's order.[72] Going to the jail in which the criminals were confined, and in the presence of two witnesses, he informed them of the sentence handed down. They expressed the proper submission and in token thereof each laid the official paper upon his head. After receiving appropriate spiritual consolation, they were shot and their bodies hanged on the royal road to serve as an example. The alcalde mayor signed the formal report of their deaths and the governor informed the commandant general that the sentence had been carried out.[73]

The type of punishment inflicted upon those convicted of crimes included the following: corporal punishment ranging from execution to floggings and impounding in stocks;[74] sentences of exile either to a town in another alcaldía mayor or out of the province; labor on public works in New Mexico or at the Obraje de Encinillas in Chihuahua;[75] and judicial fines and confiscation of property. In

71. Instructions on Civil Jurisdiction, Nava to Concha, Chihuahua, December 21, 1791, SANM, doc. 1179; and Case Against Josef Moreno, Sabinal-Santa Fe, July 11-18, 1805, SANM, doc. 1853.

72. Report of Alcalde Mayor Manuel García de la Mora, Santa Fe, August 4, 1809, SANM, doc. 2242.

73. Lansing B. Bloom, "The Death of Jacques D'Eglise," *NMHR,* II (1927), 373.

74. Ferdinand VII, by a royal order of October 20, 1820, forbade whippings as a penalty for crimes, SANM, doc. 2210.

75. The obraje or wool mill on the Hacienda de Encinillas situated along the royal road to Chihuahua was worked by prisoners from northern Nueva Vizcaya and New Mexico. It is recorded that in 1764 forty-eight families were supported by the forced labor of 137 convicts and 12 Indian prisoners of war. Moorhead, *New Mexico's Royal Road,* p. 14. Many of the Indians ended their days here miserably with the fruits of their labor being charged to

spite of the case mentioned above, death sentences were relatively rare, as the Germanic principle of compensatory damages was preferred in most cases where conviction was secured.

Persons fleeing from the law might seek refuge in churches under the ancient right of sanctuary. An alcalde mayor and his witnesses, with permission of the local minister, might enter the church to interrogate the culprit and take his declarations, but the accused could refuse to co-operate by repeating the formula "church is my name" to all questions. Under ordinary circumstances the authorities had to wait until they might catch their quarry outside his refuge before an arrest could be made.[76]

The symbol of an alcalde mayor's authority was his *bastón de justicia* or black cane with a silver tip. He carried this staff on all occasions when he acted in his official capacity as an arm of the law. Persons were often summoned to appear before an alcalde by an aide who carried the cane as assurance that the demand was genuine.

Other duties of a legal nature which fell to the alcalde mayor included notarization of official documents and wills and handling of land grants. Each district should have possessed its own escribano to certify legal papers, but, as has been seen, the provincial capital itself often lacked such a civil servant. Regarding land grants, the alcaldes investigated land requests put forth by citizens of their districts, and, in a formal ceremony, placed grantees in possession. The right itself, however, to make both Spanish and Indian land grants, was reserved to the governor who conferred title in the name of the king.[77]

The involved procedure by which grants were made has been fully described by Jenkins and is worth summarizing here for the light it sheds upon the role played by the alcalde mayor.[78] To obtain a grant, the citizen first submitted a written petition to the gov-

the accounts of the king. Thomas, "Antonio de Bonilla, Notes," p. 199; and Governor of New Mexico to the Audiencia of Guadalajara, Santa Fe, July 5, 1800, SANM, doc. 1495b.

76. Elizabeth Howard West, "The Right of Asylum in New Mexico in the Seventeenth Century," *Hispanic American Historical Review,* VIII (1928), 375.

77. Twitchell, *Spanish Archives of New Mexico,* I, 394.

78. "The Baltazar Baca 'Grant,' " p. 50.

ernor describing the lands desired and asserting that it was vacant public domain. The governor then ordered the alcalde mayor in the appropriate jurisdiction to investigate and report any irregularities or adverse claims which might affect the application, and to announce the request publicly so that others could come forward if they had a legitimate protest. A document was drawn up by the alcalde and signed by two witnesses certifying that the land was as described. This paper, together with a sketch map of the area concerned, was presented to the governor who determined if a title of possession should be granted. In a final ceremony, the alcalde mayor, with two witnesses and neighboring citizens, proceeded to the location where the boundaries were pointed out to the new grantee, who tore up grass and threw rocks. The assembled crowd shouted "Long Live the King," which signified that the new owner now held undisputed possession. All details of this final act were set down in a report to the governor.

Those who had received grants were required to remain on the land for four years to receive title. During this period, they were not permitted to obtain land elsewhere without forfeiting rights to the first grant. The alcalde mayor, at the end of four years, reported to the governor that the lands had been occupied continuously. The governor then issued the final papers.[79]

Military Duties. The perilous situation of many New Mexican towns and settlements, owing to the ferocity and frequency of Indian incursions, determined that the military duties of the alcalde mayor should be among the most important. He was designated as *capitán a guerra,* or war captain, which was the title bestowed upon a civil official who exercised military functions within his jurisdiction in the absence of an officer of the regular army.[80] The instructions to Commandant General Ugarte y Loyola make clear that each juez within the provinces was to receive the title in order

79. *Ibid.,* pp. 50-51. For further details, see Twitchell, *Spanish Archives of New Mexico,* I, 428-32.

80. Charles Wilson Hackett, *Revolt of the Pueblo Indians of New Mexico and Otermín's Attempted Reconquest, 1680-1682* (2 vols.; Albuquerque, 1942), II, 405. Often the alcalde mayor was an officer in the local militia.

that the militia and other citizens might show him the proper respect when he led them against the Indians.[81]

Following Indian attacks the alcalde mayor organized local forces and gave chase, often pursuing the fleeing enemy for a considerable distance. The alcalde of Albuquerque, in October of 1794, for example, followed a band of Apaches south into the Sierra de la Magdalena, killing three and taking a woman captive.[82] While they usually acted on their own authority with the local militia at their command, occasionally the alcaldes mayores and their troops joined with other forces in the province in a full-scale punitive expedition. At such times, the governor or one of his immediate subordinates in the presidial garrison assumed full command. A specific number of men was often levied against each alcaldía mayor for large campaigns; and if the alcalde was incapable of leading them to the predetermined rendezvous, he was required to appoint someone who enjoyed the complete confidence of the men.[83]

For a time after 1814, a yearly tax amounting to five per cent on the livestock industry was levied upon each alcaldía to aid the royal treasury in defraying expenses of the regular troops stationed at Santa Fe. The funds were to be collected by the alcalde mayor and remitted to the office of the supplymaster. There an accounting was made under supervision of the governor, who then informed the commandant general. In 1817 the accounts of a number of districts were found to be in arrears.[84] In addition, levies of grain for support of the presidial company were made against individuals, and these assessments were, likewise, collected by the alcaldes.[85]

Concerning all military matters, the alcaldes mayores kept the governor fully informed of developments within their respective dis-

81. AGN, Prov. Int. 129, art. 161.

82. Nava to the Governor of New Mexico, Chihuahua, October 8, 1794, SANM, doc. 1288.

83. Circular to the Alcaldes of New Mexico, Governor Allande, Santa Fe, January 11-September 7, 1817, SANM, doc. 2686.

84. *Ibid.* The tax was imposed in an edict of November 28, 1814. Pedro Ignacio de Gallego to Governor Allande, Abiquiú, April 17, 1817, SANM, doc. 2688.

85. Circular to the Alcaldes of New Mexico, Governor Maynez, Santa Fe, July 1, 1808, SANM, doc. 2132.

tricts. The governor in turn transmitted details to the office of the commandant general.[86] Besides conducting campaigns, the alcaldes actively worked for the establishment or preservation of peace with the hostile tribes. From time to time, the magistrate received instructions to undertake negotiations with the Indians and on some occcasions they were able to reach an accord.[87]

An edict issued from the office of the commandancy general in 1807 specified that all citizens traveling abroad were to be armed, and the alcaldes mayores and their tenientes were provided instructions as to how to enforce compliance.[88] Everyone going into the countryside was required to carry a musket, pistol, or lance, according to his means. The poor who could not purchase this class of weapon were to carry a sling and a bag of stones at the very least, and the Pueblo Indians, bows and arrows. The alcaldes in enforcing the law were to impose the penalty of one peso for the first offense and two pesos for the second; while those persons of lesser means were to be fined four reales for the first and eight for the second; and those of little means three days' labor on public works for the first and six days for the second. Indian cases of serious nature were to be referred to the commandant general.

No mule train, loaded or not, was to be permitted out on the roads unless accompanied by three servants of the owner, one with musket and the other two with lances. Whenever an alcalde chanced upon an infraction to this rule, he was to order the train to halt until the said arms were produced, and a three peso fine was to be imposed upon the owner or *mayordomo*.[89]

Police Powers. The alcalde mayor received responsibility for maintaining law and order in the executive as well as the judicial sphere. His police powers were in reality separate from his military functions; the latter pertained to relations with the hostile tribes, and the former concerned the regulation of conduct among the Spanish citi-

86. Extract of Events Occurring in the Province of New Mexico, November 20, 1803, to March 30, 1804, SANM, doc. 1715.

87. Bando of Salcedo, Chihuahua, June 16, 1807, SANM, doc. 2057.

88. *Ibid.*

89. *Ibid.*

zenry and Pueblo Indians. The alcalde was authorized to arrest persons within his district who had violated the law and to apprehend fugitives who might enter his jurisdiction from other areas.[90] After introduction of the government tobacco monopoly, he was charged with regulating the growing of the local substitute, *punche,* although the prohibition on its production was seldom strictly enforced.[91] Also, his permission was required before public dances and other celebrations of a purely secular character could take place.[92]

An important duty which involved considerable time on the part of the alcalde was the regulation of public travel. Permission to venture outside New Mexico had to be obtained from the governor, but the right to travel within the province itself was granted by a citizen's own alcalde mayor.[93] Rather extensive documentation exists regarding this matter, beginning with an order of the commandant general issued to the governor of New Mexico in 1783.

This mandate clearly reveals the rationale behind the regulations controlling movement of individuals. The commandant general noted that edicts had been proclaimed on repeated occasions in the past, though to no avail, to the effect that border ruffians, vagabonds, and other footloose undesirables should be pursued, apprehended, and punished. It was also observed that Indians were forbidden to leave their villages without proper license from either the local magistrate, or in his absence, the friar or parish priest. In spite of this, Indians commonly were forsaking their villages to wander afar and join with the floating vagabonds in committing all manner of crimes. The difficulty of ferreting out the offending parties was increased by their custom of disguising themselves as Apaches so that blame for their outrages would be laid upon that tribe. When these wanderers were encountered in the countryside and questioned, they

90. Order of the Commandant General to the Governor of New Mexico, April 18, 1808, attached to Order of Governor Maynez to the Alcaldes Mayores, Santa Fe, July 16, 1808, SANM, doc. 2137.

91. Kinnaird, "The Spanish Tobacco Monopoly in New Mexico," pp. 332-33.

92. Coan, *Shorter History of New Mexico,* I, 119.

93. *Recopilación,* lib. v, tit. 1, ley 18; and Order of Juan Bautista de Anza, Santa Fe, April 24, 1784, SANM, doc. 891.

invariably represented themselves as laborers looking for employment, and upon no other evidence than their word, they were believed and permitted to continue on their way.

In view of all the disorder, the commandant general declared that from that day forward no citizen, whether Spaniard, mestizo, or Indian, should be permitted to leave the town or mission in which he resided without the express permission of his magistrate or religious minister. Such licenses were to be issued to individuals free of charge and were to express the destination of the bearer and the dates for which the permit was valid. All persons discovered without these were to be arrested and prosecuted. So that no one might plead ignorance of the law, the official edict was to be proclaimed throughout New Mexico by both the civil and religious authorities.[94]

Seven years later, this order was reiterated and expanded under the stimulus of viceregal concern. The commandant general again directed the New Mexican governor to prohibit persons from leaving their home districts without proper credentials, and he called upon everyone to report violators to the nearest alcalde mayor so that that official might apprehend the party and through investigation discover his origin or residence and the motives which induced him to leave. Old, established, and well-known settlers in the province, however, were to be free from the encumbrance of having to obtain travel permits.[95]

Later orders to the alcaldes mayores of New Mexico charged them to be vigilant in carrying out the letter of the law. They were to prevent anyone from establishing himself in their jurisdictions who did not possess a proper certificate setting forth his place of residence, family, and reasons for coming. Also they were to check carefully on transient Indians designated as seasonal labor.[96]

Magistrates in the several districts were to co-operate with each other in enforcing the superior regulations. When the alcalde mayor of Alameda in 1805 refused to arrest a citizen of the alcaldía of

94. Neve to Anza, Arizpe, December 10, 1783, SANM, doc. 871a.

95. Bando of Ugarte y Loyola, July 2, 1790, SANM, doc. 1091.

96. Bando of Nemesio Salcedo, Chihuahua, June 16, 1807, SANM, doc. 2057.

Laguna-Acoma who had entered his jurisdiction without authorization, the magistrate of the latter district complained to the governor that his neighboring counterpart was making a mockery of justice.[97] This marks one instance of many which witnessed rivalry and dissension among the alcaldes mayors.

To assist local officials in checking on strangers, after 1792 all innkeepers were obliged to make daily reports on travelers stopping in their *posadas* or *mesones*. A listing of the individual's name, civil state, residence from which he had departed, and direction and destination of travel were to be included. Only famous persons whose business was well known could be omitted from the list. A legal copy of this regulation was to be posted on the door of each inn so that all might comply with the terms of the law.[98]

Closely related was the matter of trading permits. Small parties of citizens often petitioned their alcaldes mayores for permission to venture with the trade goods among the roving Indian tribes. The alcalde conveyed the request to the governor for his superior license, and upon receipt of the permit he reminded the prospective merchants of the various laws governing commercial dealings with the Indians.[99] This was the foundation of the so-called Comanchero trade, which endured well into the nineteenth century. Anyone who undertook a trading expedition without proper authorization was subject to arrest by the alcalde mayor on returning home.[100]

Trading fairs were common events at a number of the frontier towns and the alcaldes mayores were responsible for the good conduct of all persons attending. The annual Taos fair which was visited in the summer by the Comanches and other plains tribes became so boisterous that the local alcalde was incapable of maintaining order, and, hence, the governor or one of his immediate subordinates often led a military detachment to the fair to insure tran-

97. Aragon to Real Alencaster, Laguna, May 29, 1805, SANM, doc. 1840.

98. Nava to the Governor of New Mexico, Janos, December 4, 1792, SANM, doc. 1220.

99. García de la Mora to Manrrique, Rio Arriba, August 25, 1812, SANM, doc. 2455; and Manrrique to García de la Mora, Santa Fe, August 26, 1812, SANM, doc. 2456.

100. Sanchez Vergara to Manrrique, Jémez, January 16, 1811, SANM, doc. 2391. Permission to go buffalo hunting on the plains was obtained in the same manner as trading permits.

quility. Smaller fairs were held at Santa Clara for the Utes, at Pecos for the Jicarilla Apaches, and at Laguna and Jémez for the Navajos.

Miscellaneous Functions. A variety of petty tasks remained to engage the energies of the alcaldes mayores. One of these was the proclaiming of official edicts or royal decrees. A single copy of a new edict was circulated by the governor among the various magistrates who were named in the margin of the document.[101] Each alcalde mayor proclaimed the edict publicly and in the prescribed manner throughout his jurisdiction. When the fact was accomplished, he and two witnesses signed the original copy to that effect and passed the document on to the next district by special messenger or by the real servicio, or postal service. Eventually, the edict was returned to the governor who notified his superior that the edict had been made known in all parts of the province. It was then filed away in the provincial archives.

To make a public proclamation, a drum was sounded on the plaza of each town and village, summoning the inhabitants. When all were assembled, the order was read in a loud voice, and afterward copies were tacked up at conspicuous sites. Thus no citizen could claim he had not been made aware of the law.[102]

Another duty of the alcalde mayor involved compiling census reports.[103] He followed a specified *formulario* furnished him by the governor and was assisted by his tenientes. Persons were listed by plazas, poblaciones, ranchos, or Indian pueblos, depending upon in which of these they resided.[104] Entries were made according to age, sex, racial origin, and occasionally according to occupation or other

101. The expression used was *alcaldes de la cordillera del margen* which meant the "alcaldes [named] in the relay list in the margin" of this document.

102. Anza to the Alcaldes of New Mexico, Santa Fe, April 24, 1784, SANM, doc. 891; and Kinnaird, "The Spanish Tobacco Monopoly in New Mexico, p. 332.

103. Regulations concerning the forming of censuses by an alcalde mayor may be found in a cedula of 1741. Dublán and Lozano, *Legislación mexicana,* I, 77.

104. New Mexico Census, Santa Fe, May 19-29, 1805, SANM, doc. 1830; and Circular on General Census, Santa Fe, May 5, 1805, SANM, doc. 1822. In New Mexico, except for the four villas, the loosely grouped Spanish ranchos were generally referred to as poblaciones, or if the population consolidated for mutual defense, as plazas. The terms "plaza" and "placita," thus, were employed in New Mexico to mean a town or village. A very small place was sometimes called a *lugar.*

characteristics. Special censuses were formulated at times for various purposes as the listing of school-age children or the enumeration of survivors after a severe epidemic.[105] Demographic information assembled from the province as a whole was forwarded to the offices of the commandancy general. In submitting a census in 1805, Governor Real Alencaster warned his superior that neither it nor the one compiled by his predecessor could be considered in any way accurate owing to incompetence of the alcaldes and the indifference of the poulace to carrying out royal orders.[106]

Other tasks charged to the alcaldes mayores included collection of the donativos or "gifts" required by the king and the assembling of levies from citizens for goods to pacify the nomadic Indians. In addition, the magistrates were compelled to preach the bulls of crusade, though specific information on the sale of these is lacking.[107] Details have already been presented regarding the role played by the alcaldes in the registry of cattle brands. They recorded the brands in a special *libro de registro,* charging stock owners only the moderate fees permitted by the law. All official papers were filed and kept in the local archive under care of the alcalde.[108]

Abuses of the Alcaldes Mayores. Some passing reference has already been made to a few of the excesses committed by the New Mexican alcaldes. The general poverty of provincial justices throughout New Spain repeatedly tempted them to engage in extortion and illicit activities, provoking the censure of Viceroy Revilla Gigedo, the Elder, José de Gálvez, and other persons of importance.[109] As we have seen, the Order of Intendants was designed, in part, to curb the peculations of local officials, but the new regulations regarding this matter did not extend to New Mexico.

105. Delgado to the Governor of New Mexico, Santa Fe, May 8, 1805, SANM, doc. 1824.

106. Real Alencaster to Salcedo, Santa Fe, November 20, 1805, SANM, doc. 1925, part 22.

107. Royal Order on the Bula de la Cruzada, Governor Anza, Santa Fe, August 27, 1785, SANM, doc. 918.

108. Maynez to Gallegos, Santa Fe, March 15, 1816, SANM, doc. 2652.

109. Priestley, *José de Gálvez,* pp. 224-25; and "Instrucción del Sr. Conde de Revilla Gigedo al Sr. Marqués de las Amarillas," Mexico, November 28, 1754, in *Instruccións que los virreys de Nueva España dejaron a sus sucesores* (Mexico, 1867), pars. 36-37.

The Pueblo Indians were the chief sufferers at the hands of the alcaldes mayores. From the earliest days of the post-conquest period, royal legislation had been conscientiously issued to protect Indian vassals of the king. Just as regularly, however, governors, alcaldes, and other officials had ignored the law to exploit the natives and contribute thereby to the causes of disastrous rebellions. Conditions were perhaps ameliorated somewhat in New Mexico in the years immediately following the reconquest after the Pueblo revolt. But within a short time, the old abuses reappeared, and private citizens feared that continued oppression of the Indians would lead to renewed hostilities.[110]

The clergy were among the most consistent critics of the alcaldes. Their reports and letters of the mid-eighteenth century and afterward provide ample evidence of the manner in which a local officer could exploit the Indians if he was so inclined. Charges reveal that alcaldes mayores and their tenientes were commonly accused of the following crimes: cruel and inhuman punishments meted out for slight offenses; violation of Indian women; exacting tribute from the Pueblos; requiring subjects to go among the heathen Indians to trade on their behalf; demanding personal services of the Indians in direct violation of numerous decrees; hiring Indians under various pretenses and then refusing to pay them; encroaching upon Indian land; and obstructing the work of the missionary friars.[111]

Within the pueblos, the alcalde and missionary exercised something of a joint authority over the Indians, but in case of conflict of interest, the civil officer's will customarily prevailed.[112] A certain amount of rivalry between the two, no doubt, encouraged the bitter denunciations advanced by the churchmen, and hence it must be suspected that they did not always hew to the truth. Notwithstanding, other contemporary sources indicate that the alcaldes were naturally prone to commit mischief, and one must conclude that

110. Warner, "The Career of Martínez de Torrelaguna," p. 168.

111. Hackett, *Historical Documents,* III, 427-29; and Morfi, Desórdenes, arts. 40-44.

112. Circular to the Magistrates and Religious of New Mexico, Arizpe, March 31, 1795, SANM, doc. 1322.

strict honesty was in short supply among most of these civil servants.

An accusation often heard was that the alcaldes were mere creatures of the governor, doing his bidding, joining with him in profitable activities of an illicit nature, and spying and reporting to him on the actions of the friars.[113] While this may have been the case on occasion, the governor ordinarily was seen as an effective curb on the unwholesome inclinations of his subordinates. When authoritative complaints reached his ears, he usually ordered a full investigation by a juez comisionado. Records remain of a number of alcaldes brought to task in this way for their misdeeds.[114]

Curbing abuses of the alcaldes was the *protector partidario,* or protector of the Indians. This office had been bestowed upon leading clergymen of New Spain in the sixteenth century, but after a short time, it was suppressed. Later revived, the principal provisions governing the functions of the protector were incorporated in the *Recopilación.*[115] A protector general appointed by the viceroy was responsible for naming protectors partidarios, the officials who were to aid the natives at the local level. A provincial protector was present in New Mexico in the seventeenth and early eighteenth centuries, though sometime later the office became vacant and remained so until the first decade of the nineteenth century.[116]

With the separation of the Provincias Internas from the rest of the viceroyalty, a protector general for the new northern jurisdiction was appointed in the Audiencia of Guadalajara in the person of the crim-

113. Adams, *Bishop Tamarón's Visitation of New Mexico,* p. 106; and Twitchell, *The Spanish Archives of New Mexico,* I, 17.

114. Proceedings which may serve as an example were those conducted by the alcalde mayor of Santa Fe acting as juez comisionado against the alcalde of Alameda, who was charged with speaking disrespectfully of the provincial governor. SANM, doc. 2804. The Indians in some instances of litigation appealed to the governor to appoint an impartial judge since they did not trust their own alcalde. Sánchez Vergara to Allande, Jémez, September 12, 1816, SANM, doc. 2673.

115. Lib. vi, tit. 6.

116. Twitchell, *The Spanish Archives of New Mexico,* I, 6, 394. The viceroy in a letter of 1763 to the governor of New Mexico noted that the office of protector for this province was still vacant. SANM, doc. 571. In 1747 one Cristóbal Martínez had received a commission as protector of the Indians, but when Governor Vélez Cachupín opposed him, he renounced the post. Hackett, *Historical Documents,* III, 473.

inal attorney (*fiscal criminal*).[117] The protector general named local defenders who were nominated by the provincial governor and endorsed by the commandant general with final confirmation resting with the Audiencia as a body.

In general terms, the protectors partidarios were obligated to defend the rights of the Indians, in court if necessary; to free them from all oppressors; and to make certain the natives were receiving proper religious instruction. The Indians were not to be charged any fees for these services, but they should each contribute one-half a real yearly to defray legal expenses incurred in their behalf.[118]

In 1810 a Cochití Indian presented himself before the commandant general in Chihuahua and, speaking as a representative of the native people, he asked that a protector partidario be appointed to defend them as there was no such official in the province. Since the request was entirely proper, the commandant ordered the governor of New Mexico to investigate the qualifications of Felipe Sandoval of Santa Fe, who had been suggested by the petitioners, and to ascertain if the other pueblos of the province agreed with his selection.[119] The governor replied with a hearty recommendation of Sandoval, who subsequently received his official appointment from the protector general de indios, i.e., the fiscal, in Guadalajara.[120]

Felipe Sandoval held the office until his death in 1817, at which

117. A fiscal was the crown attorney of the superior tribunal who, among his regular duties, defended Indian rights in cases brought before the Audiencia. In the court at Guadalajara, there were two fiscales, one for criminal and the other for civil cases. It was the former who served as protector general of the Indians, at least in the years after 1810, as demonstrated by the records in the New Mexico archives. Actually, some other member of the Audiencia may have filled the post earlier as selection was left up to the president of the body. *Recopilación,* lib. vi, tit. 6, ley 5; and Haring, *The Spanish Empire in America,* pp. 61, 130.

118. *Recopilación,* lib. vi, tit. 6, ley 4; and Twitchell, *The Spanish Archives of New Mexico,* I, 6.

119. Salcedo to the Governor of New Mexico, Chihuahua, March 21, 1810, SANM, doc. 2305.

120. Order of Vicente Alonso Andrade, Guadalajara, August 20, 1810, SANM, doc. 2352; and Governor of New Mexico to the Commandant General, Santa Fe, May 31, 1810, SANM, doc. 2325(2).

time he was succeeded by Ignacio Sánchez Vergara, alcalde mayor of Jémez.[121] Sánchez Vergara maintained his post until independence. These men, while they served, were enjoined by their superiors to exercise absolute impartiality and to maintain the rights of the Indians in the manner prescribed in the *Recopilación* and in royal cedulas of September 30, 1779, and of March 11, 1781. All alcaldes were forbidden to interfere with such activities and were required to assist in seeking justice for the Indians. The clergy in particular were delegated to report to the protector any infringement upon native rights.[122] Most cases which came to the attention of the defender in New Mexico were concerned with disputed land claims involving Indian pueblos.

It may be seen from the foregoing discussion that the activities of New Mexico's alcaldes mayores were scrutinized by a number of persons: the governor, the protector of the Indians, the clergy, fellow alcaldes mayores, and individual citizens. The last three groups especially were quick to criticize the actions of a particular official. Sometimes their complaints were just, but on other occasions they were motivated solely by personal vindictiveness. Notwithstanding, they provided a much needed check on arbitrary behavior of local justices.

The Teniente Alcalde. Some attention has already been directed to the teniente alcalde, suggesting his formal relationship to the alcalde mayor and to the general scheme of local government. A brief summary of the characteristics of this office will round out the present discussion of district administration.

As disclosed previously, the jurisdictional unit under the teniente alcalde was the partido which occasionally was referred to as a tenencia. Judicially, the teniente settled minor cases verbally, referring

121. Elsewhere in Spanish America, protectors existed in most large Indian communities. It is possible that more than one of these held office at a time in New Mexico after 1810, but the present writer has uncovered no clear evidence of this. See Haring, *The Spanish Empire in America,* p. 61.

122. Order of Mariano Mendiola Velarde, Guadalajara, June 21, 1817, SANM, doc. 2692; and *Recopilación,* lib. vi, tit. 6, ley 14.

important matters to the alcalde mayor. At a later time, he was known as a *juez de paz,* and in the Mexican period, he was granted ordinary jurisdiction in the first instance.[123]

There is some question as to how a teniente alcalde was selected for his post. Most evidence indicates that he was chosen by the governor, who followed the same procedure indicated for the alcaldes mayores. In certain instances, the superior alcaldes may have named their own assistants or may have exerted influence over their final selection.[124]

The duties of the tenientes, beyond those of a judicial nature, were similar in many respects to the activities of the alcaldes mayores. The lieutenant participated in military campaigns; he assisted the superior magistrates in law enforcement, in the collection of taxes and special levies, and in the compiling of censuses; and he aided in promoting the welfare of the Pueblo Indians. Unfortunately, the documents reveal that these lieutenants abused their office or committed misdeeds against the natives as frequently as the alcaldes mayores. In one extreme case, a teniente arrested an Indian accused of horse-stealing. As punishment he placed the culprit in the stocks, but with the head and neck through one of the smaller holes intended for the leg. As a result, the unfortunate Indian was strangled.[125] Though this instance may not be considered as typical, it illustrates the lengths to which a misguided local official might go.

123. It seems fairly certain that the alcaldes or jueces de paz of the Mexican period were equivalent to the tenientes alcaldes of the colonial regime. Escudero, *Noticias estadísticas,* p. 46. For a time in the late colonial years, the term "alcalde de barrio" was used as a synonym for teniente alcalde. This question is discussed at the conclusion of the next chapter.

124. Fisher, *The Intendant System,* p. 5; and Jenkins, "The Baltasar Baca 'Grant,'" p. 53.

125. Fray Canales to the Governor, Santo Domingo, February 2, 1792, SANM, doc. 1188.

Chapter X

MUNICIPAL GOVERNMENT

New Mexican municipal government has always posed a problem for scholars—first, because of its retarded development in this province, and second, owing to the sketchy nature of the documentation presently available. Towns were founded and received their charters (*instrumentos de fundación*) according to the procedure outlined in the *Recopilación*,[1] but only for Santa Fe do we possess direct evidence that the customary municipal corporation was created.[2] Instead, the alcalde mayor exercised quasi-municipal powers in the principal town of his district, thus fulfilling in part the role ordinarily reserved for a cabildo.[3]

Municipal administration in New Mexico until the early 1700's was, as we have seen, the story of the Santa Fe cabildo—that town government composed of councilmen (*regidores*) and elected magis-

1. Lib. iv, tit. 7. The principal law governing municipalities was a royal edict of 1573, the main features of which were incorporated in the *Recopilación*. In 1789 the Plan of Pitic for establishing the new town of Pitic, Sonora, was prescribed by the crown as the model for the founding of other pueblos in the interior provinces. Actually, the Plan was merely an extension, or in some cases re-expression, of the earlier ordinances. Haring, *The Spanish Empire in America*, p. 160; and Richard E. Greenleaf, "The Founding of Albuquerque, 1706: An Historical-Legal Problem," *NMHR*, XXXIX (1946), 3.

2. Lansing B. Bloom believed that El Paso, Albuquerque, and Santa Cruz de la Cañada all possessed cabildos soon after they were founded, but he notes that there is no data to prove this. "Beginnings of Representative Government in New Mexico," *NMHR*, XXI (1964), 130.

3. The term for a municipal corporation was ayuntamiento or cabildo—the former being common in Spain and the latter being generally used in the colonies. After important legislation emanating from Spain, as the Order of Intendants of 1786 and the Constitution and subsequent Decrees of 1812 and 1813, which contained numerous provisions on "ayuntamientos," was made known in New Mexico, this word for the municipal body tended to supplant "cabildo," which had been employed earlier. In practice, cabildo, ayuntamiento, and the alternative but less frequent *regimiento* could all be used interchangeably to refer to the municipal governing body.

trates, the alcaldes ordinarios. The recent research of Ted J. Warner has thrown much light on the last days of the Santa Fe corporation and, together with documents viewed for a later period, it is possible to advance an authoritative statement on the demise of that body and its resurrection in the following century.

The Santa Fe cabildo, as observed previously, exercised a kind of general authority over the entire New Mexican province in the seventeenth and early eighteenth centuries. The wide latitude of its powers and the independent spirit of its members brought the municipal council into frequent conflict with the governor. The statement reputed to López de Mendizábal in 1661 that he considered the cabildo, his mule, and his Negress all one, suggests the degree of contempt with which individual governors might view the city fathers.[4] Friction between the provincial and municipal authorities in the early 1700's was intensified when members of the cabildo joined with factions hostile to the incumbent governors. The storm caught up with the Santa Fe body during the administration of Juan Ignacio Flores Mogollón (1712-1715). The governor ordered the cabildo abolished and appointed a subordinate as alcalde mayor to assume the functions normally delegated or reserved to the municipal officials.[5]

Fernando Ocaranza advises us that the town council was reinstituted under Félix Martínez de Torrelaguna (1715-1717) but eliminated anew with viceregal sanction when Antonio Valverde y Cossío assumed the governorship.[6] Valverde, following the precedent established by Flores Mogollón, appointed one of his close associates to serve as alcalde mayor in Santa Fe, stipulating that in this position he should exercise and conduct the affairs usually performed by the cabildo. The governor's successor, Domingo de Bustamante, failed to re-establish the council, provoking complaints that he had made himself absolute master of New Mexico.[7] The viceroy ordered the

4. Scholes, "Civil Government in New Mexico," p. 101.

5. Warner, "The Career of Martínez de Torrelaguna," p. 121.

6. *Establecimientos franciscanos en el misterio reino de Nuevo Mexico* (Mexico, 1934), p. 187.

7. Warner, "The Career of Martínez de Torrelaguna," p. 122.

election of alcaldes ordinarios in 1726, but it remains doubtful if after this date there was any semblance of a cabildo in the New Mexican capital.[8] In the years which follow, there appears to be a total lack of reference to any municipal official other than an alcalde mayor.

No historian to the present has felt qualified to declare with finality that the Santa Fe cabildo passed out of existence in the eighteenth century, although a few have intimated that such may have been the case.[9] The tribulations of the council as just outlined clearly demonstrate how its activities could be brought to an end by a strong-minded governor. It remains to be shown how a prolonged period of quiescence could be expected since decay of municipal government throughout New Spain was a common phenomenon in this period.

Herbert Ingram Priestley, in several of his works, has demonstrated the retrogressive tendency of New Spain's municipal administration in the eighteenth century.[10] The decadence of governments in such large towns as Guadalajara, San Luis Potosí, and Guanajuato was brought on, he declares, by the continual intervention of their governors, each of whom stood as the regional one-man power serving to strangle any attempt at municipal independence.[11] This closely parallels the conditions we have just described for Santa Fe.

On arriving in the viceroyalty in 1767, José de Gálvez discovered that the cabildos of cities and towns had fallen into disuse and in some provinces municipal decay was almost complete. It then became the objective of the tireless Gálvez to reinvigorate this important sphere of government, introducing at the same time reforms which would effectively remove the causes which had led to its decline.

The ideas of Gálvez were embodied in the important Order of Intendants of 1786. Reforms included therein looked particularly toward restoring town corporations and improving management of

8. SANM, doc. 341.

9. See, e.g., Coan, *Shorter History of New Mexico,* I, 107; and Bloom, "Beginnings of Representative Government," p. 131.

10. *José de Gálvez,* pp. 210-18; and "Spanish Colonial Municipalities," p. 411.

11. *The Coming of the White Man,* p. 193.

municipal finances. Article 11 of this Order is of special significance for New Mexican affairs. It declared that in the first year in which the new measure should be made effective, two alcaldes ordinarios were to be chosen in the towns which had an adequate number of inhabitants (without excepting those of the governments which were left in existence) but did not have these officials. The phrase "governments left in existence" refers to those provinces remaining under military rule and outside the jurisdiction of the new intendants. Such a province was New Mexico. Here then, as elsewhere, alcaldes ordinarios or municipal magistrates were to be selected. The Order makes clear that in choosing these officials the procedures outlined in the *Recopilación* were to be followed,[12] that is, the town judges were to be named by the regidores or councilmen of the ayuntamiento. But what of towns which possessed no such governing body? In continuing, Article 11 states that where no regular municipal council existed to perform this elective function, each political or military governor should appoint in his district alcaldes ordinarios in conformity with the spirit of the laws.[13] Here, then, was a clear mandate regarding selection of town justices.

By an official directive dated October 7, 1793, Commandant General Pedro de Nava ordered Governor Fernando de la Concha to name alcaldes ordinarios in accordance with the new law for the Villa of Santa Fe and for other places in his province which counted a sufficient number of inhabitants. This unequivocally demonstrates that no ayuntamiento then functioned in New Mexico. The governor's immediate reply presented a number of difficulties which prevented him from fulfilling the command of his superior, whereupon the Commandant General submitted Concha's answer to his assessor for a legal opinion. Apparently the governor had set forth a number of inconveniences and impediments attendant to the choosing of local magistrates. The assessor agreed that for the time being, the naming of alcaldes should be suspended for all the provincial towns except Santa Fe where they should be chosen as previously

12. As found in lib. v, tit. 3, leyes 1-9.

13. Fisher, *The Intendant System,* p. 106.

ordered. After some delay, the Commandant General advised Fernando de Chacón, who had succeeded Governor Concha, to proceed according to this judgment and to create the appropriate judicial offices for the New Mexican capital.[14]

Governor Chacón in 1797 responded by indicating such difficulties as the poverty of Santa Fe and the relatively small number of inhabitants it contained. In this respect, it should not be considered any different from other towns in the province, he pointed out. Moreover, among the better citizens of the villa, there was scarcely anyone qualified to hold the post of alcalde ordinario, this situation being the true reason for his hesitation in the matter.[15] In addition, there were numerous other factors staying the hand of the governor, but, notwithstanding, he declared that the naming of the Santa Fe alcaldes would proceed as provided in Article 11 of the Order of Intendants if the Commandant General so required it.[16]

The surviving correspondence breaks off here, but not before we have been given a fair picture of the status of New Mexican municipal affairs just before the turn of the nineteenth century. From this information we may summarize several salient points. First, neither Santa Fe nor any other town possessed a municipal corporation which could select the alcaldes ordinarios in the usual manner. Second, the governor of New Mexico was specifically empowered to make these appointments himself as the new law provided. The fact that two successive governors declined to do so, for reasons already set forth, suggests that government at the local level was at its lowest

14. Nava to Chacón, Quartel de Guajoquilla, August 23, 1796, SANM, doc. 1369.

15. Chacón uses the phrase *alcaldes ordinarios bienales* since the original Order of Intendants had stated, "Only one of the alcaldes shall be chosen in each consecutive year, in order that their offices may be biennial in all the towns." A subsequent royal cedula of September 12, 1792, annulled this provision and returned to the former practice whereby alcaldes ordinarios served for a term of one year only. Apparently Governor Chacón at the time of his writing had not been made aware of this new modification. See Fisher, *Order of Intendants,* p. 107.

16. Chacón to Nava, Santa Fe, July 13, 1797, SANM, doc. 1451. It should be mentioned in passing that here is a conspicuous example of the direct impact which the Order of Intendants had on New Mexico and serves, as does evidence presented in an earlier chapter, to refute the claim by some writers that the Order in no way affected affairs in this province.

ebb. Also it is apparent that either of these men, had they been so inclined, might have named persons who, though lacking the requisite qualifications, would have been responsive to the governor's will. Finally, the letters quoted make clear the legal basis by which a number of alcaldes ordinarios in New Mexico were appointed in the brief period from 1800 to 1812. After this latter date, the Spanish Constitution intervened by providing new regulations for organization of municipal government.

The objections to naming magistrates for Santa Fe were overcome or overruled at least by 1803 and perhaps earlier. In that year appears the first reference to an *alcalde ordinario de sequndo voto* since early in the previous century.[17] The two justices were customarily designated as senior and junior, that is, *alcalde de primer voto* and *alcalde de segundo voto* or alternately *alcalde de primera elección* and *alcalde de segunda elección.*[18] The senior magistrate ordinarily would have presided over the ayuntamiento and performed certain other functions not given to the junior alcalde. In most concerns, however, especially those related to judicial matters, the powers and authority of the two alcaldes ordinarios were the same.

In view of the fact that Santa Fe now possessed two alcaldes ordinarios, the fate of the alcalde mayor presents somewhat of a problem. It will be recalled that an officer of this title administered affairs of the capital along with those of its entire district and acted as special adviser to the governor during the long period beginning with the cabildo's demise in the early 1700's. With a partial restoration of regular municipal government in the form of the alcaldes ordinarios, it may be surmised that the alcalde mayor's activities in the villa were considerably curtailed. In the district of Santa Fe outside the limits of the town itself, his authority probably continued as before. What appears certain is the fact that an alcalde mayor for the Santa Fe jurisdiction as a whole did continue to function.[19]

17. Trial of Ramos Madrid, et. al., Santa Fe, June 11-19, 1803, SANM, doc. 1661.

18. The word "elección" in this instance should be translated as "selection" rather than "election" as may be adduced from the discussion above. The alcalde selected first was designated as the senior magistrate.

19. This is evident in a letter from Manuel Delgado to Governor Real Alencaster, Santa

By the year 1806, an alcalde ordinario is found in the Villa of Santa Cruz de la Cañada, though here, too, an alcalde mayor continued at his post.[20] Four years later, the Villa of Albuquerque had its complement of two alcaldes ordinarios, but there was still no full-fledged ayuntamiento within the province.[21]

Before proceeding, some mention of the nature of the office of alcalde ordinario should be made. The regulations regarding the foundation of municipal government in New Mexico are contained in the instruction issued to Governor Peralta in 1609.[22] This, together with subsequent royal legislation on the subject, particularly that contained in the *Recopilación,* defines the official character of the town magistrates and other municipal officers (known collectively as *capitulares*). Under ordinary circumstances, the citizens (*vecinos*) of Santa Fe, that is, property holders, each year elected the regidores (town councilmen), who in turn chose two alcaldes ordinarios from among the voters. The governor approved and confirmed these persons in office as well as the town attorney (*procurador*), a municipal secretary, the royal standard bearer or alférez real, and a constable and court bailiff (*alguacil*) named by the regidores.[23]

The prime function of the alcaldes ordinarios was to sit as judges of first instance in civil and criminal cases. Appeals from their courts ordinarily went to the governor and thence to the Audiencia of Guadalajara except in minor affairs which were carried to the

Fe, May 8, 1805, SANM, doc. 1824. Later the Constitution of 1812 provided that alcaldes mayores might be named as jueces for the new judicial districts to be set up. Dublán and Lozano, *Legislación mexicana,* I, 393.

20. Real Alencaster to the Real Audiencia, Santa Fe, November 20, 1806, SANM, doc. 2029.

21. Pino, *Exposición,* p. 29. Reference is here made by this writer to Don Cleto Miera y Pacheco as alcalde ordinario of San Carlos de la Alameda y sus partidos. Since Miera y Pacheco was the longtime alcalde mayor of this jurisdiction and as there was no villa within his district, Pino's allusion to him as alcalde ordinario would seem to be an error.

22. Bloom, "Instrucción a Peralta por vi-rey," pp. 178-88.

23. *Recopilación,* lib. v, tit. 3, ley 10. In addition to these officials, every town council was to have its *escribano de cabildo* or town clerk, who kept the minutes, drafted letters and deeds, and witnessed the signatures of the regidores. Often this office was combined with that of secretary. J. H. Perry, *The Sale of Public Office in the Spanish Indies under the Hapsburgs* (Ibero-Americana: 37; Berkeley, 1953), p. 7. Larger towns had a *mayordomo* or "city manager" who administered the resources of the cabildo. Constantino Bayle, *Los cabildos seculares en la América española* (Madrid, 1952), p. 267.

cabildo and terminated there.[24] All appeals from the judgments of the early nineteenth-century alcaldes ordinarios in New Mexico, of course, reached the governor as there were no town councils to rule on the petty cases. Jurisdiction of the Santa Fe magistrates included the villa itself and the area surrounding within five leagues. All cases involving Indians were reserved to the governor or his lieutenant.[25]

Under ordinary circumstances, the alcaldes presided over meetings of the council whenever the governor was not present to do so, and they possessed a vote equal to the regidores.[26] One of the alcaldes ordinarios was obliged to make weekly visits to the jail and prepare a monthly report of the results for the supreme court of justice, accompanying the same with a list of cases pending, with a specification of the day of commencement of the proceedings and the stages these had reached.[27]

By law, the alcaldes assisted in the supervision and preservation of the municipal archives. The town records were supposed to be kept locked, with one key in the possession of an alcalde ordinario, another to be held by a regidor, and a third by the escribano of the council. The archives encompassed the official documents of the cabildo and the *libro de acuerdos,* or book of measures, passed by that body and notarized by the escribano.[28] After the demise of the Santa Fe town council, the municipal archives were placed with those of the province under care of the governor. In the outlying districts, the alcaldes mayores maintained their own depositories for official documents.[29]

As was the custom, the ordinary magistrates of Santa Fe, together

24. Blackmar, *Spanish Institutions,* p. 290; and Priestley, "Spanish Colonial Municipalities," p. 404.

25. Bloom, "Instrucción a Peralta por vi-rey," p. 181.

26. O. Garfield Jones, "Local Government in the Spanish Colonies as Provided by the Recopilación de Leyes de los Reynos de las Indias," *Southwestern Historical Quarterly,* XIX (1916), 77.

27. Bancroft, *California Pastoral,* p. 579.

28. Ots Capdequí, *Manuel de historia del derecho español,* p. 382.

29. Removal and unauthorized use of papers in the official archives were strictly forbidden by a royal cedula of July 19, 1741. Dublán and Lozano, *Legislación mexicana,* I, 77.

with the regidores, were delegated the duty of assigning in the presence of the city attorney town lots and nearby lands to residents.[30] Each municipality, theoretically, owned a grant of land four leagues square, at the center of which was the main plaza surrounded by the house lots (*solares*). At the edge of these were the *ejidos*, or strips of commons used for various communal purposes, the *suertes* or arable fields distributed among the citizens, and the *dehesas y tierras de pasto,* or grazing grounds for livestock.[31] Beyond these land classifications, there remained the municipal grounds (*propios*) retained by the cabildo and rented out or leased as a source of town revenue.[32] Lands for agricultural purposes were divided into irrigable and non-irrigable, with each townsman receiving some of each. A person overseeing distribution of water was designated as *alcalde* or *justicia de aguas.*

Beyond the specific duties just mentioned, the alcaldes ordinarios exercised, in addition, a paternal vigilance over the affairs of their towns. An alguacil maintained order under their direction and served as executive officer of the courts. Within rather vague limits, the magistrates exerted their influence in any matter that was conducive to the local welfare.

The Spanish Reform Movement and Municipal Government

In the spring of 1808, the forces of Napoleon marched into Spain, having previously taken captive Ferdinand VII. This action initiated a series of events whch was to have a profound impact upon the

30. Bloom, "Ynstrucción a Peralta por vi-rey," p. 181. The procurador or municipal attorney was known later as the *síndico* or *procurador-síndico.*

31. Jones, "Local Government in the Spanish Colonies," p. 68; and Blackmar, *Spanish Institutions,* p. 169.

32. Supposedly, another source of local revenue came from the *arbitrios* which were the duties collected by the towns from mercantile business, trades, and products. As far as can be determined, neither the propios nor the arbitrios ever received more than a token collection by the Santa Fe authorities, and the amount of town funds as a whole remained almost nil throughout the colonial period. On these forms of taxes, see Priestley, "Spanish Colonial Municipalities," p. 406.

governmental system of the empire as a whole and which eventually led to independence for the American colonies. New Mexican officialdom and the citizenry were keenly interested in happenings unfolding in the mother country, and they were kept relatively well informed by announcements and reports originating in Spain and the Mexican capital.

A council, the *Junta Suprema de Gobierno de España é Indias,* was organized in Spain to direct the affairs of the empire in the absence of the king.[33] It called upon citizens everywhere to recognize it and to swear allegiance to Ferdinand VII. The governor of New Mexico was instructed by the commandant general to proclaim the will of the Junta, and this was done in an elaborate four-day ceremony organized in Santa Fe.[34] The populace at large was thus made aware, however vaguely, of the changes in Europe. Within a short time, contributions for the Peninsular War were requested of the citizens, bringing somewhat closer to home the meaning of otherwise remote events. The special collections were assembled by the district alcaldes and special masses to pray for Spanish victory were conducted in mission churches throughout the province. At Jémez, which was probably typical, a solemn mass initiated a three-day ceremony in which all citizens participated. Bonfires were kept burning throughout the night and many *Vivas* were shouted for the king.[35]

The contributions made by New Mexicans to the Spanish cause were by no means meager considering the relative poverty which prevailed. In the jurisdiction of Alameda alone, several hundred persons donated over 117 pesos, in addition to a large quantity of goods and 79 head of livestock.[36] In the jurisdiction of Santa Fe, the number of persons contributing came to almost five hundred.[37]

In the meanwhile, events were moving rapidly in Spain. The Central Junta issued a decree on January 22, 1809, recognizing the

33. SANM, doc. 2167, in Orders and Decrees, II, 119.

34. Order of Governor Manrrique, Santa Fe, November 8, 1808, SANM, doc. 2174.

35. Sanchez Vergara to Manrrique, Jémez, April 25, 1809, SANM, doc. 2224.

36. Alameda Accounts, April 29, 1809, SANM, doc. 2226.

37. List of Citizens Subscribing to the Donative Voluntario, Santa Fe, November 19, 1809, SANM, doc. 2271.

Spanish dominions in America as integral parts of the nation and declaring that they should have representation in the governing body. On January 31, 1810, a Regency was installed in Spain which issued a call for a meeting of the Spanish Cortes (or congress) later that same year.[38] In June, printed copies of new decrees by the Regency were received in Santa Fe.[39] One of February 14 declared that from that moment forward, all citizens should consider themselves as elevated to the status of free men.[40] Another of the same date set forth the procedure to be followed in selecting deputies to the Cortes.[41]

Representatives to the Spanish congress were to be chosen in each provincial capital by the local ayuntamiento. The municipal body was to nominate three leading citizens and from among these was to draw the name of one to serve as deputy. His expenses were to be arranged by local authorities, and he should receive instructions and suggestions from leading citizens as to the business which should be brought before the Cortes.[42]

In fulfillment of the command to elect a deputy, an assembly of the alcaldes and leading men of the province—there being no ayuntamientos—was convoked on August 11 in Santa Fe. With the governor presiding, three candidates were voted upon and from these a delegate, Pedro Bautista Pino, was chosen by lot. After receiving instructions from a number of prominent citizens, he embarked for Spain in October of 1811.[43] Although Pino was obliged to pay the expenses of his journey, the patriotic people of New Mexico contributed the equivalent of $9,000 as a donativo to the cause of Ferdinand VII.[44]

Pedro Bautista Pino's representation to the Cortes took the form of a lengthy report or *Exposición* on the internal affairs of New Mex-

38. Lucas Alamán, *Historia de México* (5 vols.; Mexico, 1849-1852), I, 272.

39. Nettie Lee Benson, "Texas Failure to Send a Deputy to the Spanish Cortes, 1810-1812," *Southwestern Historical Quarterly,* LXIV (1960), 18.

40. The Council of Regents to the Spanish Americans, SANM, doc. 2288, in Orders and Decrees, II, 136-37.

41. Real Decreto, SANM, doc. 2289, in Orders and Decrees, II, 138.

42. *Ibid.*

43. Pino, *Exposición,* p. 31.

44. Bancroft, *Arizona and New Mexico,* p. 288.

ico. The document was first published in Cádiz in 1812 and provides one of our best sources of information on the province in this period—especially as to the weaknesses and needs of the government.

A fellow delegate with Pino in the Spanish congress was Miguel Ramos de Arizpe, the representative from the eastern internal provinces.[45] He, too, prepared a report for the Cortes, outlining the defects in the government of his area, but its tone was more severe than that of Pino and it resulted later in his imprisonment by the Spanish king.[46] Of particular interest to us are his comments on the condition of municipal governments. He deplored the fact that only one city in his own province of Coahuila, the capital, Saltillo, had a regular ayuntamiento. Such cities as Parras, with ten thousand inhabitants, and Monclova, with over six thousand, had no councils. The municipalities of adjacent provinces were in similar straits. These sad conditions he attributed to the military governors who found the curbs imposed by municipal bodies distasteful and, therefore, sought to hinder their establishment.[47] These remarks forcefully demonstrate that the poor development of town government in the Provincias Internas as a whole was similar to that we have pictured for New Mexico.

About the only attention compilers of New Mexican history give to the liberal movement in Spain comes with a brief notice of Pino's activities and of the *Exposición* he presented to the Cortes. To neglect the Constitution of 1812 with its subsequent augmentive and explanatory decrees is impossible if one wishes to comprehend the fundamental alterations at all levels in the governmental structure of Spain's empire. Although New Mexico was affected by only a limited number of the new provisions, it is imperative for a full view of colonial history in this later period to consider the changes wrought—transitory though they were—by the new instrument of government.

45. Ramos de Arizpe was legally the representative only for Coahuila, but as his neighboring provinces failed to name a delegate, he undertook to speak for them all. Benson, "Texas Failure to Send a Deputy to the Spanish Córtes," p. 28.

46. Benson, *Report of Miguel Ramos de Arizpe,* p. ix.

47. *Ibid.,* p. 30.

The men of the ad interim government who assumed the direction of Spain's political affairs and of the resistance to Napoleon's armies were in the majority young liberals who had belatedly come under the influence of the Enlightenment and the doctrines of the French Revolution. It is not surprising, then, that they produced a document providing for a ministerial monarchy based on sovereignty of the people and the responsibility of the king's ministers to the Cortes.

The *Constitución política de la monarquía española* was promulgated on March 18, 1812, at the city of Cádiz. The ten titles (*títulos*) into which it was divided, defined among other things the future membership of the Cortes and provided regulations governing election of delegates; set forth the power of the Cortes and prescribed the procedure for the enactment of laws; described the authority and privileges reserved to the king; outlined forms to be pursued in the administration of justice; and dictated the provisions which should be followed in the reorganization of local government at both the provincial and municipal levels.[48]

Throughout the remainder of 1812 and during the subsequent year, a series of decrees were issued by the same Cortes which clarified some matters that had been treated only sketchily in the Constitution. Especially pertinent to later developments in New Mexico was a decree of October 12, 1812, concerning the functioning of audiencias and courts of first instance, and orders of May 23 and July 10, 1812, on the formation of constitutional ayuntamientos.[49]

That these specific decrees, the Constitution itself, and numerous other directives originating with the Cortes in Spain reached Santa Fe and were duly digested by the authorities cannot be questioned. The Secretary of State dispatched printed broadsides of the new

48. Created by the Constitution were a Council of State (*Consejo de Estado*) and offices of seven secretaries, including a Secretary of State (*Secretario de Estado*) and a Secretary for Overseas Affairs (*Secretario de Ultramar*). The Council and these two Secretariats are occasionally mentioned in the New Mexico documents of the period, but they had little direct contact with the province itself.

49. These decrees and others, together with the Constitution of 1812, are printed in Dublán and Lozano, *Legislación mexicana,* I, 349-428.

legislation to the commandant general of the Provincias Internas, who ordered his subordinates in the provinces to distribute copies to magistrates, church officers, and ayuntamientos for proclaiming, so that all would be informed of the new events.

From all indications, only the new ruling regarding creation of constitutional ayuntamientos was widely followed in New Spain.[50] In February of 1813, Commandant General Salcedo sent to the governor of New Mexico the decree of July 10 on this subject, and presumably the decree of May 23 concerning the same topic was dispatched earlier, though it is not presently in the archives.[51] Taken together, these two pieces of legislation, along with Title 6 of the Constitution, supply the legal basis for the municipal development soon undertaken by the New Mexican authorities.

According to the laws proclaimed by the Cortes, all towns of one thousand inhabitants or larger were to have ayuntamientos composed of alcaldes constitucionales, regidores, a *procurador-síndico* (attorney) and a secretary.[52] Towns with a smaller population, but of special economic importance, might also select municipal councils. Villages unable to maintain a government of their own were to be attached to the nearest ayuntamiento. The old municipal administrations, wherever they existed, were to be swept aside and replaced by newly elected officers. In December of every year the citizens of each town should gather to choose by a plurality vote the electors, who would in turn select the municipal magistrates, the councilmen, and lesser officers. The alcaldes, as in the past, should serve one-year terms. The regidores filled their offices for two years,

50. This point is stressed by José Bravo Ugarte in his *Historia de México* (3 vols.; Mexico, 1941-1946), III, 41.

51. Salcedo to the Governor of New Mexico, Chihuahua, February 13, 1813, SANM, doc. 2445.

52. An order of the Cortes, February 2, 1813, provided that the new terminology introduced in the Constitution and Decrees should henceforward be employed in all official papers. Thus, for example, *alcalde constitucional* was intended to supplant the older usage of alcalde ordinario. See Salcedo to Manrrique, Chihuahua, February 2, 1813, SANM, doc. 2476. A decree of October 9, 1812, declared that the constitutional alcaldes should maintain the same jurisdiction and powers as formerly exercised by the alcaldes ordinarios. Dublán and Lozano, *Legislación mexicana,* I, 395.

half of the membership being elected every other year. All municipal officials, in order to qualify for election, were required to be at least twenty-five years of age and to have resided in their towns for a minimum of five years.[53]

By 1814, a number of the larger towns in New Mexico, including Albuquerque, Belén, Bernalillo, El Paso, Santa Cruz de la Cañada, and Santa Fe had complied with the Constitution and created full ayuntamientos.[54] In addition to the alcaldes constitucionales and regidores, most or all of these bodies had an elected secretary who kept the minutes of the council meetings in a *libro de sesiones* and the record of resolutions in the *libro de actos*. The El Paso ayuntamiento listed the following documents as comprising its archives in 1815: one copy of the Spanish Constitution; a copy of the decree of May 23, 1812; the libro de actos or acuerdos; and a tax schedule (*plan de arbitrios*) for a common fund for El Paso.[55]

It may be assumed that the printed Constitution was fairly widely distributed throughout the provinces as it is frequently quoted by local officials. The governor besought the commandant general in 1814 to supply him with six copies of the document for distribution to magistrates in New Mexico who were still in need of them.[56]

Before turning to the events following upon the restoration of Ferdinand VII to the Spanish throne, it will be well to mention in specific terms another section of the Constitution of 1812 which was at least partially applied in New Mexico. This reference is to Title 3 which detailed the procedure for the election of future deputies to the Cortes. Electoral juntas were to be conducted in three stages or levels: parochial (*de parroquia*), district (*de partido*), and provincial (*de provincia*). *Juntas electorales de parroquia* were to be attended by all citizens in each parish who should assemble in the

53. Dublán and Lozano, *Legislación mexicana,* I, 373-75; 380-82.

54. The commandant general ordered the governor in September of 1814 to inform him of the New Mexican towns which had erected governments. SANM, doc. 2560. Unfortunately, we do not have the governor's reply.

55. Index of Documents, El Paso del Norte Archives, May 1, 1815, SANM, doc. 2595.

56. Index of Correspondence, 1814, Governor of New Mexico to Bonavia, Santa Fe, SANM, doc. 2554.

casa consistorial (any house where community meetings were customarily held). With the local alcalde presiding and with the assistance of the parish priest, officials called *compromisarios* were to be selected who would in turn choose the parroquial electors by a plurality vote. There was to be one of these latter named for every two hundred inhabitants counted in the parish. If the local population was small, eleven compromisarios would be elected to choose one elector. If the parish was entitled to two electors, then twenty-one would be the number of compromisarios. Named also was a secretary to record the business of the junta and persons to count the votes (*escrutadores*).

The parochial electors all convened in the chief town of their district to select from their number *electores de partido,* who in turn proceeded to the capital of the province for the final election of a deputy to the Cortes.[57] A rather lengthy document of approximately sixty-five pages in the Spanish Archives of New Mexico clearly indicates that in the first half of 1814 the important towns of the province convoked juntas electoriales to name parochial electors.[58] The procedure followed adhered closely to that laid down by the Constitution in Title 3. Further, the district juntas also convened and carried out their missions of choosing electors to the provincial junta. This documentation demonstrates that the parochial electoral districts corresponded in New Mexico to the smallest political jurisdictions commanded by a teniente alcalde and known here as partidos or tenencias. The district juntas (labeled by the Constitution as juntas de partido) corresponded to the New Mexican alcaldías mayores.

Until now it has remained uncertain if the provincial junta ever assembled. The present writer, however, discovered a document in the Santa Fe archives which clears up this matter.[59] On March 13 and 14 of 1814, the provincial junta convened in El Paso, rather than Santa Fe, and was composed of delegates from northern Nueva Viz-

57. Dublán and Lozano, *Legislación mexicana,* I, 352-57.

58. Collected Documents on Constitutional Elections, January 10 to June 14, 1814, SANM, doc. 2528.

59. Results of the Electoral Junta, El Paso, 1814, unnumbered printed document following SANM, doc. 2573.

caya as well as from New Mexico.[60] Presiding was the ad interim lieutenant governor in El Paso, Don Rafael Montes. Francisco José de Juáregui, first alcalde of the Villa of Chihuahua, was named deputy to the Cortes, and Simón de Ochoa, regidor of the same city, was chosen as alternate (*suplente*). Elections for two deputies and an alternate to the provincial deputation, that is the provincial assembly or congress, of the Provincias Internas de Occidente as specified by the Constitution were also held. One of the representatives (*vocal*) and the alternate were citizens of New Mexico—Juan Rafael Ortiz and Francisco Xavier Chaves, respectively. These elections were voided, however, by subsequent events in Europe.

On the continent, Napoleon had been defeated and Ferdinand VII had regained his throne. The king immediately dissolved the Cortes and began undoing its liberal work by revoking the Constitution and decrees and by returning the empire, governmentally speaking, to the status quo ante bellum.

On July 2, 1814, Ferdinand issued an order from Madrid, re-establishing the old Council of the Indies (Consejo de Indias), which had been the chief body in Spain concerned with colonial affairs. In this cedula, he spoke of the disorder and confusion reigning in the government, particularly in administration of justice, during the period of his absence.[61] This observation foreshadowed his order of the following July 30, which extinguished the constitutional ayuntamientos and directed that the old officials which had preceded them be returned to office.[62] In February of the following year, the commandant general instructed Governor Maynez of New Mexico to comply with this order and dissolve the existing municipal councils.[63]

This mandate was apparently carried out in all towns within two months, although we have records showing the abolition only of the

60. The reasons for this state of affairs are suggested later in this chapter when a similar junta held in El Paso in 1820 is discussed.

61. SANM, doc. 2546 (part 1).

62. Montoya to Maynez, La Cañada, April 3, 1815, SANM, doc. 2586; and Cedula of Ferdinand VII, December 28, 1814, SANM, doc. 2570.

63. SANM, doc. 2586.

ayuntamientos at El Paso del Norte in early March of 1815[64] and at Santa Cruz de la Cañada on or about April 3.[65] In addition, there remains in the archives a letter from the governor to the constitutional alcalde of Laguna referring to the decree of July 30. The governor declares in part:

> I didn't relieve you [the alcalde] from office immediately because of the shortage of someone to take your place; but having now considered that José Vicente Ortiz, citizen of Acoma, can fulfill the charge of alcalde mayor of Laguna, I name him to serve. You will recognize him handing over the corresponding archive and official papers, and you will cease exercising the functions of your office.[66]

This suggests that in the jurisdiction of Laguna-Acoma, which was largely Pueblo Indian, no ayuntamiento had been created and the governor, instead, had replaced the alcalde mayor with a constitutional alcalde, which meant in truth merely a change in name to conform to the new law. A similar circumstance may have existed in other predominantly Indian districts such as Zuñi and Jémez.

With the end of the period of expanded municipal government in 1815, the administration of local affairs was returned again to the alcaldes mayores and their tenientes. It may be recalled that along with these, alcaldes ordinarios appointed by the governor had existed in the pre-Constitution days in at least Santa Fe, Santa Cruz de la Cañada, and Albuquerque. With resumption of the old forms of government, only the alcaldes ordinarios for the city of Santa Fe seem to have been returned to office.[67] In Santa Cruz and Albuquerque, the alcaldes mayores once again directed the affairs of their respective communities.

This situation prevailed only a few years, however, for in 1820 a liberal revolution in Spain forced the king to restore the Constitution of 1812 and to recall the Cortes. By a decree dated April 15,

64. Quiñones to the Governor, El Paso, March 13, 1815, SANM, doc. 2582.
65. Montoya to Maynez [Santa Cruz], September 3, 1815, SANM, doc. 2586.
66. Maynez to Gallego, Santa Fe, March 15, 1816, SANM, doc. 2652.
67. Index of Municipal Documents, Santa Fe, May 10, 1818, SANM, doc. 2720.

1820, the laws of the first Cortes were declared re-established and in force in America.[68] The first order of business confronting New Mexicans in view of these developments was the election of a deputy to the new Cortes. On July 5, 1820, a preliminary council (*junta preparatoria*) was convened in the city of Durango to formulate a set of instructions on the necessary parochial, district, and provincial elections for the western internal provinces.[69] Nueva Vizcaya was to select two congressional deputies and one alternate, the province of Sonora and Sinaloa the same number, and New Mexico one deputy and one alternate. Since New Mexico, according to the latest census, did not have the ten thousand inhabitants necessary to qualify for a deputy under the Constitution, the junta ordered that several jurisdictions in Chihuahua should be attached to it for the moment and all district electors would then assemble in the city of El Paso del Norte on a date designated by the governor to conduct the final election. Other provisions of the junta followed closely the electoral procedure set down in the Constitution.

The parochial and district (de partido) elections were held in the manner described earlier and in the final meeting of provincial electors, Pedro Bautista Pino was once again named New Mexico's representative to Spain.[70] His election, doubtless, occurred in El Paso as recommended by the junta, since this had been the location of similar activity in 1814. Pino started for Spain, but only reached Vera Cruz where a shortage of funds forced him to abandon his journey. In writing to the Cortes in 1821 to explain his nonattendance, he complained that reforms he had urged in his earlier *Exposición,* though adopted by an order of May 9, 1813, had not been carried into effect.[71] New Mexico went through the form of electing a deputy to Spain for the years 1822 and 1823 and traveling expenses

68. Proclamation of Ferdinand VII, SANM, doc. 2887.

69. SANM, doc. 2903.

70. The only returns which have survived are those of the Santa Fe parochial election, August 6, 1820. Pino's name appears first on the list. SANM, doc. 2910.

71. Bancroft, *Arizona and New Mexico,* pp. 289-90. Among the measures passed had been provision for the establishment of a bishopric and seminary in Santa Fe. AGI, Audiencia de Guadalajara, leg. 561. Letters of Pino relative to this subject are contained herein.

were even appropriated, but by this time independence had become a reality and hence these acts were meaningless.[72]

Bancroft has declared that no ayuntamientos existed in New Mexico in the period prior to independence. Recent writers have accepted this at face value without taking into consideration the fact that Bancroft's source was Pino's *Exposición* written in 1812. In the years which followed this date, as we have seen, ayuntamientos were created and then abolished again except in Santa Fe. After viewing some of the evidence presented above, Bloom rather timidly asserted that "Bancroft's statement is too sweeping and must be modified" and acknowledged that New Mexico appeared to have several ayuntamientos by 1821.[73]

The fact is, as unchallengeably demonstrated by surviving documents, at independence most New Mexico towns and even Indian pueblos possessed their own ayuntamientos.[74] Article 309 of the Spanish Constitution explicitly provided that all towns should have municipal governments with the appropriate alcaldes and regidores together wth an attorney and a secretary. Governor Facundo Melgares, carrying out the law in 1820, ordered that communities under his jurisdiction should elect an alcalde de barrio, two regidores, and an attorney (procurador síndico).[75]

The use of the term alcalde de barrio here when the meaning intended is alcalde constitucional is somewhat confusing. Customarily the former designation applied to magistrates who exercised authority over the wards or barrios of the larger colonial towns and were subordinate to the municipal council.[76] Mexico City, after the reforms of José de Gálvez, possessed four such alcaldes. The ayunta-

72. Bloom, "New Mexico under Mexican Administration," p. 45; and Garcia Conde to Melgares, Durango, July 10, 1821, SANM, doc. 2993.

73. Bloom, "New Mexico under Mexican Administration," p. 44.

74. A document of 1823 refers to thirteen alcaldías in New Mexico plus the jurisdiction of El Paso. Account Received by José Antonio Vizcara, Santa Fe, December 31, 1823, Bancroft Library, Pinart Col., P-E 59. The basic law of the new Republic of Mexico remained until 1824 the Spanish Constitution with a few modifications. The provisions in this document regarding municipalities continued in force untl 1850. Blackmar, *Spansh Institutions,* p. 190.

75. Melgares to Salasar, Santa Fe, December 27, 1820, SANM, doc. 2947.

76. *Recopilación,* lib. v, tit. 12.

miento of the Villa of Chihuahua in 1793 selected four magistrates to fill posts in the barrios of that city, and this action was approved by the commandant general.[77]

From these and other instances it is apparent that alcaldes de barrio were usually confined to larger towns divided into wards. However, while it is true that barrio ordinarily signified a ward or district of a city, an alternate meaning could be a small village or town dependent upon a larger one.[78] Seemingly it was in this latter sense that the term was used by New Mexican officialdom. Since the Constitution required that each town have its own local government, this meant that the partidos in New Mexico, which as shown were composed of a single community and the surrounding countryside, were now to select their lawful officials. Alcalde de barrio thus may seem to have been a logical title for the new magistrates who were to preside over the old partidos.[79] Alcalde constitucional, as already noted, however, was by far the more common term used for these officers.

Governor Melgares apparently interpreted the new law regarding the creation of municipal governments as extending to the Pueblo Indians. Although native towns elsewhere in New Spain had long maintained cabildos with alcaldes and regidores, the practice had not been extended to the Indian communities of New Mexico. Since the Constitution declared residents of the New World to be Spanish citizens, the Governor understood this to include the Pueblo people. Therefore, he announced that the "minority" of the Indians was ended and, henceforward, they should be regarded "as Spaniards in all things, exercising especially their rights to vote and to stand as candidates for office." As a result, by late 1820 most of the Pueblos had installed formal municipal governments.[80]

77. "Efemérides Chihuahuenses,' *BSCEH,* II (1939), 32.

78. The *Diccionario histórico de la lengua española* (2 vols.; Madrid, 1936), II, 134, defines barrio as "un grupo muy apartado de casas que con otros forma un pueblo a aldehuela dependiente do otra población."

79. Substantiating this assumption is a document of 1814 which refers to the partidos or alcaldías de barrio of Albuquerque. Indian Fund Accounts, Albuquerque, July 2, 1814, SANM, doc. 2545.

80. Draft of a Letter by Facundo Melgares, Santa Fe, April 18, 1821, SANM, doc. 2974. On the ayuntamiento established at the small Pueblo of Pecos, see Durán to Melgares, Bado, January 3, 1821, SANM, doc. 2954.

Chapter XI

CONCLUSION

The foregoing study has attempted to reconstruct a picture of Spanish government in New Mexico during the late colonial period. Throughout, the emphasis has been on the presentation of simple fact; subjective interpretation has entered only incidentally. The scarcity of specific information on political institutions in the latter phase of colonial development has hitherto hindered full understanding of New Mexican affairs. So, too, has the lack of articles and monographs on economic and social conditions in the same period. These last topics offer a rich field for the resolute student who might wish to carve out a home in a little-explored wilderness.

Although the present description of Spanish government makes no pretense of offering other than a factual account of political institutions, it is possible to detect in the particular details certain general trends. Comment upon these may serve as a handy summation of the study as a whole, conveying a notion of the problems solved and those remaining, and suggesting a new point of departure for future research.

In the past there has been an unfortunate tendency on the part of scholars to consider New Mexico as essentially isolated from the main current of events transpiring in New Spain. There is obviously some logic in steering such a course, given the province's geographical remoteness, but carried to an extreme it ultimately may cause the historian's ship to founder.

As the preceding chapters have amply demonstrated, New Mexico was closely tied to the central government in the South and, through it, to the mother country. The province's immediate responsiveness to changes in the central authority is nowhere more apparent than in the period of revolutionary reform beginning in 1810, when the welter of new laws and decrees produced something of a scramble as New Mexican officials hastened to comply with these measures. A fact which is clearly expressed in Part One and which is at least implied in Parts Two and Three is the close dependence of provincial political officers upon their superiors in Mexico. This argues that New Mexico was fundamentally an extension of the southern government, and if data were available it could, no doubt, be shown that economic and social patterns here were essentially copies of those prevailing elsewhere in the commandancy. If this is accepted, then the illogic of regarding New Mexico as an isolated component in the total machinery of government becomes apparent. By way of conspicuous example, we may cite the Gálvez visita which initiated basic reforms in a number of areas of New Spain. Without reference to this event and the results which it produced, a proper understanding of subsequent developments in New Mexico cannot be achieved.

With regard to the functioning of provincial government here, the current study has attempted to offer an over view of Spanish administration during the last half-century of the colonial era. As pointed out in the preceding chapters, political activity was stimulated in this period by an increasing concern on the part of the central authorities for the improvement of local affairs. The new legislation which came as a result of this interest and the comment which it evoked from administrators at all levels brought forth, beginnning about 1770, a wealth of documentary materials. Students viewing these sources today in archival collections may readily observe their abundance, and by comparison may note the relative scarcity of papers on the subject of political administration earlier in the eighteenth century.

Thus, one characteristic of government which may be noted is the expanding complexity of basic institutions. In the military system, to cite one instance, a series of reglamentos and cedulas initiated programs looking toward the amelioration of the effectiveness and morale of the royal troops. In another area, that of the administration of justice, fundamental reforms were introduced through the Order of Intendants, the Constitution of 1812, and other measures which sought to establish the proper local courts, so that all citizens might easily have recourse to the law. New Mexico, therefore, may be viewed as something of a case study—an example of how the new laws relating to the military, judiciary, and other areas were applied.

The intensive use of hitherto neglected documents and the description of several previously unstudied aspects of government shed light on and raise questions about facets of New Mexican history properly outside the scope of an institutional survey. Those persons interested in economic development, for instance, should take note of that material which conveys the impression that New Mexicans were not so universally penurious as has been believed. Specie imported to pay the troops, to supply them, and to fill the coffers of the fondo de aliados suggests the source of hard cash, while extensive returns for the numerous donativos indicate that such money did filter down to people below the rico class.

Review of the entire subject of the local economy, taking these and other points into consideration, may reveal that some of the early writers, as Pedro Bautista Pino, exaggerated or distorted the picture of conditions prevailing in New Mexico in an effort to win concessions from the Spanish government. In this and other efforts to achieve a more balanced perspective of colonial New Mexican history, the subject of provincial government must figure as an integral part.

APPENDIX

Chronology of Administrative Changes in Northern New Spain

1728-1730 Pedro de Rivera's inspection of the frontier.

1766 Inspection of the Marqués de Rubí.

1772 New Presidial Reglamento published.
Hugo O'Conor appointed Commandant Inspector.

1776 Commandancy General of the Internal Provinces established.
Teodoro de Croix becomes first Commandant General.

1783 Felipe de Neve succeeds Teodoro de Croix.

1784 José Antonio Rengel becomes ad interim Commandant General upon the death of Neve.

1785 Jacobo Ugarte y Lotola becomes Commandant General.

1786 Reorganization of the Internal Provinces to form three departments dependent upon the Viceroy of New Spain. Establishment of the Intendancy System.

1787 Internal Provinces reorganized and a second commandant general appointed: Ugarte y Loyola, Commandant General of the Western Provinces; Juan Ugalde, Commandant General of the Eastern Provinces.

1788 Office of commandant inspector merged with that of commandant general of the West.
Ugarte y Loyola transfers his headquarters from Arizpe to Chihuahua.

1790 Antonio Cordero becomes ad interim Commandant General of the Western Provinces.

1791 Pedro de Nava appointed Commandant General of the Western Provinces.

1792	Internal Provinces reunited under Nava. Chihuahua declared the official capital.
1800	Nemesio Salcedo y Salcedo named to succeed Nava.
1802	Salcedo takes command of the Internal Provinces.
1812	Order of the Spanish Regency dividing the Internal Provinces into Eastern and Western Commandancies.
1813	Bernardo Bonavía succeeds Salcedo as Commandant General of the Western Provinces.
1814	Joaquín de Arredondo, Commandant General of the Eastern Provinces.
1817	Alejo García Conde succeeds Bonavía.
1818	Royal order curtails powers of the commandants general.
1821	Plan of Iguala and Mexican independence.

GLOSSARY

Acordada. A rural police force and court concerned with crimes committed on the king's highways.

Administrador de rentas. A superior treasury officer responsible for administration of government monopolies.

Alcabala. A special form of sales tax applied by the colonial government on certain commodities at both first and later sales.

Alcalde. In general, a civil official with judicial, executive, and legislative functions.

Alcalde mayor. A superior alcalde governing a district.

Alcalde ordinario. A municipal magistrate.

Alcaldía mayor. The district of an alcalde mayor.

Almacen de aliados. A special warehouse which held goods destined as gifts to allied Indians.

Almacen de la tropa. The storehouse of a military company.

Almud. A measure of grain, from 3 to 23 liters according to locality.

Asesor general. A legal adviser in matters of civil and criminal jurisdiction.

Asesoría general. Central office of government legal advisers.

Audiencia. A high appelate court presided over by a president.

Auditor de guerra. A legal adviser in matters of military jurisdiction.

Ayudante inspector. An adjutant inspector. The subordinate of a commandant inspector.

Ayuntamiento. A municipal council.

Bando. An official edict or proclamation.

Bastón de justicia. A black cane with a silver tip which symbolized the authority of an appointed official.

Cabecera. The principal town and administrative seat of a political jurisdiction.

Cabildo. 1) A municipal council. 2) The meeting hall of a municipal council. 3) A cathedral chapter.

Cajas reales. Treasury offices or branches of the real hacienda.

Capitán a guerra. The title bestowed upon a civil official, usually the alcalde mayor, who exercised military functions in the absence of an officer of the regular army.

Casa consistorial. Any house where community meetings are held.

Casa de monedu. A mint.

Casa real Any government building, but more particularly the official residence of the governor.

Cédula. A dispatch of the king, executed by some superior council, in which a grant is conceded or a judgment taken.

Cédula de premio. A military service award.

Ciudad. A city. The formal title of an important municipality which carries exceptional legal and honorific privileges.

Comandancia general. A military-political district under a commandant general.

Comandancia inspección. The district or jurisdiction of a commandant inspector. (See Inspección.)

Comandante de armas. In general, any commander of military forces.

Comisario de justicia. In New Mexico this term referred to the teniente alcalde.

Contador. An accountant.

Cordón. 1) A military cordon formed by a line of troops or forts. 2) A caravan.

Correo mayor. A private mail contractor who purchased his office from the crown.

Cortes. Senate and congress of deputies in Spain.

Cruzada. A special tax raised by the sale of indulgences.

Cuerpo de inválidos. The retired and disabled list of a military company.

Curador. A defender of Indians in legal cases.

Defensor. A crown-appointed defender of the Indians in legal cases.

Diario de novedades. A day-by-day report of an expedition or other military activity.

Dictamen. A formal legal opinion delivered by a person trained in law.

Donativo. A form of "voluntary" tax.

Encomenderos. Holders of encomienda grants.

Encomienda. A formal grant of Indians entrusted to the care of a Spaniard.

Ensayador. An assayer.

Escribano. A notary.

Estanco de tabaco. The government tobacco monopoly.

Fanega. A dry measure varying from 1.5 to 2.5 bushels depending upon the locality.

Fiel administrador. An administrator of a government monopoly at the local level.

Fiscal civil. A civil attorney.

Fondo común. The common fund of the enlisted men of a military company.

Fondo de aliados. A special expense fund to supply gifts and rations to Indian allies.

Fondo de gratificación. Officer's reserve fund of a military unit.

Fondo de inválidos. The retired and disabled fund of a military company.

Fondo de retención. A mustering-out reserve fund for military personnel.

Fuero. A privileged judicial jurisdiction or court which functioned independently of ordinary civil tribunals.

Genízaros. Indians of nomadic tribes surrounding New Mexico who, after ransom or capture, were incorporated into colonial society.

Graduado. Brevet.

Habilitado. A presidial supplymaster.

Hacendado. Owner of an hacienda or large landed estate.

Hacienda. 1) Landed property as an estate or ranch. 2) A treasury.

Hoja de servicio. The service record of a military officer.

Inspección. That department of the military concerned with supply and discipline.

Instancias. Litigation or prosecution of a suit.

Instrucción. 1) A set of orders. 2) Court proceedings.

Inválidos. Retired or disabled soldiers.

Jefe de alcaldes. A chief alcalde; an official, as a provincial governor, who held jurisdiction over alcaldes.

Jefe político. A political or civil administrative chief.

Juez comisionado. A magistrate whose commision was limited to a single case.

Juez de primera instancia. A judge of first instance.

Juez de residencia. Magistrate designated by royal commision to conduct the residencia of a retiring official.

Juez de segunda instancia. A judge of second instance.

Junta superior de real hacienda. The governing council of the royal treasury in Mexico City.

Jurisdicción eclesiástica castrense. A special legal jurisdiction and body of privileges applied to those who came under both the military and ecclesiastical fueros.

Justicia mayor. The highest judicial officer in a particular jurisdiction.

Justicia ordinaria. The regularly established courts with jurisdiction over ordinary civil and criminal cases.

Justicia privilegiada. A term applied to all special courts operating under their own fueros.

Letrado. Any person formally trained in law.

Libro de filiaciones. A military company roster.

Licencia absoluta. Military discharge.

Mayordomo. 1) A supervisor of an organized activity. 2) A city manager. 3) A religious steward or head of a church society.

Media anata. Half of the first year's salary of a newly appointed official which was collected by the government as a tax.

Monte-pio militar. A military pension fund for the widows and orphans of officers dying in service.

Oficiales. Officers in general. Or specifically military or treasury officers.

Pagaduría. A paymaster's office.

Paraje. An official campsite on a road or trail.

Partido. 1) A district or territorial division. 2) The jurisdiction of a teniente alcalde. 3) A sheep contract.

Patronato real. The body of rights which the sovereigns of Spain possessed over the Catholic Church in America and which derived from papal grants of the early sixteenth century.

Penas de cámaras. Judicial fines.

Plaza. 1) The open "square" in the center of a town. 2) A village or community. 3) An enlisted man.

Pliego. 1) A parcel of letters enclosed in a single cover. 2) A single sheet of paper folded once to form a two-page writing folder which was the unit sold as stamped paper.

Preeminencias. A body of special privileges and exemptions awarded to deserving soldiers.

Premios. Military service awards.

Portes. Postal revenues.

Procurador-síndico. The attorney of a municipal corporation.

Propuestas. Nominations for a civil, military, or religious office.

Protector partidario. A protector of the Indians appointed at the local level.

Punche. A low grade of tobacco raised in New Mexico.

Real. 1) Coin valued at one-eighth of a peso. 2) A military camp.

Reales efectivos. An expression meaning "in cash."

Real hacienda. The royal treasury.

Real provisión. A decree made in the name of the king by a council, audiencia, or other governing body.

Real servicio. The royal postal service.

Regidor. A member of a municipal council.

Reglamento. A body of regulations or ordinances.

Reservada. Confidential.

Residencia. The official investigation of political officer's conduct at the end of his term of administration.

Revista de armas. A military review of arms and troops.

Secretario de visita. A secretary or clerk who serves as official recorder during a visita.

Servicio nacional. The Mexican postal service after independence.

Síndico. The attorney of a municipal corporation.

Sínodo. The stipend for missionaries provided by the government.

Subdelegados. The agents or assistants of a political officer, particularly of a governor intendant.

Teniente alcalde. The subordinate of an alcalde mayor.

Testigos de asistencia. Witnesses to a legal case or to the signing of an official document.

Tribunal de cuentas. An accounting office and court of audit.

Vara de justicia. Staff of justice and symbol of office.

Visita. 1) A formal inspection of a department of government. 2) A Church without a resident priest, but which is regularly "visited" by a priest who conducts services.

Visitador. An inspector who is formally commissioned to conduct a visita.

BIBLIOGRAPHY

I. Manuscript Materials

Manuscript source materials utilized in the preparation of this study have come principally from the Spanish Archives of New Mexico located in the State Records Center, Santa Fe. These documents include the official colonial records which have survived, and special collections of related papers acquired by the Archive. The official records have been listed and annotated by Ralph Emerson Twitchell in *The Spanish Archives of New Mexico,* Vol. II, and the numbers cited in the footnotes of this study correspond to those used by Twitchell.

In addition, microfilm and photoprints of documents from various sections of the Archivo General de Indias, Sevilla, and the Archivo General de la Nación, Mexico City, have been employed. These copies are available in the Coronado Room of The University of New Mexico Library. Some related materials, both manuscript and printed, were viewed at the Bancroft Library, Berkeley.

II. Primary Sources (*Printed*)

Adams, Eleanor B. *Bishop Tamarón's Visitation of New Mexico, 1760.* Albuquerque, 1954.

Alessio Robles, Vito. *Diario y derrotero de lo caminado, visto y observado en la visita que hizo a los presidios de la Nueva España septentrional el Brigadier Pedro de Rivera.* Mexico, 1946.

Benson, Nettie Lee (tr.). *Report that Dr. Miquel Ramos de Arizpe Presents to the August Congress.* Austin, 1950.

Bloom, Lansing B. (tr.). "A Campaign Against the Moqui Pueblos," *NMHR,* VI (1931), 158-226.

———. (tr.). "The Death of Jacques D'Eglise," *NMHR,* II (1927), 369-79.

———. (ed.). "Early Vaccinations in New Mexico," Hist. Soc. of New Mexico Publ. 27 (1942), 2-12.

———. (ed.). "A Glimpse of New Mexico in 1620," *NMHR,* III (1928), 357-80.

———. (ed.). "Instrucción a Peralta por vi-rey," *NMHR,* VI (1929), 178-86.

Carroll, H. Bailey, and J. Villasana Haggard (eds. and trs.). *Three New Mexico Chronicles.* Albuquerque, 1942.

Concha, Fernando de la. "Advice on Governing New Mexico, 1794," *NMHR,* XXIV (1949), 236-54.

Dominguez, Fr. Francisco Atanasio. *The Missions of New Mexico, 1776.* Tr. by Eleanor B. Adams and Fr. Angélico Chavez. Albuquerque, 1956.

Dublán, Manuel and José María Lozano. *Legislación mexicana.* 2 vols. Mexico, 1876.

Escobar, Rómulo. "La feria de Paso del Norte," *BSCEH,* II (1939), 131-33.

Hackett, Charles W. (ed.). *Historical Documents Relating to New Mexico, Nueva Vizcaya, and Approaches Thereto, to 1773.* Collected by Adolph and Fanny R. Bandelier. 3 vols. Washington, D.C., 1923-37.

Hackett, Charles Wilson, and Charmion C. Shelby (eds. and trs.). *Revolt of the Pueblo Indians of New Mexico and Otermín's Attempted Reconquest, 1680-1682.* 2 vols. Albuquerque, 1942.

Hammond, George P. and Agapito Rey (eds.). *Don Juan de Oñate, Colonizer of New Mexico, 1595-1628.* 2 vols. Albuquerque, 1953.

Humboldt, Alexander von. *Ensayo político sobre el reino de la Nueva España.* 4 vols. Mexico, 1941-1947.

Informe general que entregó el Señor Marqués de Sonora al virrey D. Antonio Bucareli y Ursua, Dec. 31, 1771. Mexico, 1867.

Instrucciones que los vireyes de Nueva España dejaron a sus sucesores. 2 vols. Mexico, 1867.

Kinnaird, Lawrence (ed.). *The Frontiers of New Spain: Nicolás de Lafora's Description, 1766-1768.* Berkeley, 1958.

———. "The Spanish Tobacco Monopoly in New Mexico, 1766-1767," *NMHR,* XXI (1946), 328-39.

Mendinueta, Pedro Fermín. *Indian and Mission Affairs in New Mexico, 1773.* Trs. by Marc Simmons. Santa Fe, 1965.

Notas de la legislación mexicana. Mexico, 1854.

Recopilación de leyes de los reynos de las Indias. 4 tomos. Madrid, 1756.

Reglamento de sueldos para los oficiales y demas clases del ejército de América que se retiran del servicio. Mexico, 1817.

Reglamento e instrucción para los presidios que se han de formar en la linea de frontera de la Nueva España. Mexico, 1834.

Revilla Gigedo, Conde de. *Instrucción reservada que dío a su sucesor en el mando, Marqués de Branciforte sobre el gobierno de este continente en el tiempo que fue su virrey.* Mexico, 1831.

Rodríquez de San Miguel, Juan N. *Pandectas Hispano-Megicanas.* 2 vols. Mexico, 1852.

Thomas, Alfred B. (ed. and tr.). *Forgotten Frontiers: A Study of the Spanish Indian Policy of Don Juan Bautista de Anza, Governor of New Mexico, 1777-1787.* Norman, Oklahoma, 1932.

———. (ed. and tr.). *The Plains Indians and New Mexico, 1751-1778.* Albuquerque, 1940.

———. (ed. and tr.). *Teodoro de Croix and the Northern Frontier of New Spain, 1776-1783.* Norman, Oklahoma, 1941.

———. (ed.). "An Anonymous Description of New Mexico, 1818," *Southwestern Historical Quarterly,* XXXIII (1929), 50-80.

———. "Antonio de Bonilla and Spanish Plans for the Defense of New Mexico, 1772-1778," in *New Spain and the Anglo-American West.* 2 vols. Lancaster, Pa., 1932.

———. "Governor Mendinueta's Proposals for the Defense of New Mexico, 1772-1778," *NMHR,* VI (1931), 21-39.

Villa-Señor y Sanchez, Joseph Antonio de. *Teatro americano.* Mexico, 1748.

Worcester, Donald E. (ed. and tr.). *Instructions for Governing the Interior Provinces of New Spain, 1786.* Berkeley, 1951.

III. Secondary Sources

A. Books

Alamán, Lucas. *Historia de México.* 5 vols. Mexico, 1849-1852.

Alcàzar Molino, Cayetano. *Los virreinatos en el siglo XVIII.* Barcelona, 1945.

Alessio Robles, Vito. *Coahuila y Téxas en la época colonial.* Mexico, 1938.

Ayala, Joseph de. *Diccionario de qobierno y legislación de Indias.* 2 vols. Madrid, 1929.

Bancroft, Hubert H. *Arizona and New Mexico, 1530-1888.* San Francisco, 1889.

———. *California Pastoral, 1769-1848.* San Francisco, 1888.

———. *History of Mexico.* 5 vols. San Francisco, 1886-1888.

———. *North Mexican States and Texas.* 2 vols. San Francisco, 1884-1889.

Banegas Galván, Francisco. *Historia de México.* 3 vols. Mexico, 1938-1940.

Blackmar, Frank W. *Spanish Institutions of the Southwest.* Baltimore, 1891.

Bloom, Lansing B. and Thomas C. Donnelly. *New Mexico History and Civics.* Albuquerque, 1933.

Bobb, Bernard E. *The Viceregency of Antonio María Bucareli in New Spain, 1771-1779.* Austin, 1962.

Bolton, Herbert Eugene. *Guide to Materials for the History of the United States in the Principal Archives of Mexico.* Washington, D.C., 1913.

Bravo Ugarte, José. *Historia de México.* 3 vols. Mexico, 1941-1946.

Carmen Velázquez, María del. *El estado de guerra en Nueva España, 1760-1808.* Mexico, 1950.

Castañeda, Carlos Eduardo. *Our Catholic Heritage in Texas, 1513-1936.* 7 vols. Austin, Texas, 1936-1957.

Chapman, Charles E. *A History of California: The Spanish Period.* New York, 1921.

Chávez, Angélico. *Archives of the Archdiocese of Santa Fe, 1678-1900.* Washington, 1958.

Coan, Charles F. *A Shorter History of New Mexico.* 2 parts. Ann Arbor, 1928.

Diccionario histórico de la lengua española. 2 vols. Madrid, 1936.

Diccionario universal de historia y de geografía. 7 vols. Mexico, 1853-1855.

Escriche, Joaquin. *Diccionario razonado de legislación y jurisprudencia.* Paris [1834].

Escudero, José Agustín de. *Noticias estadísticas del estado de Chihuahua.* Mexico, 1834.

Fisher, Lillian Estelle. *The Intendant System in Spanish America.* Berkeley, 1929.

Fonseca, Fabián de, y Carlos de Urrutia. *Historia general de real hacienda.* 6 vols. Mexico, 1849.

Guest, Florian Francis. "Municipal Institutions in Spanish California, 1769-1821." Unpublished Ph. D. Dissertation, University of Southern California, 1961.

Hallenbeck, Cleve. *Land of the Conquistadores.* Caldwell, Idaho, 1950.

Haring, C. H. *The Spanish Empire in America.* New York, 1947.

Jones, Oakah L. Jr. *Pueblo Warriors and Spanish Conquest.* Norman, 1966.

McAlister, Lyle N. *The "Fuero Militar" in New Spain, 1764-1800.* Gainesville, Fla., 1957.

Moorhead, Max. *New Mexico's Royal Road. Trade and Travel on the Chihuahua Trail.* Norman, 1958.

Navarro García, Luís. *Intendencias en Indias.* Sevilla, 1959.

———. *José de Gálvez y la comandancia general de las Provincias Internas.* Sevilla, 1964.

———. *Las Provincias Internas en el siglo XIX.* Sevilla, 1965.

Ocaranza, Fernando. *Establecimientos franciscanos en el misterio reino de Nuevo México.* Mexico, 1934.

Ots Capdequí, José María. *Instituciones.* Barcelona, 1959.

———. *Manuel de historia del derecho español en las Indias.* Buenos Aires, 1945.

Parry, J. H. *The Sale of Public Office in the Spanish Indies under the Hapsburgs.* Ibero-Americana: 37. Berkeley, 1953.

Priestley, Herbert Ingram. *The Coming of the White Man.* New York, 1929.

————. *José de Gálvez, Visitor-General to New Spain, 1765-1771.* Berkeley, 1916.

————. *The Mexican Nation.* New York, 1935.

Ponce de León, José M. *Reseñas históricos del estado de Chihuahua.* Chihuahua, 1913.

Powell, Philip Wayne. *Soldiers, Indians and Silver: The Northward Advance of New Spain, 1550-1600.* Berkeley, 1952.

Read, Benjamin M. *Illustrated History of New Mexico.* Santa Fe, 1912.

Reeve, Frank D. *History of New Mexico.* 3 vols. New York, 1961.

Reynolds, Matthew G. *Spanish and Mexican Land Laws, New Spain and Mexico.* St. Louis, 1895.

Richman, Irving Berdine. *California under Spain and Mexico, 1535-1847.* Boston, 1911.

Scholes, Frances V. *Church and State in New Mexico, 1610-1650.* Albuquerque, 1937.

————. *Troublous Times in New Mexico, 1659-1670.* Albuquerque, 1942.

Smith, Donald E. *The Viceroy of New Spain.* Berkeley, 1913.

Twitchell, Ralph E. *The Leading Facts of New Mexico History.* 5 vols. Cedar Rapids, Iowa, 1911-1917.

————. *Old Santa Fe.* Santa Fe, 1925.

————. *The Spanish Archives of New Mexico.* 2 vols. Cedar Rapids, Iowa, 1914.

Wagner, Henry R. *The Spanish Southwest, 1542-1794.* 2 vols. Albuquerque, 1937.

Warner, Ted. J. "The Career of Don Félix Martínez de Torrelaguna, Soldier, Presidio Commander, and Governor of New Mexico, 1693-1726." Unpublished Ph.D. Dissertation, University of New Mexico, 1963.

White, Joseph M. *A New Collection of Laws, Charters and Ordinances of the Governments of Great Britain, France, and Spain together with the Laws of Mexico and Texas.* 2 vols. Philadelphia, 1839.

Velasco Ceballos, R. *La administración de D. Frey Antonio María de Bucareli y Ursua.* 2 vols. Mexico, 1936.

B. Articles

Almada, Francisco R. "Los Apaches," *BSCEH,* II (1939), 7-9.

————. "La comandancia general de Provincias Internas," *BSCEH,* I (1938), 36-41.

Benson, Nettie Lee. "Texas Failure to Send a Deputy to the Spanish Cortes, 1810-1812," *Southwestern Historical Quarterly,* LXIV (1960), 14-35.

Bloom, Lansing B. "Early Bridges in New Mexico," *El Palacio,* XVIII (1925), 163-82.

———. "The Governors of New Mexico," *NMHR,* X (1935), 152-57.

———. "New Mexico under Mexican Administration, 1821-1846," *Old Santa Fe,* I (1913), 3-49.

Bose, Walter B. L. "Origenes del correo terrestre en México," *Revista de historia de América,* XXIII (1947), 87-98.

Boyd, E. "Troubles at Ojo Caliente, A Frontier Post," *El Palacio,* LXIV (1957), 349-51.

Christiansen, Paige W. "The Myth of Robledo," *El Palacio,* LXXI (1964), 30-34.

Greenleaf, Richard E. "The Founding of Albuquerque, 1706: An Historical-Legal Problem," *NMHR,* XXXIX (1964), 1-15.

Grivas, Theodore. "Alcalde Rule: The Nature of Local Government in Spanish and Mexican California," *California Historical Society Quarterly,* XL (1961), 11-15.

Jenkins, Myra Ellen. "The Baltazar Baca 'Grant': History of an Encroachment," reprinted from *El Palacio,* LXI (1961), 47-64.

Jones, Oakah L. Jr. "Pueblo Indian Auxiliaries and the Reconquest of New Mexico, 1692-1704," *Journal the West,* II (1963), 257-80.

Jones, O. Garfield. "Local Government in the Spanish Colonies as Provided by the Recopilación de Leyes de los Reynos de las Indias," *Southwestern Historical Quarterly,* XIX (1916), 65-90.

Moorhead, Max. "The Presidio Supply Problem in New Mexico in the Eighteenth Century," *NMHR,* XXIV (1961), 210-29.

———. "The Private Contract System of Presidio Supply in Northern New Spain," *Hispanic American Historical Review,* XIL (1961), 31-54.

Priestley, Herbert Ingram. "Spanish Colonial Municipalities," *California Law Review,* VII (1919), 397-416.

Reeve, Frank D. "Navajo-Spanish Diplomacy, 1770-1790," *NMHR,* XXXV (1960), 200-35.

Sandoval, Fernando B. "El correo en las Provincias Internas," *Boletín del archivo general de la nación,* XVIII (1948), 320-339.

Scholes, France V. "Civil Government and Society in New Mexico in the Seventeenth Century," *NMHR,* X (1935), 71-111.

———. "Problems in the Early Ecclesiastical History of New Mexico," *NMHR,* VII (1932), 32-74.

Simmons, Marc. "Tlascalans in the Spanish Borderlands," *NMHR,* XXXIX (1964), 101-10.

West, Elizabeth Howard. "The Right of Asylum in New Mexico in the Seventeenth Century," *Hispanic American Historical Review,* VIII (1928), 357-91.

White, Leslie A. "Punche Tobacco in New Mexico History," *NMHR,* XVIII (1943), 386-93.

Wuthenau, A. von. "The Spanish Military Chapels in Santa Fe and the Reredos of Our Lady of Light," *NMHR,* X (1935), 175-94.

INDEX